ORDINATION

ORDINATION
A Biblical–Historical View

by
MARJORIE WARKENTIN

WILLIAM B. EERDMANS PUBLISHING COMPANY
GRAND RAPIDS, MICHIGAN

For Ed
in appreciation

Copyright © 1982 by Wm. B. Eerdmans Publishing Co.
255 Jefferson Ave. S.E., Grand Rapids, MI 49503

Library of Congress Cataloging in Publication Data

Warkentin, Marjorie, 1921–
Ordination, a biblical-historical view.

Bibliography: p. 189
Includes indexes.
1. Ordination.   I. Title.
BV664.5.W37 1982   234'.164   82-8908
ISBN 0-8028-1941-9

CONTENTS

PREFACE

When the German Baptist leader and evangelist J. G. Oncken visited the Southern Ukraine in October 1869, he was asked by the newly established Mennonite Brethren congregation at Chortitza if he would ordain Abraham Unger as elder, Aron Lepp as minister, and two men as deacons. Since the Brethren could not very well call upon the "old" Mennonites, from whom they had just separated, to perform this function, Oncken complied with their request. In the controversy that resulted, some of the Brethren claimed that since Oncken was a Baptist, those ordained by him were now also Baptists. To add to the difficulty, a Baptist had ordained a Mennonite elder, even though at that time Baptist polity admitted of no such office. Obviously, the act of the laying on of hands in ordination was believed to have affected the candidate in some way. No one seemed to be quite sure what had happened, if indeed anything had happened at all. Over one hundred years later, evangelicals still have no carefully articulated doctrine of ordination, though traditionally they lay hands on their candidates for office in the church. Why they do so and what the rite is intended to signify is the theme of this inquiry.

It is generally assumed that ordination with the imposition of hands for induction to the office of pastor or elder has both scriptural warrant and practical merit. It has been customary in the history of the church, and is the accepted practice throughout Christendom. "Whom should we ordain?" is the question discussed—a question based on the assumption that the rite has biblical precedent, if not command. But has it? Has the church in fact laid hands on its officers since apostolic times?

Ordination could hardly be termed a major doctrine of the faith. When it is recalled, however, that the "hand" of God signifies his power, and that the symbolic act of the imposition of hands is invariably a part of ordination, the implications for the doctrine of the church become apparent. A reexamination of the assumptions that underlie this rite of the church may well help to clarify many of the issues that have arisen in connection with spiritual gifts and their relationship to ministry as a whole. May God give us the grace and courage to bring our forms and traditions under the surveillance of Scripture, so that the "hand" of God may again move mightily through his divine agency, the church, to redeem for himself a people to his glory.

It is difficult to express adequately my thanks to those who have graciously encouraged me in this venture in spite of the topic chosen, and in spite of the fact that I cannot claim professional status as a theologian. It is even more difficult to express gratitude to those whose coolness heightened my interest in the subject of ordination. Through it all, the study has proved most rewarding personally. I feel that through their writings, I have been privileged to make the acquaintance of Christians whose love for the truth of God has surpassed all denominational and temporal barriers. It is fitting also that I acknowledge Professors Larry Perkins and Jack Graham, who provided valuable assistance in the initial stages of this work at the thesis level, and to Pat Doidge and Claudia Tinck, who helped with the typing. My deepest gratitude is reserved for my husband Ed; without his loving support and persistent encouragement this book would not even have been attempted.

—MARJORIE WARKENTIN

ABBREVIATIONS

BAG	*A Greek-English Lexicon of the New Testament and Other Early Christian Literature*
Ant	Josephus, *Antiquities of the Jews*
b	Babylonian Talmud
CQR	*Church Quarterly Review*
DCA	*Dictionary of Christian Antiquities*, vol. I
E.H.	Eusebius, *Ecclesiastical History*, vols. I and II
E.T.	English translation
EvanQ	*Evangelical Quarterly*
ExposT	*Expository Times*
HERE	*Hastings' Encyclopedia of Religion & Ethics*
HTR	*Harvard Theological Review*
Institutes	John Calvin, *Institutes of the Christian Religion*
Int	*Interpretation*
j	Jerusalem Talmud
JE	*Jewish Encyclopedia*
JEH	*Journal of Ecclesiastical History*
JETS	*Journal of the Evangelical Theological Society*
JSS	*Journal of Semitic Studies*
JTS	*Journal of Theological Studies*
Judaica	*Encyclopedia Judaica*
KJV	King James Version
LXX	*Septuagint*
m	*The Mishnah*
ME	*Mennonite Encyclopedia*
MT	Massoretic Text
NASB	New American Standard Bible
NBD	*New Bible Dictionary*
NCE	*New Catholic Encyclopaedia*
NEB	New English Bible

NIDNTT	*The New International Dictionary of New Testament Theology*
NIV	New International Version
ODCC	*Oxford Dictionary of the Christian Church*
RSV	Revised Standard Version
SacraM	*Sacramentum Mundi*
Sanh.	Sanhedrin (Mishnaic tractate)
Seeburg	*The History of Doctrines*, vols. I and II
Sir.	Sirach (Apocrypha)
SJT	*Scottish Journal of Theology*
TDNT	*The Theological Dictionary of the New Testament*
Theol	*Theology*
ZPEB	*The Zondervan Pictorial Encyclopedia of the Bible*

INTRODUCTION

The reader who has glanced at the table of contents of this book may well wonder with what he or she is getting involved. From Moses to Timothy? From Sinai to the present? Perhaps an explanation is in order.

The author has deliberately chosen an interdisciplinary approach to the subject of ordination as the only procedure likely to be able to bring to light the assumptions that lie under a rite that has been practiced in the Christian church for almost two thousand years. All kinds of suppositions about ordination abound. It is thought that Jesus ordained his disciples, that the rite has been practiced continuously since apostolic times, that it has scriptural warrant, that it confers on the recipient a special "character" that remains with him or her for life, that it protects the church from heresy, that only the ordained should administer the ordinances, that it transmits "grace" for office, that it does *not* transmit "grace" for office, that it conveys authority, that it conveys nothing whatsoever, and so on. The Scriptures of the New Testament are called upon to substantiate many of these assumptions, but contradictory doctrines continue to coexist. For example, a strong case can be built for the transmission of "grace" for office in the church through prayer and the laying on of hands if we select our Scripture carefully (2 Tim. 1:6), remove the text from its historical setting (the Paul/Timothy relationship), and then view it through the ecclesiologies of the later Fathers and Thomas Aquinas. Should the times and circumstances dictate, however, the doctrine can be modified, as happened following the Reformation. The Reformers claimed 1 Tim. 4:14 as an indication that ordination was a function of the presbytery. This did not satisfy the Separatists, and so a totally different rationale for the ordination of church officers emerged. Acts 13:1–3 was the text chosen, and there was, for the most part, silence on 1 Tim. 4:14 and 2 Tim. 1:6. Paul and Bar-

1

nabas were already prophets and teachers in the church at Antioch
(Acts 13:1) and were about to set out on a different type of service.
It is now possible, it was said, to see ordination as merely "recognition" or "commissioning." There is, therefore, no transmission of
"grace" in the laying on of hands. It is not asked why there is no
mention of hands being laid on others who go out on similar missions; rather, it is sufficient that a theology of ordination has been
formulated that is compatible with a truly Protestant doctrine of
the ministry. Results achieved by such selectivity leave much to
be desired.

This book, then, attempts a synthesis of the evidence from
historical, exegetical, and theological sources. The imposition of
hands for induction to office originated in the time of Moses and
was (apparently) becoming customary in first-century rabbinic Judaism. The New Testament rite can be understood only if these
factors are taken into account. So also, the use (and abuse) of the
rite of ordination throughout the history of the church has much
to teach us. It is hoped that the convergent testimony from these
sources may help to separate fact from fiction. This inquiry makes
no claim to being exhaustive.[1] If it can clarify the relationship
between ordination, the laying on of hands, and office, it will have
achieved its purpose.

Ordination is accepted almost universally as a legitimate rite
of the church, but attempts to define its significance reveal the
uncertain foundations on which it is based. Among Baptists it is
"the setting apart of a person divinely called to a work of special
ministration in the church,"[2] it "empowers a man to administer the
ordinances,"[3] it is recognition of a call,[4] or it "commissions him for
service."[5] Others define it as "an impressive sign of the apostolic

---

1. The details of ritual and some of the finer theological distinctions have
been omitted. So also have the rites of the eastern churches, since the influence
of their ritual on western ordination practices has been negligible. The Pauline
origin of the so-called Pastoral Epistles has been assumed. The texts that mention the laying on of hands in 1 and 2 Tim. can be elucidated without arguing
the question of authorship.

2. A. H. Strong, *Systematic Theology* (Old Tappan, NJ: Fleming H. Revell,
1907), p. 910.

3. W. R. McNutt, *Polity and Practice in Baptist Churches* (Philadelphia:
Judson Press, 1935), p. 81.

4. Robert G. Torbet, *A History of the Baptists*, rev. ed. (Valley Forge:
Judson Press, 1969), p. 56.

5. "Guidelines for Uniform Procedure Concerning Ordination and Recognition for North American Baptist General Conference Churches," *North
American Baptist General Conference Handbook* (n.p., n.d.).

succession of the pastorate,"[6] or as that which "confers spiritual authority which limits the ecclesiastical theologumenon of the priesthood of all believers,"[7] or simply as that which "qualifies a man for office in the church."[8] For our purposes, ordination will denote installation in office (i.e., a position of responsibility) accompanied by the imposition of hands on the head of the candidate. Since (with a few minor exceptions) the laying on of hands has been a part of ordination throughout history, this motif will be permitted to limit the treatment of the subject matter.[9]

The English word "ordain" may be traced to the Latin *ordo* (which translates the Greek τάξις), through the late Latin *ordinare*,[10] the Old French *ordener*, and then to the *ordeinen* of Middle English.[11] In secular use τάξις frequently implies orderly succession. In the New Testament it occurs only at Luke 1:8 in this sense. Its frequent use in Hebrews does not connote degree of authority[12] but refers to the difference in kind of the priesthoods of Aaron and Melchizedek (Heb. 5:6, 10; 6:20; 7:11, 17, 21). A distinction between the *ordinatio* of the priest and the *consecratio* of the bishop was not made until the twelfth century.

The term "church" will be used to designate a visible com-

---

6. Hans Küng, *The Church* (E.T., New York: Sheed & Ward, 1967), p. 433.

7. Eric Wolf, "Church Constitutions: Protestantism," *SacraM*, p. 1302.

8. *ODCC*, p. 1005.

9. H. Bender, "Ordination," *ME* IV:73. According to Edward T. Hiscox (*The New Directory for Baptist Churches* [Philadelphia: American Baptist Publication Society, 1894], p. 364), Thomas Hall, Jr., was ordained by his father and others by the lifting up of their right hands and prayer. In Hutterite ordination, hands were sometimes placed on the shoulder of the candidate "as evidence in the name of our Lord Christ and the power of God, that the office and the duty to serve in the word of the Lord will be trusted on you and burdened on you" (John A. Hostetler, *Hutterite Society* [Baltimore: Johns Hopkins Univ. Press, 1974], p. 344). Deviations from the customary mode of the imposition of hands will not be discussed in this work. "Consecration," a term used in the induction of a bishop, also included the laying on of hands and prayer and so will be treated as roughly synonymous with "ordination."

10. *Ordinare* and *ordinatio* were Roman technical terms for the appointment of civil functionaries; Tertullian (c. A.D. 160–230) used these terms of the appointment of clergy, monks, and abbots. See E. Hatch, "Ordination," *DCA*, p. 1502.

11. "Ordain," *The Random House College Dictionary*. "Ordain" was used in two senses in Middle English: (1) to put in order, arrange; (2) to appoint, decree, destine. By the middle of the sixteenth century, meaning (1) had become obsolete. Of the seven variations of meaning (2), most had fallen into disuse by the end of the seventeenth century. Those with a religious or ecclesiastical connotation have been kept alive to the present. Consult the *Shorter Oxford English Dictionary*, "ordain."

12. *BAG*, p. 811.

munity of those who profess to be followers of Christ, or an organized group of such communities. Since this term has such a wide
spectrum of meanings, the context must determine the shade of
meaning intended.

Due to the nature of the subject matter, it has been difficult
to avoid what may be, for some, emotionally loaded terms. "Sacrament" is a case in point, especially when used in connection with
ordination. Seeburg defines a sacrament as any symbolic act in
which the recipient is the object of "real objective exertions of divine energy."[13] This is a valid theological concept and expresses a
truth with which we must concern ourselves, though "sacrament"
may not be a biblical term.

Anachronisms have not been entirely unavoidable, either. To
speak, for example, of the ordination of Timothy in reference to
the events of 1 Tim. 4:14 and 2 Tim. 1:6 may, for the modern reader,
introduce connotations not justified by the texts; ordination is,
however, a brief and convenient way of speaking of these events.
In this connection it should also be pointed out that familiarity
among English readers with the KJV tends to color the whole
subject of ordination. The translators of this version have used
"ordain" for twenty-one different Hebrew and Greek words.[14] It is
quite evident that seventeenth-century ecclesiastical understanding influenced the choice of "ordain" in some of these instances. In
1 Tim. 2:7 Paul is said to have been "ordained" (ἐτέθην) a preacher.
This is the common verb τίθημι, to put or place. Also, our Lord is
said to have "ordained" the Twelve (Mark 3:14), but this is the verb
ποιεῖν, to make or do. Modern translators have avoided "ordain"
in these instances but the influence of the old translation persists.

Further confusion has been introduced into the understanding
of ordination by the use of "ordain" (RSV; KJV has "consecrate")
to translate יָד מִלֵּא, millē' yāḏ, "to fill the hand" (Exod. 28:41; 29:29,
33, 35; Lev. 8:33; Num. 3:3, etc.), a phrase used in the consecration
of Aaron to the priesthood,[15] but never used in connection with the
ordination of the Levites or other ceremonies involving the laying
on of hands. The use of "ordain" or even "consecrate" in this context
tends to blur the distinction between the rites of induction of the
priests and the rites of induction of the Levites, so that any distinction between the two is seen as one of degree rather than one
of kind. Since the laying on of hands did not occur in the instal-

---

13. Seeburg I:322.
14. "Ordain," *Young's Analytical Concordance to the Bible*.
15. T. F. Torrance, "Consecration and Ordination," *SJT* 11 (1958), p. 226.

lation of the priests, yet is a practice associated with ordination, the use of "ordain" for *millē' yāḏ* by the translators of the RSV (and the NASB) has contributed to the assumption that the priests of the Old Testament cult were ordained, i.e., that hands were laid on them in induction to office. Since the Old Testament priesthood has been consummated in Jesus Christ, the distinction is an important one. In assuming that hands were laid on Aaron in ordination, the laying on of hands is seen as incorporated in the Aaronic priesthood, and hence also in Christ's. Even though hands were not laid on the apostles (except Paul in Acts 13:1–3), this element is appropriated as that which gives apostolic authority to ordained church officers. In other words, a measure of Christ's mediatorial office is transferred by the laying on of hands to "the ministry." Thus, a mediatorial office is introduced between the believer and his Lord.[16]

This inquiry follows an historical-exegetical-theological sequence. Part I traces the history of ordination from the time of Moses to the present.[17] It explores the uses of the laying-on-of-hands motif in connection with office in the Old Testament, notes the purposes for which the rabbis later used this symbolic act, and then traces the rite through those confessions in the history of the church whose theology and traditions are germane to practices in twentieth-century Protestantism. In Part II the New Testament texts that have a bearing on the imposition of hands in induction to office are examined in their historical settings, and their function as part of the whole witness of Scripture to this subject is assessed. The theological questions anticipated in the historical and exegetical sections constitute Part III. Present ordination practices are discussed in the light of the findings of Parts I and II, and are evaluated in the context of a doctrine of the church that sees διακονία, service, as the guiding principle in the structuring of New Covenant communities. There remains much to be done, however. It is hoped that this study will serve as a catalyst to stimulate others to carry on where it has left off.

---

16. *Ibid.,* p. 229.
17. The laying on of hands in the apostolic age is omitted in the historical survey but is examined in detail in Chapters 7–11.

Part I

HISTORICAL OVERVIEW

Chapter 1

ORDINATION: OLD TESTAMENT ORIGINS

Old Testament references to the laying on of hands occur in various contexts: in blessing (Gen. 48:14 MT, שִׁית, *šît*); in sacrifice (Lev. 4:4 etc., MT, סָמַךְ, *sāmak*); in stoning for blasphemy (Lev. 24:14 MT, *sāmak*); in induction into office (Num. 8:10 MT, *sāmak*); and in commissioning for a special task (Num. 27:23; Deut. 34:9 MT, *sāmak*). Unlike the New Testament, the Old Testament references do not occur in the context of healing. The imposition of hands does, however, play an indispensable role in the sacrifices of the cult.

The basic meaning of the act of laying on of hands is demonstrated in the ritual performed on the Day of Atonement (Lev. 16). Aaron lays both hands on the head of the scapegoat and confesses over it all the sins of the people (Lev. 16:21). The goat then bears away all these sins. Thus there is a real transference of the confessed guilt through the laying on of hands. This is also seen in Israel's act of blessing his grandsons (Gen. 48:8–22), where the distinction between his right hand and his left hand indicates a real transference from Israel to Ephraim and from Israel to Manasseh. A comparison with other instances (e.g., Lev. 24:14; Num. 8:10; 27:18) shows us that the laying on of hands in the Old Testament always symbolizes a real transfer from one person to another, with the thing transferred depending on the occasion.[1]

The Old Testament gives us many examples of the various procedures that characterize the induction into office of priests, kings, prophets, and other leaders. Aaron and his sons were consecrated to the priesthood according to the regulations given to

---

1. Note also the interpretative activity: Num. 27:20 *hôḏ*, majesty (MT); Deut. 34:9 *ḥāḵām*, wisdom (MT); Num. 27:20 δόξης, glory (LXX); Deut. 34:9 συνέσεως, knowledge (LXX).

Moses at Sinai: ritual washings, the donning of special garments, anointings, and the accompanying sacrificial rituals (Exod. 29). The priests pressed their hands on the heads of the animals, but they themselves did not receive the imposition of hands, although the expression "to fill the hand" (*millēʾ yāḏ*) is often used in induction to priestly office.[2] Kings were anointed as part of the enthronement ceremony (1 Sam. 9:16; 10:1; 15:1, 17; Judg. 9:8, 15), but although the anointing signified the communication of authority (כָּבֹד, *kāḇôḏ*), the laying on of hands was not a part of the making of a king. The prophets often received their call to office directly from Yahweh. Jeremiah's call took the form of a dialogue with Yahweh, who told him that his mission was foreordained. "Before you were born I consecrated you," says Yahweh, who then touches Jeremiah's mouth. In addition, the prophet received two confirmatory visions (Jer. 1:5, 9, 10, 11–13). Yahweh also spoke to Moses when he commanded him to gather together seventy elders (Num. 11:16ff.) in order to fulfill an administrative need. "The LORD came down to him in the cloud and spoke to him, and took some of the spirit that was upon him, and put it upon the seventy elders; and when the spirit rested on them they prophesied. But they did so no more" (Num. 11:25). We do not read that prophets, priests, kings, or elders received the laying on of hands for the purpose of either endowment or installation into office. This rite was reserved for practice only within the Old Testament cult. There is one exception to this, however—Moses' ordination of Joshua.

THE ORDINATION OF JOSHUA

Joshua, "the son of Nun, a young man" (Exod. 33:11), stood in very special relationship to Moses, a relationship intimately connected with the giving of the Law at Sinai. "So Moses rose with his servant Joshua, and Moses went up into the mountain of God" (Exod. 24:13; cf. 32:17). When the Lord spoke to Moses in the tent of meeting Joshua was there (Exod. 33:11), and he was with Moses when the elders prophesied (Num. 11:28–30).

When the time came for Joshua to assume leadership, Moses

2. For example, 1 Kgs. 13:33. The failure to make a distinction between ordination with the laying on of hands and other forms of induction to office such as the priestly rite of the "filling of the hand" causes confusion. "Ordain" is often used when nothing more than "appointment" is meant; cf. Mark 3:14; Tit. 1:5.

laid hands on him.[3] This act had cultic overtones, though Joshua was not a Levite (Num. 13:8). It was, however, facing a task of critical importance in the history of redemption, a task that would require great courage (Josh. 1:6, 7; cf. 1 Tim. 6:12; 2 Tim. 2:1, 3). At the command of God, Moses was to appoint Joshua to oversee[4] the congregation, and to indicate this by placing his hand on him in their presence (Num. 27:17-19). Joshua was to lead his nation into the Promised Land, a commission distinct from Moses', even though implicit in his responsibility of leading the people was the prophetic function of custodian of the covenant mediated through Moses (cf. Josh. 24). Joshua was not *the* lawgiver, nor would he speak face to face with God (Deut. 34:10); the Deuteronomist takes pains to preserve the primacy of Moses. Joshua would "go out before them and come in before them" and "lead them out and bring them in" that they be not like "sheep which have no shepherd" (Num. 27:17). These expressions connote military leadership (cf. 1 Sam. 18:13-16; 1 Kgs. 22:17; cf. Acts 1:21). Joshua was a kairotic figure, a man with a momentous task.

By the imposition of hands, Moses gave public testimony to the divine appointment of Joshua as Israel's leader, that the people might obey him (Num. 27:20). Joshua, already a man of spiritual endowment (Num. 11:25; cf. Gen. 41:38), received some of Moses' majesty (הוד, *hôḏ* MT; δόξα, glory, LXX).[5] Moses' majesty is, perhaps, a reference to the divine authority conferred on Moses at Sinai when God gave him the Law for Israel.[6] "Majesty" (*hôḏ*) refers to kingly position (Ps. 45:3, 4 MT; Jer. 22:18 MT),[7] and de-

---

3. In Num. 27:18 the Lord instructs Moses, "Take Joshua ... and lay your hand upon him," but in Num. 27:23 and in Deut. 34:9 Moses is said to have laid his "hands" upon Joshua. Apparently, there is no distinction being made between the singular and the plural in this case. A distinction arises when "right" or "left" hand is specified (see Gen. 48:13-20).

4. Num. 27:16 (LXX), ἐπισκεψάσθω, a word denoting service. See L. Coenen, "Bishop, Presbyter, Elder," *NIDNTT* II:189.

5. Ben Sirach says of the famous men of Israel, "The Lord apportioned to them great glory, his majesty from the beginning" (Sir. 44:2). The Lord made Moses "equal in glory to the holy ones" (45:2), and Joshua is said to have been "the successor of Moses in prophesying" (46:1); he was "glorious ... when he lifted his hands and stretched out his hands against the cities" (46:2). Philo (*On the Virtues* xi:68) quotes Moses as saying to the congregation, "here is a successor to take charge of you."

6. Exod. 34:29-35; 2 Cor. 3:7; Moses' face shines with the "glory of God."

7. "Majesty" (*hôḏ* MT) is used in Zech. 6:13 in reference to Joshua, the priestly Messiah. The veneration that surrounded the figure of Moses is evident in the writings of Philo of Alexandria. To Philo, Moses is the perfect God-king who can not in himself be diminished. See David R. Cartlidge and David L. Dungan, eds., *Documents for the Study of the Gospels* (Philadelphia: Fortress Press, 1980), pp. 253ff.

notes the authority by which a king rules. It is used in parallel with עֹז, 'ōz and כֹּחַ, kōaḥ ("strength," "power") in contexts suggesting the might of God, expressing God's power in creation (Ps. 104:1; 148:13 MT), and characterizing his work (Ps. 45:4; 111:3; 145:5 MT). It is transferable to his creatures (Hos. 14:6; Zech. 10:3 MT). Thus David rejoices in the hôḏ that God has given him (Ps. 21:5 MT). The writer of Deut. 34:9 interprets the hôḏ Joshua receives from Moses as none other than "wisdom," חָכָם, ḥāḵām, the characteristic of the prophets, the חֲכָמִים, ḥᵃḵāmîm, the wise men of Israel who spoke by inspired utterance.[8] Joshua was already a man "in whom is the spirit"; this was additional power to lead the Israelites into the Promised Land. The Covenant people publicly witnessed God's choice; Joshua's authority to wield power was divinely authorized. When Moses instructs Joshua to stand before the high priest Eleazar, in the presence of the people (Num. 27:22), the dualistic character of his ordination is demonstrated. Joshua is responsible to Yahweh through Eleazar; he also bears responsibility to the people. The "church in the wilderness" is now prepared to take Canaan (Acts 7:38).

Moses placed his hands on Joshua to equip him for a unique task, one that would be required of no one else in the history of the Old Covenant peoples. Through the hands of Moses Joshua received grace, divine enablement, that he might be instrumental in the salvation of Israel. The imposition of hands was not mere symbolism; God chose to bestow his grace through the hands of Moses.[9]

There is no evidence that Joshua laid hands on a successor or that Moses was establishing a pattern of office.[10] In the Old Testament narratives, kings and prophets may be mediators of the Covenant, but the laying on of hands is not an indication of this office. Joshua's ordination was unique, and was for a specific his-

8. N. Hillyer, "Scribe," NIDNTT III:479.

9. "Hand" is paralleled with "spirit," "understanding," and "power," in Job 26:12, 13. "Hand" and "spirit" become synonymous in Ezekiel. "He put forth the form of a hand, and took me by a lock of my head; and the Spirit lifted me up between earth and heaven ..." (Ezek. 8:3).

10. Lloyd Neve (The Spirit of God in the Old Testament [Tokyo: Seibunsha, 1972], p. 87) comments: "Joshua is provided with the divine charisma which means the ability and insight necessary to carry out his assigned task. Because Num. 27:13 [sic] does not speak of his receiving the spirit but assumes that Joshua already possesses it, one may conclude that the Biblical writer considered Joshua to be one of the seventy elders in Num. 11:25 who had received the spirit (cf. Num. 11:29)."

torical purpose at a critical moment in the progress of salvation history.

THE ORDINATION OF THE LEVITES

The Levites were the priestly tribe of the sons of Jacob, though not all Levites were priests (Judg. 19:1). They had no inheritance in the land, for the Lord was their inheritance (Deut. 10:9). The Levites were chosen by God to replace the firstborn in the stream of redemption, thus placing them at the very core of salvation history. Again and again we read that it is Yahweh, the God of the Covenant, who has taken the Levites from among the people of Israel to be his own special possession (Num. 3:12, 41, 45; 8:14, 16; 18:6). "Behold, I have taken the Levites from among the people of Israel, instead of every firstborn that opens the womb among the people of Israel. The Levites shall be mine" (Num. 3:12). This statement is repeated when they are ordained to service.

In the ordination, the Levites are first cleansed: "sprinkle the water of expiation upon them," Yahweh instructs Moses (Num. 8:7). Actually, this is "water of sin," that is, water to remove sin;[11] the cleansing (טָהַר, *tihar*) of the Levites is a cultic expression signifying ceremonial purity. The congregation is then to place (*sāmak*) their hands on them. By this act, the obligation of the whole people to serve Yahweh is transferred to the Levites. The Levites in turn accept the responsibility for serving the people. Atonement is then made for the sins of the Levites. Through the imposition of hands on the sacrificial animals, the Levites present themselves to the Lord as a living sacrifice well pleasing to him. It is only by presenting an offering for their own atonement[12] that the Levites can then be presented as a wave offering, that is, as a gift to Yahweh. The service that the Levites are now ready to perform has a dual application. They serve Yahweh through the high priest Aaron, and they perform a priestly service for the Covenant people (Num. 3:5–7; 18:3ff.). The Levites are scattered throughout the tribes that they might teach the law to all Israel.[13]

Thus, in ordination the Levites assumed the responsibilities of the firstborn. Their service was priestly service to Yahweh the

11. C. F. Keil and F. Delitzsch, *Commentary on the Old Testament*, vol. I: *The Pentateuch* (Grand Rapids: Eerdmans, 1971 reprint), III:47.

12. Martin Noth, *Numbers, A Commentary* (Philadelphia: Westminster Press, 1968), p. 68.

13. Deut. 33:10; Num. 35:1ff. See also T. F. Torrance, "Consecration and Ordination," *SJT* 11 (1958), p. 226.

ruler of the theocracy, and to his subjects. This service could only be performed in conjunction with their own atonement, for only then were they and the service they performed acceptable to Yahweh. Through them, as the sacrificial offering of the congregation, the Covenant people were also accepted. The laying on of hands is an indispensable part of this pericope. Because of it, the Levites could function vicariously for the congregation as a whole.[14]

SUMMARY

Induction into office in the theocracy of the Old Testament took diverse forms. In only two instances was the imposition of hands a component of investiture: in Moses' ordination of Joshua and in the consecration of the Levites. In both cases, hands are laid on at the express command of God.

Through the hand of Moses Joshua was inbued with power from on high to lead the Israelites in taking the Promised Land. The occasion is historically unique and the act is sacramental. The Levites also accepted responsibility when hands were laid on them by the people of God. Through them the nation as a whole was sanctified and made acceptable to Yahweh. Not only were the sins of the Levites themselves atoned for in the sacrificial ritual involving the laying on of hands for the transfer of guilt, but through them the whole nation was cleansed. The Levites became representatives of the firstborn of Israel.

Levites did not ordain more Levites; the office was theirs by birth. Neither did Joshua ordain a successor; the essence of his commissioning lay in its temporal and historical significance. There is no laying on of hands for succession in the Old Testament.

For the people of the Old Covenant, the primary reference of the laying on of hands consisted in its function in the atonement for sin. So long as the Temple stood and sacrifices were continued, the Israelites would associate the rite first of all with the cult. The fact that the Levites and Joshua had received the imposition of hands was secondary, though the latter incident may have been kept alive by the traditions of the rabbis. These facts need to be kept in mind when we meet this motif in the Book of Acts and the Pastorals. The question of the observance of the Law was a burning issue in the early churches and underlies much of what Luke has to say. Our concern with the laying on of hands for office holding

14. J. K. Parratt, "The Laying on of Hands in the New Testament," *ExposT* 80 (1968–1969), p. 213.

in the church must not be permitted to exclude what was the primary import of the rite in the Old Testament. Furthermore, since the thought-world of the New Testament writers was permeated by the rabbinic traditions of their day, we must next inquire whether the imposition of hands for office holding was a practice in first-century Judaism.

Chapter 2

ORDINATION: RABBINIC TRADITIONS

Ordination practices in rabbinic Judaism are difficult to trace. We know that hands were laid on scribes in ordination, but whether this was customary in the first century is a matter of dispute. Did the imposition of hands always accompany the rite? What class of people was ordained, and what did ordination signify in Judaism?

EVIDENCE FOR FIRST-CENTURY ORDINATION

Many scholars believe that when scribes had attained a high level of proficiency in the interpretation of the Torah and the oral traditions they were ordained and became known as sages, and were then eligible for office in the Sanhedrin. Our sources, mainly the Mishnah and its codifications, permit us to speak only of the "scribes of the Pharisees" (Acts 23:9). The Sadducees also had their scribes, but the strength of this party rested in the lay and priestly aristocracy who, to a diminishing extent, made up the controlling element in the Sanhedrin. With the ascendancy of the Pharisaic party during the period 76 B.C. to A.D. 70, and with their growing popularity with the general public, the scribes became more and more influential. When had they felt the need for the "authority of Moses" that ordination would imply?

Modern authors usually place the origin of rabbinic ordination before the birth of Christ, though Newman would argue for the late fourth century A.D.[1] Lauterbach suggests that it became cus-

1. Leon Morris, *Ministers of God* (Downers Grove: InterVarsity Press, 1964), p. 70, n. 2, quoting J. Newman, *Semikhah* (Manchester: Manchester University Press, 1950), p. 102. Dr. Eduard Lohse has given us a thorough study of the early rite of rabbinical ordination in *Die Ordination im Spätjudentum und im Neuen Testament* (Göttingen, 1951). He argues that the early church

tomary during the reign of Alexander Janneus (103–76 B.C.).[2] Writing in *Judaica*, Rothkoff traces the tradition back to Moses' ordination from that time.[3] Ehrhardt asserts that rabbis were installed by an enthronement ceremony, and the laying on of hands, if practiced at all, was at least kept in the background.[4]

As we can see from these various views, a careful assessment of the available evidence is essential. In spite of the tradition of Maimonides quoted in *Judaica*,[5] there is no evidence that ordination was practiced successively from the time of Moses. In fact, the class of theological scholar that we meet in mainstream Judaism, the scribe (of whom Ezra was the prototype),[6] originated during the Babylonian captivity, and gradually gained power and influence during the centuries following the building of the Second Temple. The Old Testament Scriptures appealed to in support of the succession tradition are Num. 11:16–17, 24–25 (Yahweh's selection of the seventy elders); Num. 27:22–23; Deut. 34:9 (Moses lays hands on Joshua). Moses says, "Bring to me seventy of Israel's elders who are known to you as leaders and officials among the people" (Num. 11:16 NIV). The LXX translates שֹׁטֵר, *šōṭēr* (official), as γραμματεύς, scribe. The laying on of hands is not mentioned in this incident, but under the terms of midrashic exegesis this omission is not a serious difficulty. That is, in two analogous texts, a particular consideration in one may be extended to the other as a general principle.[7] By this exegetical device, the laying on of hands becomes part of the ordination of elders, thus establishing a link with Moses.[8] According to Daube, "The idea evidently was that the chain linking each generation of Rabbis to the preceding one should under no circumstances be allowed to break—else tradition would never recover its full value."[9] The laying on of hands was, of course,

---

adopted the custom of the laying on of hands in ordination from the rabbis, filling it with new content. Arnold Ehrhardt takes issue with his contention in "Jewish and Christian Ordination," *JEH* 5 (1954), pp. 125–138. Until such time as ordination in early Judaism can be dated more exactly the question must remain open.

2. J. E. Lauterbach, "Ordination," *JE* IX:428f.

3. Aaron Rothkoff, "Semikhah," *Judaica* XIV:1139.

4. Ehrhardt, "Jewish and Christian Ordination," p. 130.

5. Maimonides, Yad Sanh. 4:21, quoted by Rothkoff in "Semikhah," p. 1139.

6. N. Hillyer, "Scribes," *NIDNTT* III:480.

7. Richard Longenecker, *Biblical Exegesis in the Apostolic Period* (Grand Rapids: Eerdmans, 1975), p. 34; Middoth #5, כְּלָל וּפְרָט, *kᵉlāl ûpᵉrāṭ*: the general and the particular; a particular rule may be extended into a general principle.

8. Everett Ferguson, "Jewish and Christian Ordination: Some Observations," *HTR* 56 (1963), p. 17.

9. D. Daube, "'Ἐξουσία in Mark 1:22, 27," *JTS* 39 (1938), p. 47.

an essential part of the cultic sacrificial ritual, and had been since the giving of the Law. Yet, as we have already seen, there is no evidence (except in the laying on of hands on the Levites and Joshua) that it was a part of induction into office, not even of the elders.

We are almost totally dependent on the talmudic literature for information on ordination in the intertestamental period. Yet these sources are notoriously difficult to evaluate.[10] As they represent only the Pharisaic stream of Judaism, it is necessary to be alert to the possibility of theological bias.[11] During this time Jewish society was threatened by the infiltration of Hellenism, and by the political domination of Rome. In the Pharisees' struggle for the control of the Sanhedrin, ordination, representing a link with the authority of Moses, was a valuable asset to claim. For all its concern with the minutiae of the Law and ritual purity, the priesthood was corrupt. Ignorance,[12] nepotism, and violence[13] were rife. Under such circumstances, one might expect the traditions to reflect a disproportionate emphasis on the credentials of the leaders of the Pharisaic bloc in the Sanhedrin. Actually, however, mention of ordination in either the Mishnah or the Talmud is rare, and the laying on of hands occurs as often in the context of sacrifice as of ordination.

Several references to appointment to office with the laying on

10. Adin Steinsaltz (*The Essential Talmud* [E.T., New York: Bantam, 1976], p. 37) claims that "Many *halakhot* and *mishnayot* were introduced into the new compilation [R. Judah Ha-Nasi's, c. A.D. 200] in their original form, sometimes accompanied by a later explanation and sometimes unchanged."

11. Ehrhardt ("Jewish and Christian Ordination," p. 127) comments: ". . . the Jewish scholars, the only surviving group from which members of the Sanhedrin were elected, obtained the leadership in the Synagogue, very largely because of the genius of one man, Aqiba, and the school which he founded. . . . For this reason it becomes necessary to test carefully the accounts of early ordinations in the Talmud to see whether they have the purpose of safeguarding Aqiba's line of succession. For, if such be the case, they may be suspected of introducing the paraphernalia of a later ordination rite into this early period in order to enhance in this way the impeccability of Aqiba's succession line." Jacob Neusner warns that the Mishnah has "a vigorous polemic, an urgent apologetic, which it proposes to set forth. Everything is subordinated to the polemic and apologetic" ("The Use of Later Rabbinic Evidence for the Study of First Century Pharisaism," in *Approaches to Ancient Judaism: Theory and Practice*, ed. William S. Green [Missoula: Scholars Press, 1978], p. 222).

12. M. Yoma 1:6.

13. Joachim Jeremias, *Jerusalem in the Time of Jesus* (E.T., London: SCM Press, 1969), p. 99.

of hands (סְמִיכָה, $s^e mik\bar{a}h$) are of particular interest.[14] A typical admission into the Sanhedrin prior to A.D. 70[15] is described in m. Sanh. 4:4:

> Before them [the Sanhedrin] sat three rows of disciples of the Sages, and each knew his proper place. If they needed to appoint [sāmak] another as judge they appointed him from the first row, and one from the second row came into the first row, and one from the third row came into the second. . . .

The b. Sanh. 13b mentions the סְמִיכוּת זְקֵנִים, $s^e mik\hat{u}t$ $z^e q\bar{e}n\hat{i}m$. This is generally taken as a reference to ordination by elders,[16] not ordination to create elders.[17] Ordination of elders became customary after the destruction of Jerusalem. "Elder" then became a title of honor for theologians, and implied ordination.[18]

Evidence that ordination was an early occurrence is derived from the account of the ordination of the five pupils of R. Johanan b. Zakkai.[19] Even though some of the events in the life of R. Johanan have acquired a legendary aura, the pupils he is said to have ordained are historical persons who lived before A.D. 70.[20] One of these, Joshua b. Hananiah, was a chorister in the Temple, and later gave an eyewitness account of its destruction.[21] Another, Simon b. Nethaniel,[22] married the daughter of Gamaliel the Elder.[23]

---

14. *Sāmak* was not just a technical term for appointment, but included the laying on of hands. See Daube, "'Εξουσία in Mark 1:22, 27," p. 46, n. 1. Also, in b. Sanh. 13b discussion centers on how many are needed for the laying on of hands in a proper ordination ceremony.

15. Ferguson, "Jewish and Christian Ordination: Some Observations," p. 17.

16. Eduard Schweizer, *Church Order in the New Testament* (London: SCM, 1965), p. 190, n. 812; Ferguson, "Jewish and Christian Ordination," p. 14, n. 8.

17. Herman L. Strack and Paul Billerbeck, *Kommentar zum Neuen Testament aus Talmud und Midrash*, vol. II (Munich: C. H. Beck'sche, 1974), pp. 653ff., and David Daube, *The New Testament and Rabbinic Judaism* (London: Athlone Press, 1956), p. 244, both interpret this expression as ordination *to* eldership.

18. L. Coenen, "Bishop, Presbyter, Elder," *NIDNTT* I:196.

19. J. Sanh. 11:3.

20. According to Louis Finkelstein (*Pharisaism in the Making* [New York: Ktav, 1972], p. 122), these disciples are known to have contributed several *mishnayot* to the Pirke Aboth collection. This is not to say, however, that the account of their ordination in j. Sanh. 11:3 was not the addition of a later redactor.

21. C. Roth, "Joshua b. Hananiah," *Judaica* X:279.

22. Israel Burgansky, "Simon b. Nethaniel," *Judaica* XIV:1562.

23. Jeremias, *Jerusalem*, p. 219. Jeremias says "granddaughter." There is some confusion as to the identity of the Gamaliel involved.

The other pupils whom R. Johanan ordained are known to have been his disciples before the destruction of the Temple.[24]

Hugo Mantel describes two judiciary bodies in existence during the period of the Second Temple.[25] Into one of these, the Sanhedrin, the scribes (sages) were ordained. Mantel suggests that the laying on of hands was a form of blessing that the sage might be successful.[26] The word "sage" (ḥākām) was an official term used of an ordained teacher. M. Yoma 1:16 reads: "If he is a sage he may expound." This throws light on Mark 1:22: "Those in the synagogue were astonished at his [Jesus'] teaching, for he taught them as one who had authority, and not as the scribes." Daube interprets "scribes" as a reference to the unordained scholars, the γραμματεῖς, those not yet proficient in the Torah and the oral traditions.[27] When Jesus exorcises the man with the unclean spirit, they are again amazed. "What is this? A new teaching with authority?"[28] According to Daube, this expression is a reference to "the privilege, enjoyed only by a proper Rabbi, of introducing novel doctrines."[29] Perhaps also Matt. 11:25 refers to these ordained teachers, the ḥᵃkāmîm. At that time Jesus declared, "I thank thee Father, Lord of heaven and earth, that thou hast hidden these things from the wise and understanding and revealed them to babes." Again, Jesus says, "The scribes and the Pharisees sit on Moses' seat, so practice and observe whatever they tell you, but not what they do. . . . They bind heavy burdens hard to bear . . ." (Matt. 23:2, 3). This may possibly refer to the "binding and loosing" that was part of the official function of the ordained rabbis in the Sanhedrin.[30] Daube comments:

> The Midrash [on Num. 27:18ff.] explains that Joshua was thereby permitted to enunciate teachings, deliver judgments and sit on a special chair like Moses—obviously the privileges resulting from ordination in New Testament times.[31]

This may, of course, have been some kind of "enthronement," and not necessarily ordination with the laying on of hands. We read in

24. C. Roth, "Johanan b. Zakkai," *Judaica* X:147.

25. Hugo Mantel, "Ordination and Appointment in the Period of the Temple," *HTR* 57 (1964), p. 328.

26. *Ibid.*, p. 340.

27. Daube, "Ἐξουσία in Mark 1:22, 27," p. 45, but see also Hillyer, "Scribes," *NIDNTT* III:480.

28. Mark 1:27 (NASB). The RSV has "What is this? A new teaching! With authority he commands the unclean spirits and they obey him."

29. Daube, *New Testament and Rabbinic Judaism*, p. 206.

30. Jeremias, *Jerusalem*, p. 236; G. C. Berkouwer, *The Church* (Grand Rapids: Eerdmans, 1976), p. 211, n. 34.

31. Daube, *New Testament and Rabbinic Judaism*, p. 208.

John 7:14ff. that the Jews were amazed when Jesus taught in the Temple, being an unlearned man, a μὴ μεμαθηκώς. According to Jeremias "a man who had not completed a rabbinic education was known as μὴ μεμαθηκώς (John 7:15) and he had no right to the privileges of an ordained teacher."[32] Thus, it cannot be proved from the New Testament that there was rabbinic ordination in the first century. There was, apparently, an authority structure of some kind, but the part that formal ordination played, if indeed it was used at this time, cannot be declared with certainty on the basis of present evidence.

Another possible witness to first-century rabbinic ordination with imposition of hands is linguistic in nature. Sāmak was a term used in the cult for the laying on of hands in animal sacrifice; it is unlikely that a society that knew it in this context would also use it for "appoint" unless the term included the idea of the laying on of hands.[33] In the Mishnah, sāmak was used in two contexts: in animal sacrifice[34] and in the ordination of a rabbi.[35] Although not in itself conclusive, mishnaic evidence cannot be totally discounted. Although this material was not codified until the end of the second century, it had, nevertheless, existed as a fixed oral tradition well before R. Judah the Patriarch put it in written form.[36] Sāmak was not used for the appointment of the delegate (שָׁלִיחַ, šālîaḥ) of the elders, or the "seven of the city,"[37] though one might well expect it in such contexts. If the rabbinic literature can be depended on, there is nothing anachronistic about the laying on of hands in appointment to office in first-century rabbinic Judaism. We should also note that sāmak was not used in connection with proselyte baptism, or in judicial appointment to the Beth-Din.[38] The sᵉmîkāh was, apparently, the prerogative of rabbinic ordination.

FIRST-CENTURY SCRIBES AND RABBINIC ORDINATION

The scribes first became a cohesive group in the second century B.C. through the pressure of Hellenization on Jewish culture and religion. At first, many of the priests were scribes,[39] but gradually

---

32. *Ibid.*, p. 236.
33. There were other terms used for appointment: פָּקַד, *pāqaḏ*, Num. 1:50; 3:10; or שִׂים, *sîm*, Num. 4:19.
34. M. Betzah 2:4; m. Hagigah 2:2; m. Menahoth 9:7ff.; etc.
35. M. Sanh. 4:4.
36. Steinsaltz, *Essential Talmud*, p. 37; H. Danby, "Introduction," *The Mishnah*, p. xxii.
37. T. F. Torrance, "Consecration and Ordination," *SJT* 11 (1958), p. 236.
38. Daube, *New Testament and Rabbinic Judaism*, p. 228.
39. Jeremias, *Jerusalem*, p. 133.

the division between the priesthood and the lay theologians wid-
ened. Soldiers, merchants, and even proselytes could become scribes
if they were zealous for the Law and were willing to devote themselves to it wholeheartedly.[40] A scribe attached himself to a teacher,
and when he was proficient in both Torah and traditions, and could
argue the *halakah* or the *haggadah* after the customary fashion,
his teacher could ordain him into the company of the scribes as an
ordained scholar or sage.[41] He became a teacher, a "servant of the
Torah."[42] He could also decide matters of a legal or ritual nature
and financial cases not involving fines.[43] The decisions of the sages
had the power to "bind or loose for all time."[44] "Rabbi," at first a
term of respect for one well versed in the Law, later became the
formal title of the sage.[45] Along with the priestly (Sadducean) and
lay aristocracy (the Elders), ordained scribes occupied seats in the
Sanhedrin. They were not a clerical group; they played no role in
the liturgical or sacerdotal life,[46] though they might be called on
to read the Torah in the synagogue.[47] Dimitrovsky says that these
rabbis

> appear to have been most reluctant to exert their influence in
> the area of worship and synagogue practice. ... The sages
> tended to worship and pray in the *yeshivot* rather than the
> synagogues, asserting that a place where Torah is studied has
> greater importance than one reserved only for prayers.[48]

For a rabbi, to be a Jew meant Torah and the traditions of
Torah. But even more than that, being a rabbi meant being a
successor of the prophets, and above all, a successor of the great
prophet Moses. The rabbis were not only custodians of the Law,
but also the possessors of the esoteric knowledge of the mysteries

40. *Ibid.*, pp. 234f.

41. M. Yoma 1:6; Ehrhardt ("Jewish and Christian Ordination," p. 113) expresses the opinion that such private ordination was a transient practice between A.D. 70 and A.D. 135 and was not the true origin of rabbinical ordination.
The "seventy" of the Sanhedrin would suggest that Jewish ordination has a
basis in the midrashic exegesis of Num. 11:16.

42. Strack-Billerbeck II:647.

43. Mantel, "Ordination and Appointment in the Period of the Temple,"
p. 328.

44. Jeremias, *Jerusalem*, p. 236.

45. Hershel Shanks, "Is the Title of 'Rabbi' Anachronistic in the Gospels?",
in *Exploring the Talmud*, ed. H. Dimitrovsky (New York: Ktav, 1976), p. 165.

46. Mantel, "Ordination and Appointment," p. 340.

47. Jacob Neusner, *There We Sat Down* (Nashville: Abingdon, 1972), p. 101.

48. Dimitrovsky, *Exploring the Talmud*, pp. xxf.

of God.[49] They looked upon themselves as the saviors of society,[50] the stewards of the secret revelations, to be administered by them only to the extent that the common folk had the capacity for understanding them.[51] The rabbis' stress on Torah led to the development of customs, rites, and practices unique to the rabbinical estate, thus setting that state apart as one enjoying special privileges and bearing special responsibilities.[52] Many of the rabbis abused the privileges of their office, so much so that Jesus could say of them:

> Woe to you, scribes and Pharisees, hypocrites! because you shut the kingdom of heaven against men; for you neither enter yourselves, nor allow those who would enter to go in. (Matt. 23:13)

The Judaism of the Pharisaic scribes was, in an age of messianic expectation, an alternate means of reconciliation between God and Israel. The scribes were concerned with ritual purity outside the Temple "as if they were priests."[53] " 'You shall be a kingdom of priests and a holy people' was taken literally."[54] Both the Torah and the oral Torah had been given to Moses at Sinai; the scribes were his successors and the interpreters of all Torah.[55] Thus after the fall of the Temple, the rabbis were ready to take over the role of the "new priests"[56] of Israel.

> Rabbinic Judaism claimed that it was possible to serve God not only through sacrifice, but also through study of Torah. A priest is in charge of the life of the community, but a new priest, the rabbi. The old sin-offerings still may be carried out through deeds of loving-kindness; indeed, when the whole Jewish people will fully carry out the teachings of the Torah, the Temple itself will be rebuilt.[57]

Study thus became the new ritual of Israel, and the *yeshivot* the new centers of the religious community. The rabbis had become the mediators of the revelation of God.

49. Jeremias, *Jerusalem*, p. 237. It was to these traditions that Paul fell heir; cf. Exod. 20:22 and 2 Cor. 12:1–4.

50. Nathaniel L. Gerber, "The Wise Man in Rabbinic Judaism and Stoic Philosophy," in *Exploring the Talmud*, ed. H. Dimitrovsky, p. 105.

51. Jeremias, *Jerusalem*, p. 239.

52. Neusner, *There We Sat Down*, p. 90.

53. Jacob Neusner, *Between Time and Eternity* (Encino, CA: Dickenson, 1975), p. 29.

54. *Ibid.* (Exod. 19:6).

55. *Ibid.*, p. 70.

56. *Ibid.*, p. 43.

57. *Ibid.*

What did scribes believe they received when hands were laid on them? The question has been much debated. The insistence that the hands be bare in the laying on of hands in animal sacrifice so that nothing was interposed between the hands of the one sacrificing and the head of the beast[58] would imply a sacramental understanding of the rite. Gavin observes that

> ... rudimentary and germinal sacramentalism in fact, even if it be not explicitly stated and formulated in theory, not only existed but flourished, as an essential part of the Jewish religion, from the Old Testament into Rabbinism.[59]

The use of material means was basic to Jewish religious practices. By means of externals, God initiated, achieved, and maintained the proper relationships between himself and man.[60] That is not to say, however, that the laying on of hands was thought to convey the divine Spirit:

> It is unlikely that the laying on of hands at Rabbinic ordination was commonly associated with possession of the Spirit. If so, the categorical saying about the cessation of the Spirit with the last prophets would be inexplicable.[61]

The important element in the ordination was the connection with Moses, who spoke "mouth to mouth" with Yahweh (Num. 12:8). The rabbis believed that Moses imparted some of his wisdom to Joshua in ordination, and that through succession they also received some of this Moses-wisdom. "Moses received the Law from Sinai and committed it to Joshua, and Joshua to the Elders, and the Elders to the Prophets"[62] and thence to themselves, the $h^a\underbar{k}\bar{a}m\hat{i}m$. Thus the rabbis, the ordained scribes, were the successors of Moses, the bearers of Torah and tradition. It was *they* who possessed the Moses-wisdom.

Ordination in early rabbinic Judaism had become a rite ad-

58. Rothkoff, "Semikhah," *Judaica* XIV:1140.

59. F. Gavin, *The Jewish Antecedents of the Christian Sacraments* (New York: Ktav, 1969), p. 5.

60. *Ibid.*, p. 24.

61. E. Sjöberg, "πνεῦμα," *TDNT* VI:386.

62. M. Aboth 1:1. An expanded version (R. Nathan's) based on oral tradition reads: "Through Moses the Torah was given at Sinai ... Joshua received it from Moses as it is written 'and thou shalt put some of thine honor upon him (Num. 27:20)' ... The elders received it from Joshua; the judges received it from the elders as it is written 'and now it came to pass in the days when the judges ruled' (1:1). The prophets received it from the judges ... Then Haggai, Zechariah and Malachi" (Finkelstein, *Pharisaism in the Making*, p. 146).

ministered to rabbinic scholars on the basis of intellectual proficiency, qualifying them for authoritative judicial and religious office. With ordination, the number of scholars increased—as did their status.[63] As those who interpreted both Torah and tradition, the rabbis became the mediators of the will of God to all Israel.

FROM BAR KOCHBA TO THE PRESENT

After the Bar Kochba revolt (A.D. 132–35) the Romans forbade Jewish ordination.

> The Roman Emperor Hadrian attempted to end the spiritual authority still wielded by the Sanhedrin, which had been shorn of all government support, by forbidding the granting of *semikhah* to new scholars. It was declared that "whoever performed an ordination would be put to death, the city in which the ordination took place demolished, and the boundaries wherein it had been performed uprooted."[64]

R. Judah b. Baba defied the edict, thus continuing the line of ordination, so that the succession from Moses could still be claimed.[65] The practice of ordination was resumed after the Hadrianic Wars. For some time, the patriarchs of the House of Hillel, who claimed Davidic descent,[66] headed the Jewish community in Israel, and no ordination was considered valid without their approval. Later, consent of the Sanhedrin was also required.[67]

With the adoption of ordination as a Christian rite in the third century,[68] the Palestinian Jews abandoned the *sᵉmîķāh*. They substituted the מִנּוּ, *minnu*, "appointment," discarded the laying on of hands, and emphasized instead the pronouncement of the Name.[69] The *sᵉmîķāh* was retained for some time in the diaspora, but seems to have been discontinued there by the fourth century, also.[70] From the fifth century on, appointment to office was accomplished by

63. Steinsaltz, *Essential Talmud*, p. 25.
64. Rothkoff, "Semikhah," *Judaica* XIV:1142.
65. Gavin, *Jewish Antecedents*, p. 102.
66. H. H. Ben-Sasson, ed., *The History of the Jewish People* (Cambridge, MA: Harvard Univ. Press, 1976), p. 339.
67. Rothkoff, "Semikhah," *Judaica* XIV:1142.
68. See Chapter 3.
69. Lauterbach, "Ordination," *JE* IX:429.
70. Rothkoff, "Semikhah," *Judaica* IX:1142. This point is disputed; some claim that traditional *sᵉmîķāh* continued to the time of Maimonides, but this may be an attempt to claim authority on hereditary principles in imitation of Christian ways. See Ben-Sasson, *History of the Jewish People*, p. 597.

giving a document conferring certain powers, but the sacral element was never present to the same extent as that involved in ancient $s^e mik\bar{a}h$. Furthermore, the jurisdiction of the rabbi who was installed by this neo-$s^e mik\bar{a}h$ was limited to the local congregation.[71]

Attempts were made from time to time to restore the traditional $s^e mik\bar{a}h$, for example, in Palestine in A.D. 1083, and in Franco-Germany following the Black Death in A.D. 1348–49.[72] After suffering waves of persecution, the Jews had a desperate need to stabilize their social structure; this, they felt, could best be accomplished by elevating the status of the scholars and sages.[73] The $s^e mik\bar{a}h$ was thus used to distinguish the scholar who was qualified to instruct in accordance with the *halakah*; he was given the title מָרֵנוּ, *mōrēnû* (our teacher), was accorded great respect, and could head a *yeshivah*.[74] Up to this time there had been no need for scholars to carry a patent of $s^e mik\bar{a}h$; their authority had rested on personal rather than institutional grounds. Now formal $s^e mik\bar{a}h$ became a necessity for safeguarding academic standards when the dispersal of most of the scholars and academies endangered the continuity of academic traditions. As soon as $s^e mik\bar{a}h$ was formalized, a process of institutionalization set in, thus making it possible for lesser types of scholars to obtain rabbinical authority and privileges.[75]

> As time went on, an aura of hallowed authority attached itself to the act of ordination. R. Moses Mintz maintained that "every rabbi and expert has been ordained a rabbi by a preceding rabbi all the way back to Moses our Master . . . no householder may in any case question the words of the rabbi." . . . Thus a virtual *halakhah* on the chain of ordination arose and had considerable influence, even if it had no historical base.[76]

This "Ashkenazi ordination" was resented by other scholars, especially the exiles from Spain, for they recognized that it was being used to strengthen and centralize the authority of the rabbinate in Franco-Germany, who then considered themselves superior to the others. The Spanish Jews looked on ordination as evidence of improper pride and an imitation of Christian ways.[77] There was

71. Isaac Levitats, "Ordination," *Judaica* XIV:1143.
72. *Ibid.*
73. Ben-Sasson, *History of the Jewish People*, p. 597.
74. *Ibid.*, p. 598.
75. Rothkoff, "Semikhah," *Judaica* XIV:1146.
76. Ben-Sasson, *History of the Jewish People*, p. 598.
77. Levitats, "Ordination," *Judaica* XIV:1143.

another reason behind this interest in restoring $s^e mik\bar{a}h$, however. Maimonides had taught that the renewal of the sacral chain of ancient $s^e mik\bar{a}h$ could lead to the restoration of the Sanhedrin, and thus pave the way for national repentance and the coming of the Messiah.[78] Messianic hope also underlay the attempt to reinstate the $s^e mik\bar{a}h$ in Safed (Galilee) in A.D. 1538. R. Jacob Berab, on the authority of the teachings of Maimonides, was the first so ordained, and he then ordained four sages who in time ordained seven more, the idea being to reestablish the Sanhedrin.[79] The rabbis in Jerusalem strenuously opposed this, as they believed that such an act must await the divine initiative.[80] After R. Jacob's death, the $s^e mik\bar{a}h$ again lapsed into obscurity.[81]

With the rise of rationalism in the nineteenth century, drastic changes occurred in Jewry; Reform Judaism gained great strength, especially in Germany. This meant even less emphasis on traditional forms. It is significant that the plea made for the reinstatement of the Sanhedrin in Israel in 1948 met with strong opposition in the Knesset and came to naught. However, $s^e mik\bar{a}h$ has now been revived in the *yeshivot* in Israel. In some of the Jewish seminaries in the United States, ordination is conferred on the completion of rabbinic studies.

SUMMARY

In rabbinic Judaism, the Moses-Joshua $s^e mik\bar{a}h$ lost its intrinsic temporal character and became instead the badge of office and authority. Only later, in the teaching of Maimonides, do we see any recognition of the eschatological dynamic of the $s^e mik\bar{a}h$, a theme picked up again in modern Israel but with little success.

The strength of rabbinic ordination lay in the succession motif, and in the privilege this conferred on the rabbis of being the mediators of God's will as expressed in his revelation. The Jews wanted to keep their practices distinct from those of the Christians, but they found that the laying on of hands could be dispensed with in induction to office only at the expense of a loss of authority. Ordination with the imposition of hands did not create the professional religionist as such, but it did foster professionalism in religious matters. It also did much to insure that the dichotomy

78. *Ibid.*, 1144.
79. Ben-Sasson, *History of the Jewish People*, p. 664.
80. Levitats, "Ordination," *Judaica* XIV:1143.
81. *Ibid.*

between the "lay" person and the spiritual leaders remained permanent and intact. The actual laying on of hands played no small part in this process. Ordination encouraged individualization;[82] the edict of a Shammaite or a Hillelite carried much more weight because he participated in the wisdom of Moses.

82. Steinsaltz, *Essential Talmud*, pp. 24, 25.

Chapter 3

ORDINATION: EARLY
CHURCH ADAPTATIONS[1]

> Then Peter and John placed their hands on them and they
> received the Holy Spirit.
>   When Simon saw that the Spirit was given at the laying
> on of the apostles' hands, he offered them money and said,
> "Give me also this ability so that everyone on whom I lay my
> hands may receive the Holy Spirit." Peter answered: "May
> your money perish with you, because you thought that you
> could buy the gift of God with money! You have no part or
> share in this ministry. . . . (Acts 8:17–21 NIV)

Simon Magus was the first of many throughout the centuries to
misunderstand the gift of the Spirit to the Samaritans. Few, perhaps, have thought that they could purchase the ability to confer
the Spirit, but many indeed have believed that it was in their
power to pass on the gift of the Spirit to others through the laying
on of hands. Two New Testament texts have shaped the understanding of all the rites in which the laying on of hands has been
used.[2] In Acts 8:14–17 the Samaritans received the Holy Spirit
when Peter and John laid hands on them; in Acts 19:1–7 Paul
conferred the Spirit on the twelve at Ephesus in a similar manner.
We should note that both events occurred in the context of baptism.
As the imposition of hands came to be seen as a sacramental act

1. The New Testament texts on which the laying on of hands in ordination
has been based will be discussed in Part II of this study.
2. Tertullian, for example, in *On Baptism* 6.10, interprets the reception
of the Spirit as a result of the laying on of hands. Unless otherwise noted, all
references to the works of the Fathers are from Alexander Roberts and James
Donaldson, eds., *Ante-Nicene Fathers* (Grand Rapids: Eerdmans, 1951) and
Philip Schaff and Henry Wace, eds., *Nicene and Post-Nicene Fathers* (Grand
Rapids: Eerdmans, 1952).

in baptism, it fostered a similar interpretation when used in induction to church office.

THE LAYING ON OF HANDS IN BAPTISM

As we have just noted, the earliest postapostolic evidence for the laying on of hands occurs in the context of baptism. The doctrine of the bestowal of the Spirit by the imposition of hands was nurtured in this context, so that when we read in the fourth-century *Apostolic Constitutions* that hands are laid on in ordination, it is no surprise to find that a sacramental understanding of the rite is evident in this setting, also. It is necessary, then, to trace briefly the role that the laying on of hands played in the baptismal rites of the first three centuries.

On the assumption that the imposition of hands in Heb. 6:2 refers to Christian baptism, Beasley-Murray is certain that such a rite was "an unquestionable feature of Christian baptism."[3] It is quite possible, however, that the writer to the Hebrews may not be referring to Christian rites at all.[4] In fact, if the laying on of hands had regularly accompanied baptism, it is remarkable that reference to it in the New Testament (apart from the exceptional events of Acts 8 and Acts 19)[5] is nonexistent. There is no record of the laying on of hands in the baptism of the eunuch (Acts 8:38), when many were baptized after Peter's sermon on Pentecost (Acts 2:41), or when the members of Cornelius' household were baptized (Acts 10:48). If the imposition of hands was normally conjoined with baptism, surely Philip would have laid hands on the Samaritans (Acts 8:12) as a matter of course. As White says, "It is hard to believe that either Paul or Luke could have written as they did if the imposition of hands had formed an integral part of the initiation rite in the pre-literary period."[6] Silva New's dictum that such a rite is to be assumed, even if not always specifically mentioned,[7] is a questionable method of overcoming the silence of

3. G. R. Beasley-Murray, *Baptism in the New Testament* (Grand Rapids: Eerdmans, 1962), pp. 243f.

4. Arthur W. Pink, *An Exposition of Hebrews* (Grand Rapids: Eerdmans, 1954), p. 278; see also Chapter 8, "An Elementary Doctrine."

5. See Chapter 8.

6. R. E. O. White, *The Biblical Doctrine of Initiation* (London: Hodder & Stoughton, 1960), p. 146.

7. Silva New, "The Name, Baptism, and the Laying on of Hands," in *The Beginnings of Christianity*, vol. V, ed. F. J. Foakes Jackson and Kirsopp Lake (Grand Rapids: Baker, 1966), p. 135.

Scripture on this subject. For one thing, it would have to be assumed that the baptism of Acts 19:5 was analogous to other baptismal rites in Acts, an assumption ruled out by the context. Nor is there any evidence whatsoever for such a ceremony in the century following the death of Paul, a remarkable situation if it had been common practice in the first century.[8] In the *Didache*,[9] the emphasis is on baptism in the Name; for Justin Martyr, the importance of baptism lies in the cleansing and the remission of sins.[10] Irenaeus alludes to the bestowal of the Spirit in the laying on of hands in Acts 8:17,[11] but makes no mention of it as a church practice.

The first postapostolic mention of the laying on of hands as a church practice occurs late in the second century, at a time when infant baptism was becoming customary.[12] It occurs in conjunction with other rites such as chrismation.[13]

> The importance attached to the imposition of hands at Baptism by such authors as Tertullian is directly due to their reading of Acts [8:9–17 and 19:1–7], and their assumption that it taught that the Christian experience of the Spirit, in the full sense in which St. Paul had spoken of it, was really mediated to the faithful in every case through the imposition of hands. They felt obliged to try to reconcile what they took to be the meaning of Scripture in these texts in Acts with the entirely different doctrine of the Spirit's bestowal which they found elsewhere in the New Testament. . . .[14]

However, Clement of Alexandria does not mention it when he speaks of baptism, and Origen treats the imposition of hands as a subordinate aspect of the rite.[15] Hippolytus, in the *Apostolic Traditions*, generally associates both remission of sins and the reception of the Spirit with baptism, though he also emphasizes anointing

8. G. W. H. Lampe, *The Seal of the Spirit*, 2nd ed. (London: SPCK, 1967), p. 79.

9. *Didache* 7.

10. Justin Martyr, *Apology*, I, 61.3–8.

11. Irenaeus, *Against Heresies* 4.38.2.

12. Paul K. Jewett, *Infant Baptism and the Covenant of Grace* (Grand Rapids: Eerdmans, 1978), pp. 20ff.; A. W. Argyle, "Baptism in the Early Christian Centuries," in *Christian Baptism*, ed. A. Gilmore (London: Lutterworth Press, 1959), pp. 404f.; Beasley-Murray, *Baptism*, pp. 310ff.; *contra*, Joachim Jeremias, *The Origins of Infant Baptism* (London: SCM, 1963).

13. J. N. D. Kelly, *Early Christian Doctrines*, rev. ed. (San Francisco: Harper and Row, 1978), p. 208.

14. Lampe, *Seal of the Spirit*, pp. 79f.

15. Origen, *Principles* 1.3.7.

and the laying on of hands.[16] Archeological finds in Rome (third century)[17] illustrate baptism as accompanied by the laying on of hands, with the dove (representing the Holy Spirit) about to descend on the young baptismal candidate. Cyprian and his fellow bishops, meeting in council in A.D. 256, decided that the proper outward sign of the bestowal of the Spirit was the imposition of hands.[18] The baptism of infants led to the need for confirmatory rites such as anointing with oil and making the sign of the cross on the forehead of the candidate, and then to the later rite of confirmation. Whichever rite or aspect of a rite received the emphasis, some of the Fathers considered human agency essential to the reception of the Spirit, the human agent being the "priest." Basil of Caesarea, writing in the fourth century, justifies these practices on the basis of secret traditions, traditions reserved for the hierarchy and hidden from the eyes of "inquisitive meddlers."[19] Neither Athanasius, Cyril of Jerusalem, nor Hilary, however, attributed the gift of the Spirit to the laying on of hands,[20] nor did Chrysostom.[21] Augustine taught that baptism received outside the church was incomplete, and that "baptism administered in schism has to be made effective by the imposition of hands within the true church before the schismatically baptized can be incorporated in the fellowship of the Spirit."[22] In reference to the gift of the Spirit in Acts 8:14ff. he says: "For not one of his disciples gave the Holy Spirit, since they prayed that He might come upon those upon whom they laid their hands; they did not give Him themselves."[23] The efficacy of the rite was operative through the prayer to the giver of the Spirit—God himself.

As infant baptism replaced adult baptism, especially in the west, confirmation assumed greater importance. In the laying on of hands, the bishop conferred the Spirit through his special apostolic powers received at his ordination. According to Cyprian (third century), this authority was derived not only through succession, but because every bishop is inducted into his office by

16. *Apostolic Traditions* 8.3.15.

17. See, for example, *Eerdmans' Handbook to the History of Christianity* (Grand Rapids: Eerdmans, 1977), pp. 114, 117.

18. Lampe, *Seal of the Spirit*, p. 186.

19. Basil of Caesarea, *On the Holy Spirit* 66, quoted in *The Later Christian Fathers*, ed. Henry Bettenson (Oxford: Oxford Univ. Press, 1970), pp. 59, 60.

20. Kelly, *Early Christian Doctrines*, p. 433.

21. Argyle, "Baptism in the Early Christian Centuries," p. 206.

22. *Ibid.*, p. 216.

23. Augustine, *On the Trinity* 15.46.

God's special decree[24] and receives special revelations of the Spirit.[25] Since only the bishop could confirm, and only the confirmed could partake of the Eucharist, the central rite of the church, the bishops quickly gained control over the lives of the faithful, for to rebel against the bishop was to rebel against God.[26] The suppression of the historical frame of reference of Acts 8:14–17 and 19:1–7[27] helped to foster a sacramental understanding of the laying on of hands. Social, political, and religious pressures contributed to the growth of an impregnable religious hierarchy. The imposition of hands was a visible reminder of the unassailable authority of the prelacy. In the coming struggles with the so-called heretics and the secular princes, those who could claim custody of the power of God had an invaluable asset.

THE LAYING ON OF HANDS IN ORDINATION

Installation into office in the early postapostolic period apparently involved little in the way of ceremony or protocol. This was to be expected in view of Jesus' teaching about the relationship between brother and brother. "You are not to be called rabbi. . . . Call no man your father on earth. . . . Neither be called masters" (Matt. 23:8–10). "You know that those who are supposed to rule over the Gentiles lord it over them. . . . But it shall not be so among you" (Mark 10:42, 43). In the light of these and many other similar instructions, it is not surprising that in the writings of the subapostolic age we see the simple vocabulary of the New Testament still being used for appointment to office.

Χειροτονεῖν, "to appoint," is used in Acts 14:23 of the choice of elders. In 2 Cor. 8:19, Titus is appointed by the churches (χειροτονηθεὶς ὑπὸ τῶν ἐκκλησιῶν) to travel with Paul and others. The original meaning of χειροτονεῖν, "to choose, to elect by raising hands,"[28] is seldom seen in the literature of the first few centuries. Χειροτονεῖν is used of election in Josephus, but it is divine election: Saul is said to be king by the appointment of God (ὑπὸ θεοῦ χειροτονηθείς).[29] Josephus also employs it in speaking of appointments to the priesthood.[30] Philo uses χειροτονεῖν of the selection

24. Cyprian, *Epistles* 59.5.
25. *Ibid.*, 11.3.4; 57.5; 73.26.
26. *Ibid.*, 66.1.
27. Kelly, *Early Christian Doctrines*, p. 434; Tertullian, *On Baptism* 6.
28. *BAG*, p. 889.
29. Josephus, *Antiquities* VI.13.9.
30. *Ibid.*, IV.2.4; IV.3.4; etc.

of jurymen,[31] and of Pharaoh's appointment of Joseph as governor.[32] The religious use of χειροτονεῖν prepared the word for its use in Christianity;[33] the association with divine choice was an important factor in the gradual replacement in ecclesiastical literature of καθίστημι with χειροτονέω.[34] Thus we read in the *Didache*: "Appoint [χειροτονήσατε] therefore for yourselves bishops and deacons. . . ."[35] Ignatius used χειροτονεῖν of the selection of officials to go on a mission to Antioch.[36] There is no suggestion in any of these texts that the laying on of hands occurred in connection with these appointments.

The earliest evidence we have for the laying on of hands in the induction to church office comes from the documents underlying the *Apostolic Constitutions*. The earliest of these, *Church Order #1* and the *Apostolic Traditions* of Hippolytus (late second or early third century), both show evidence of later interpolations. Frere describes these texts as "disorderly."[37] For example, in the middle of a description of an ordination service, the compiler of *Church Order #1* starts to defend certain "orthodox" practices, perhaps in answer to the attacks of some group such as the Montanists.[38] A later document, *Church Order #2* (fourth century), which also underlies the *Apostolic Constitutions*, does not even mention the imposition of hands.[39] At best, any evidence for the laying on of hands in ordination from the *Apostolic Constitutions* can only indicate possibilities. Exact dating of the onset of this practice cannot be deduced from either the *Constitutions* or the sources underlying the *Constitutions*.

The laying on of hands seems to have been understood sacramentally from the inception of the rite.

> . . . There had been from the first a connexion between the imposition of hands and the χαρίσματα, or "spiritual gifts"; and under the influence of the sacerdotal ideas of the 4th cen-

31. Philo, *Quod Deus* XX.112. References to Philo are from the Loeb Classical Library edition, trans. F. H. Colson and G. H. Whitaker (Cambridge, MA: Harvard Univ. Press, 1942).

32. Philo, *Praemiis et Poenis* 9.

33. Everett Ferguson, "Eusebius and Ordination," *JEH* 13 (1962), p. 143.

34. *Ibid.*, p. 144.

35. *Didache* 15.1.

36. Ignatius, *To the Philadelphians* X.1; *To the Smyrnaeans* XI.2.

37. W. H. Frere, "Early Ordination Services," *JTS* 16 (1915), p. 349.

38. *Ibid.*, p. 348.

39. *Ibid.*, pp. 331f. It should be noted that the *Traditions* survive in fragmentary form in various Latin, Greek, Coptic, and Syriac church orders. The textual tradition dates only to the latter half of the fourth century, however.

tury this connexion became so strong that Basil, speaking of some schismatics, says: παρὰ τῶν πατέρων ἔσχον τὰς χειροτονίας καὶ διὰ τῆς ἐπιθέσεως τῶν χειρῶν αὐτῶν εἶχον τὸ χάρισμα τὸ πνευματικόν. ... This led to a restriction of the rite of imposition of hands to the higher orders of clergy. It ceased to be part of the ceremony of admitting deaconesses ... or subdeacons ... or readers.[40]

The "grace" bestowed was related to both the accompanying prayer[41] and the rank of the one who ordained.[42] The hierarchy of the Old Testament priesthood was being used deliberately as a pattern for church office.[43]

By the fourth century, the terms used for appointment to office and for ordination start to coalesce. This can be seen in the *Apostolic Constitutions* (c. A.D. 350–375). A comparison of the underlying Latin text of the *Didascalia* with the *Apostolic Constitutions* (2.2.3) shows τὴν χειροτονίαν λαμβανῶν (those receiving the appointment) paralleling the Latin *cum manus impositionis accepit*.[44] A discussion of the installation in office of the major and minor orders shows that χειροθεσία (the laying on of hands) is included in χειροτονία. Χειροτονία, appointment, has now (in these documents at least) become "ordination," and consists of a visible sign—the laying on of hands—and the prayer to God for the person on whom office is being conferred.[45] Only the major orders are of divine origin; they must be conferred by the hands of a bishop.[46] In the *Apostolic Constitutions*, χειροθεσία, although only a varia-

40. E. Hatch, "Ordination," *DCA*, p. 1508; the Greek translates: "He had the appointment from the fathers, and was receiving the spiritual gift through the laying on of their hands."

41. Book VIII of the *Apostolic Constitutions* details the prayers and ceremonies for each order. A presbyter was not to perform ordination, for "God is not the God of confusion" (1 Cor. 14:23).

42. C. H. Turner, "χειροτονία, χειροθεσία, ἐπίθεσις χειρῶν," *JTS* 24 (1923), p. 501. One outcome of the Donatist controversy was the decision that the personal worth of the one ordaining was independent of the effect of the rite. See Seeburg I:314.

43. *Apostolic Constitutions* VIII.23.6.

44. Turner, "χειροτονία...," p. 497.

45. *Apostolic Constitutions* VIII.16.2; VIII.17.1; VIII.21.2. In the eighth book of the *Constitutions*, which is based on Hippolytus' *Traditions*, the presbyters, deacons, and subdeacons receive χειροτονία, but the virgins, widows, and those in other minor orders do not; cf. VIII.24.2; VIII.25.2. See also Walter Bauer, *Orthodoxy and Heresy in Earliest Christianity* (Philadelphia: Fortress Press, 1971), pp. 244–257.

46. F. E. Brightman, "The Sacramentary of the Serapion of Thmuis, Part III, Ordinations," *JTS* 1 (1900), p. 258.

tion of ἐπίθεσις χειρῶν, is contrasted with χειροτονία. A presbyter may lay hands on but not ordain (χειροθετεῖ οὐ χειροτονεῖ),[47] his authority evidently limited to baptism, confirmation, or the restoration of a sinner, at least according to the *Constitutions*. Turner[48] is of the opinion that the compiler of the *Constitutions* deliberately introduced a distinction between these two terms in an attempt to give precision to the terminology of the church. Thus the compiler of the *Constitutions* never used χειροτονεῖν and χειροτονία of any rite but ordination.

> Under the term χειροτονία are included in fact the whole of the conditions which constitute a regular ordination, and of those, the two most important were the election by the people and the laying on of hands by the bishops. Sometimes the people's share may be the prominent thought—the man "ordained" was the real choice of the local church: much more often the emphasis is on the rite by which the gift of the Spirit is invoked with the laying on of hands.[49]

The canons of the church councils (such as those of Neocaesarea and Nicea) do not show this precise use of terms.[50] In fact, the general practice seems to have been that the laying on of hands and the prayer invoking the Spirit were reserved for the bishop, even if the presbyter (priest) performed other parts of the rites of baptism or the restoration of sinners.[51]

The writings of Eusebius illustrate the wide range of the use of χειροτονεῖν in the fourth century. Thus, he says that the Seven of Acts 6:1–6 are "appointed" (καθίστημι) to the diaconate by prayer and the laying on of hands (δι' εὐχῆς καὶ χειρῶν ἐπιθέσεως),[52] while in the same context we read that Stephen was ordained (ἡ χειροτονία). Obviously ἡ χειροτονία included the laying on of hands. Sometimes Eusebius uses χειροτονία and χειροθεσία interchangeably. For example, he says that Origen gave public lectures at Caesarea "though not yet ordained [χειροτονία] to the presbyterate,"[53] although later he was ordained presbyter, πρεσβείου χει-

47. *Apostolic Constitutions* VIII.28.3.

48. Turner, "χειροτονία...," p. 205.

49. *Ibid.*, pp. 499f.

50. *Ibid.*, pp. 501f.

51. A. H. Couratin, "Liturgy," *The Pelican Guide to Modern Theology*, vol. II: *Historical Theology*, ed. R. P. C. Hanson (Harmondsworth: Penguin Books, 1969), pp. 202ff.

52. *E.H.* 2.1.1.

53. *E.H.* 6.19.16.

ϱοθεσίαν ... ἀναλαμβάνει.[54] The same parallel can be seen in other ancient documents.

> ... It is difficult to determine accurately the time at which χειϱοθετεῖσθαι came into general use in reference to ordination, because the texts of the MSS., especially of writers and councils of the 4th century, vary so much between χειϱοτονία and χειϱοθεσία as to make the determination of the reading ... a matter of great uncertainty.... No doubt, after χειϱοθεσία was once introduced, χειϱοτονία tended to be identified with it....[55]

In Serapion's *Sacramentary* (A.D. 350), χειϱοθεσία is used with κατάστασις (appointment) in the ordination of bishops, presbyters, and deacons.[56] This document demonstrates the growing importance of the rite of the imposition of hands in induction to office.[57]

Προχειρίζεσθαι was also used in the third and fourth centuries as a designation for ordination. It is used synonymously with χειϱοτονεῖν in Canon 3 of *Ancyra* with Canon 10 of *Nicea*.[58] Καθίστημι (appoint) and its Latin equivalent *constituere*, which reveal nothing about any ceremonial in induction to office, were still common, too.[59] Various other designations were also used: προσελθεῖν, προσάγεσθαι, implying promotion to dignity; ἱεροῦσθαι, with sacramental connotations; κληροῦσθαι, which emphasized the office itself. At this time there was no distinction between "consecration" and "ordination," nor is this distinction made in eastern rites today. Later, in the west, bishops were "consecrated" and other orders "ordained."

MINISTRY IN THE POSTAPOSTOLIC PERIOD

The vocabulary of ordination tells only part of the story. Even when the *Didache* was written, a dichotomy had begun to develop among the people of the New Covenant. Side by side with the mutual ministry of one believer to another (15.3) was the need for leadership to control false and greedy teachers (15.1; 11.1, 3, 4). A

54. *E.H.* 6.23.4.

55. E. Hatch, "Ordination," p. 1502.

56. Turner, "χειϱοτονία...," p. 503.

57. A. J. Maclean, "Ordination: Christian," *HERE* 9:541. According to this author, χειϱοθεσία is used in the present-day Greek Orthodox churches for ordination to the minor orders, and χειϱοτονία for the ordination of bishops, presbyters, and deacons.

58. Ferguson, "Eusebius and Ordination," p. 142.

59. Hatch, "Ordination," p. 1502.

cleavage was occurring between those who were "able to bear the whole yoke of the Lord" (6.2) and those who were not so able. The prophets were to be looked upon as chief priests (13.3). Schweizer sees here the beginnings of a rift between the bearers of the Spirit and the ordinary church members. "This is something quite new and foreign to the New Testament: it is the distinction between priests and laity."[60]

The process continues to be noted in the writings of Clement of Rome. In response to the threat of disorder, office was elevated and fixed after the pattern of the Old Testament priesthood.[61] Order was above all to be desired and leadership to be strengthened by the attitudes of the ordinary believers.[62] "Let us reverence our rulers; let us honor our elders" (*To the Corinthians* 21.7). A military-type hierarchy was held up for emulation.[63] Furthermore, Old Testament cultic terminology was creeping into use. Those who had been thrust out of office in Corinth were denied their λειτουργία, not their διακονία; the language of sacrifice was used to describe episcopal duties.[64] Clement establishes clerical order on the basis of Israel as a type.

> Clement sets forth a striking theory of church office. He theorizes that the structure of authority in Israel, and specifically the priestly orders—high priests, priests, Levites and people—furnish the types that find their fulfillment in the authority structure of the Christian community.[65]

Those who followed Clement carried the trend further. Ignatius parallels the local church hierarchy with the divine order: "I advise you, be ye zealous to do all things in godly concord, the bishop presiding after the likeness of God and the presbyters after the likeness of the council of the apostles."[66] The bishop is "your revered bishop"[67] and a "type of the Father."[68] By the second century, when Irenaeus wrote *Against Heresies*, the ecclesiastical hierarchy was thoroughly entrenched and the cleavage between the clergy

60. E. Schweizer, *Church Order in the New Testament* (London: SCM, 1961), p. 145.

61. *To the Corinthians* 44.1; 47.6, 7; 40.5, 6; 41.1.

62. *Ibid.*, 40.1, 2; 41.1; 65.1.

63. *Ibid.*, 37.1–4.

64. *Ibid.*, 44.4.

65. Elaine H. Pagels, "The Demiurge and His Archons," *HTR* 69:3–4 (July–October 1976), p. 304; cf. *To the Corinthians* 40.5, 6.

66. Ignatius, *To the Magnesians* 6.1.

67. *Ibid.*, 13.1.

68. Ignatius, *To the Trallians* 3.1.

and the laity was sharp. The clergy were fast becoming the guardians of orthodoxy, and were teachers, rulers, and celebrants, possessing graces and gifts not available to the mass of believers.[69] Irenaeus' concept of the apostolic succession was not from ordainer to ordained, but from one holder of the teaching chair to the next.[70] Occupying the καθέδρα (chair) also takes a prominent place in the *Pseudo-Clementines*, and precedes the laying on of hands.[71] More and more the vocabulary of the "ministry" reflected the trend to Old Testament terminology. Tertullian called the Christian leadership the *sacerdotium*, although still asserting the priesthood of all believers.[72] Cyprian (third century)

> applies all the privileges, duties, and responsibilities of the Aaronic priesthood to the officers of the Christian church, and constantly calls them *sacerdotes* and *sacerdotium*. He may therefore be called the proper father of the sacerdotal conception of the Christian ministry as a mediating agency between God and the people.[73]

The threat of Gnosticism further aggravated the growing authoritarianism of the clergy. With a dozen or more Gnostic sects breaking away from Christianity between A.D. 80 and A.D. 150, a succession theory was essential to the very existence of the church. In answer to the Gnostics' claim to their "mysteries," the Fathers' appeal to an ongoing apostolic tradition, represented especially in an orderly ministry and the rule of faith, provided an historical-geographical basis for the authenticity of orthodox teaching, and a useful hermeneutical principle in meeting the Gnostic interpretation of Scripture.[74] Later, Basil of Caesarea (fourth century) says of the schismatics:

> Those who apostatized from the Church no longer had upon them the grace of the Holy Spirit, since the gift ceased to be imparted when the continuity was interrupted. The original separatists had received ordination from the Fathers, and pos-

---

69. Janet K. and Thomas F. O'Dea, "Christianity in Historical Perspective," in *Religion and Man: An Introduction*, eds. W. R. Comstock *et al.* (New York: Harper and Row, 1971), p. 455.

70. Irenaeus, *Against Heresies* 4.12.1.

71. Ferguson, "Eusebius and Ordination," p. 140.

72. Philip Schaff, *History of the Christian Church*, vol. II (Grand Rapids: Eerdmans, 1935), p. 126.

73. *Ibid.*, p. 126.

74. Geoffrey W. Bromiley, "Authority and Scripture," in *Scripture, Tradition, and Interpretation*, eds. W. Ward Gasque and William Sanford LaSor (Grand Rapids: Eerdmans, 1978), p. 15.

sessed the spiritual gift through the laying on of their hands. But those who break away become laymen, lacking authority to either baptize or ordain, because they cannot confer on others a gift of the Holy Spirit.[75]

The fourth-century Donatist controversy was aggravated by a dispute over this matter. Seventy bishops of the church, meeting in Carthage in A.D. 312, declared the ordination of one Caecilian invalid because he had been ordained by a bishop whom they considered schismatic, and hence "unworthy." A decision of the Council of Arles (A.D. 316) declared, however, that the validity of an ordinance (whether baptism or ordination) is not dependent on the worthiness of the administrator. But, according to the church, the layman needed a mediator, an ordained bishop or priest, an ἀρχιερεύς or ἱερεύς,[76] one of the κλῆρος (the clergy), one who belongs to the *ordo sacerdotalis*.[77]

Nor was the separation of the clergy and the laity merely in the cult; in time the rift permeated all spheres of life, extending to social relationships (e.g., marriage) and life in general. The sacred was the sphere of the clergy, the secular that of the laity. Christianity became identified with an institution and its cultic observances; "church" had become an organization. Liturgy and theology became the province of bishops and priests; the world of work and war belonged to the laity—not as autonomous agents, but as a potent force to be used by the clergy in the power struggles with the political rulers. The practice of infant baptism had done much to rob the community of the New Covenant of its distinctive character as a people set apart, a royal priesthood to serve God in all aspects of life, cultic and cultural. As the gateway to the sacerdotal realm, it was inevitable that ordination should become the keystone of the hierarchical structure. By the early fifth century, Chrysostom could say of the priest who performs the mass:

> The priest as he stands there brings down not fire, but the Holy Spirit . . . it is by priests that these things are accomplished, and others of no less importance, that concern our redemption and salvation. . . . What is given to them is nothing less than heavenly authority. "If you forgive man's sins, they are forgiven . . ." [John 20:23]. What greater authority could there be? "The Father has entrusted all judgment to the

---

75. Basil of Caesarea, *Epistolae* 188, *The Later Christian Fathers*, ed. and trans. Henry Bettenson (Oxford: Oxford Univ. Press, 1970), p. 86.

76. "High-priest," "priest"; *Apostolic Constitutions* terminology.

77. These terms were in common use by the time of Tertullian.

Son": and here I see the Son giving it all into the hands of his priests.[78]

"Orders" are central to ecumenical discussion today. Piet Fransen expresses the Roman Catholic view when he says, "Ordination is the basis of all other powers."[79] So it became in the early centuries of the church.

ORDINATION IN THE EARLY CENTURIES

The earliest record of an ordination rite is found in the *Apostolic Traditions* of Hippolytus (A.D. 200–220).[80] By the fourth century there are many references to such a ceremony, particularly in the *Apostolic Constitutions*, which are in part based on the *Traditions* of Hippolytus and the *Didascalia*. There is frequent mention of ordination in Eusebius' *Ecclesiastical History*. Ordination as a rite with the laying on of hands was also known in Egypt by the fourth century.[81] There is no extant literature that gives information on Roman ordinations until the sixth century, but Maclean believes that a common form of church order originated there in the third century.[82] The prayer of consecration for a bishop found in the *Traditions* shows that in Syria, even by the early third century authority was centralized in the bishop. Prayer is made that he receive gifts for shepherding the flock, for high priesthood and propitiation, and for him as official representative of the church; that he remit sins in the high-priestly Spirit; for his distributions of offices; and that he may "loose all bonds after the authority of the apostles."[83] Evidently these gifts were then believed to be conferred in the laying on of hands. From the first, these were the essential elements in ordination; later additions were of secondary importance.

It is apparent from the consecration prayers that from the beginning there was a connection between the imposition of hands

78. Chrysostom, *De Sacerdotio*, in Bettenson, *Later Christian Fathers*, pp. 175f.

79. Piet Fransen, "Orders and Ordination," *SacraM*, p. 1139.

80. That is, induction into church office with the laying on of hands. See Henry Chadwick, *The Early Church* (Grand Rapids: Eerdmans, 1967), p. 49. Such indications may have been later interpolations; see James Donaldson, *The Ante-Nicene Fathers* VII:389, "Introductory Notes to the Constitutions of the Holy Apostles."

81. Serapion, *Sacramentary*.

82. Maclean, "Ordination: Christian," *HERE* 9:543.

83. C. H. Turner, "The Ordination Prayer for a Presbyter in the Church Order of Hippolytus," *JTS* 16 (1915), pp. 542f.

and the χάρισμα (gift) for office. The sacerdotal ideas of the fourth century reinforced the connection and led the church to restrict the imposition of hands to the higher orders of the clergy. Previous to this restriction, singers, exorcists, readers, and some other categories of church office-bearers had been ordained by the laying on of hands.[84] In the east, ordination of deaconesses was customary and included "a laying on of hands, clothing with the deacon's vestments, and the delivery of the chalice, offering remarkable parallels to the ordination of men."[85] However, the sacramental understanding of the laying on of hands meant that ordination was forbidden to readers, deaconesses, and subdeacons.[86]

Augustine believed that, since the gifts received in ordination were from God, the character or even the spiritual condition of the ordainer could not detract from the value of the gifts conveyed. Ordination confers a *character indelibilis* on the recipient; there remains in him something sacred, a *sanctum*. The Spirit is preserved to him, not in a moral sense, but in the sense of official equipment.[87] Thus the sacramental acts of a "heretical" bishop are effective, though he himself may be under the displeasure of God. For Augustine the sacraments were symbolical, but they were the signs of an invisible content, and became effective through faith. "The sacraments are purely symbols, but the reception of the sacraments brings real objective exertions of divine energy."[88] In spite of the formulations of Augustine, popular belief obviously did not make such distinctions, but instead leaned toward a sacramentalism that finally found its full flowering in the Middle Ages.

> In many instances, it is possible to see that centuries before the theologians attempted to define and establish a particular doctrine, the majority of believers within the church had already accepted it and had included it in the folklore of the church. . . . The final theological formulations of the sacraments show many signs of having been influenced by beliefs which originated among the masses.[89]

Candidates for ordination were examined as to their qualifications for office. The *Constitutions* say, with reference to the ordination

84. Hatch, "Ordination," p. 1508; Maclean, "Ordination: Christian," p. 540.

85. Jean Daniélou, *The Ministry of Women in the Early Church*, 2nd ed. (Leighton Buzzard, Beds.: Faith, 1974), p. 31.

86. Hatch, "Ordination," p. 1508.

87. Seeburg I:319.

88. *Ibid.*

89. Clarence L. Lee, Introduction to H. J. Carpenter, *Popular Christianity and the Early Theologians* (Philadelphia: Fortress Press, 1966), pp. ixf.

of a bishop, "Search diligently for all the faults of him who is to be ordained for the priesthood" and "Let him therefore if it is possible be well educated; but if he be unlettered, let him at any rate be skilful in the word and of competent age."[90] In the case of presbyters, Theophilus of Alexandria (c. A.D. 400) writes:

> The whole clergy agree and choose; the bishop scrutinizes (δοκιμάζει) the character and qualifications of the candidate; and then in open church, by way of guarding against clandestine ordinations, the bishop proclaims (προφωνεῖ) the elect that the people may testify to him; and lastly, the clergy consenting, the bishop ordains (χειροτονεῖ) in the midst of the church.[91]

Although it seemed that the church requested the concurrence of the people in this decision, the choice of candidate was the clergy's alone. The testifying to which Theophilus refers was no more than tacit approval.[92] The *Apostolic Constitutions* stipulates that after a person has been elected bishop (by the clergy) and is presented for ordination, the question is to be put as to "whether he is attested by all as being worthy."[93] The people as witnesses then shout "He is worthy" three times, signifying their approval, a custom still prevailing in the eastern rites. The expression "he is worthy" has not so much to do with the dignity of office as to "a kind of worthiness that God would honor."[94] That is to say, it is an acknowledgment of the divine choice of the candidate, and does not attribute worth to him personally. Whether this was the understanding of the ordinary believer is another matter. Certainly the writers of the day were not adverse to ascribing worth to bishops and priests.

> The bishop, he is the minister of the word, the keeper of knowledge, the mediator between God and you in several parts of your divine worship. . . . He is your ruler and governor, your king and potentate; he is next after God your earthly god, who has a right to be honored by you. For concerning him and such as he, it is that God pronounces "I have said 'Ye are gods, and ye are all children of the most High' and 'Ye shall not speak evil of the gods.' "[95]

90. *Apostolic Constitutions* II.1.3.
91. Canon 6, quoted in Brightman, "The Sacramentary of Serapion," p. 258.
92. Hatch, "Ordination," p. 1504.
93. *Apostolic Constitutions* II.4.26.
94. Ferguson, "Eusebius and Ordination," pp. 140f.
95. *Apostolic Constitutions* II.4.26.

The Council of Arles in A.D. 314 addressed the bishop of Rome as "most glorious," a secular title reserved for persons second only to the imperial family.[96]

As the bishops acquired social rank and wealth, many of them exhibited the vices that go with power. It was no easy matter to dislodge them from office once ordained. For example, Paul of Samosata was accused of heresy at Antioch by about seventy bishops (c. A.D. 265). The catalogue of his supposed sins have a ring of exaggeration to them;[97] there is no doubt that the bishops were out to get him. As Chadwick remarks, the bishops found it easier to condemn Paul than to get rid of him, for he retained control of his church with the enthusiastic support of his congregation.[98] The combination of a charismatic personality and the extensive powers bestowed at ordination were more than the synod could handle; the only way the bishops could oust him was by appeal to the pagan emperor Aurelian. Obviously, ordination needed controls. The traditional methods of ensuring good order, the enactment of canons by the synod,[99] was not the whole answer, as the prolonged strife over the Arian controversy well demonstrated. If ordination conferred a *character indelibilis*, and the Holy Spirit (or at least a χάρισμα for office) was then received, there was, in theory, little to limit the power of a bishop—except the power of other bishops. The "historic episcopate" thus gave rise to the papal system.

The parallels between political and ecclesiastical authority patterns are strikingly evident throughout the early centuries. The most common mode of appointment to office in the earlier empire, as under the Roman republic, was that of popular election. Candidates were required to meet certain standards for eligibility, and were examined by a presiding officer, on whose authority the candidate was finally admitted to office. Gradually, free elections by the people were superseded by election by the senate, subject to formal approval by the people. In course of time, the part that the senate played in the selection of candidates was no more decisive than that of the ordinary people. Similarly, selection of a church officer by the people did not guarantee his appointment; his accep-

96. Chadwick, *Early Church*, p. 163.

97. *E.H.* 7.30.2–13.

98. Chadwick, *Early Church*, p. 114.

99. *Ibid.*, p. 131. *The Nicene Code of Canon Law* directed that a bishop should be consecrated by all the bishops of his province, and in no case by less than three; it also placed a power of veto in the hands of the provincial metropolitans. This last rule accelerated the process whereby authority was increasingly concentrated in the hands of the metropolitans.

tance was subject to approval by the hierarchy of the church.[100]
Acts 6:1–6 was claimed as justification for this procedure. It was
said that though the Seven were chosen by the church, their appointment had to be authorized by the apostles. It is thus evident
that by this time the loss of the historical context of the biblical
text was complete, permitting the use of proof-texting methods to
justify organizational structures that those who held the power in
the church deemed necessary. The pattern was now set: the eschatological orientation of Luke's account was abandoned for the sake
of a church triumphant, whose security rested on an authority
structure patterned in clear contravention of Scripture (Matt.
20:25f.). The erosion of what little power the laity had, continued
apace. The outcome was that appointment by election was ultimately replaced by nomination by either the bishop or the civil
power.[101] Since church office could only be held through the rite
of ordination, the power to ordain was the crucial issue in the
establishment of religious authority. The limitation of popular
power was hastened by reaction to the Arian problem.

> . . . It is clear from the synodical letter of the council of Nicaea
> to the church of Alexandria, that in that church the right of
> the people to elect was limited by the right of the clergy to
> propose names. . . . In the course of the next quarter of a cen-
> tury the council of Laodicaea (c. 13) expressly enacted that the
> elections of those who are to be appointed to the priesthood
> . . . are not to be entrusted to popular assemblies.[102]

When Constantine proclaimed Christianity as the religion of the
state, church leadership patterns were buttressed by political sanction. Heresy consisted in anything that threatened this, the kingdom of God on earth. The forms of the Old Testament sacrificial
system combined with elements of Hellenistic hierarchicalism were
now thoroughly entrenched: the church was secure at last.

LATER DEVELOPMENTS

The church accommodated its structures to the rise of feudalism
as well as possible, but power struggles with the secular rulers
became inevitable. Although first claiming equality with the emperor, the popes soon claimed the divine right to direct him. Pope
Nicholas I (A.D. 858–867), for example, claimed papal authority not

100. Hatch, "Ordination," p. 1503.
101. *Ibid.*, p. 1504.
102. *Ibid.*

only over his own bishops, but over the imperial crown as well. This authority went virtually unquestioned: "The church in general believed in the papal idea and the popes themselves believed in it."[103] By the time of Pope Gregory VII (eleventh century), the hierarchy was well-nigh impregnable and the church supreme. The bishop of Rome had authority over all other bishops, whom he could appoint or remove at will; they were merely his substitutes. He had authority to establish new ecclesiastical laws; anyone opposing him was a heretic. Canonical ordination gave him sanctity: "by the merits of the blessed Peter he is infallibly made holy."[104]

> The infallible pope has authority over body and soul, the world and the church, time and eternity. . . . All these claims rested in the last analysis upon the objective effect of the sacrament of ordination.[105]

The Pontiff delegated his authority to "bind and loose" to his bishops in ordination,[106] and since such authority was ultimately from Christ, no one had the right to take the bishop to task no matter what he did, for he was accountable only to the pope, and the pope was accountable only to God. The bishop in turn presided at the Eucharist, and it was through him that the bread and wine became the body and blood of Christ. He received this awesome power when hands were laid on him in consecration. In the fifteenth century, the conciliar movement challenged the excessive authority of the popes, but authority once conferred is difficult to remove.

During the Middle Ages the church was engaged in a constant struggle with the secular powers for the control of ecclesiastical appointments.

> The papal attempt to control the whole medieval ecclesiastical system and at one time or another every interest and power in Europe, is drawn into its unfolding plot . . . the principle behind the struggle—an essential one in the ruling of the Christian church from the beginning—is that the ministers of the church at every level are the representatives of the communities for which they speak and act.[107]

Once power, by means of ordination and the canon law that buttressed it, was concentrated in an elite in the church, the step from

103. Seeburg II:40.
104. Gregory VII in the *Dictatus*, quoted in Seeburg II:50.
105. Seeburg II:51.
106. See Fransen, "Orders and Ordination," p. 1145.
107. R. W. Southern, *Western Society and the Church in the Middle Ages* (Harmondsworth: Penguin Books, 1969), p. 151.

representation to mediation was easily taken. Full of power, the medieval bishops modeled their lives after Samuel, concerning themselves with both spiritual and temporal affairs.[108] Invulnerable behind their ordination vows and safely entrenched in what they considered was a divinely ordained hierarchy, they fell victim to the vices that such a position bred. Anything that questioned or threatened their authority was considered heresy; if a doctrinal issue could be raised, so much the better—but the real issue was authority. Wisely, the church managed to incorporate some of the inevitable dissent into its own structure. Monastic orders were the answer for some, but there were also others who would not conform to the restrictions that the monastic life required. The only way to deal with them was by bloody persecution, torture, and death.

Many small (and to the church, irritating) "heretical" sects appeared in Europe during the eleventh and twelfth centuries. Unauthorized preaching by these "heretics" was a plague to the "orthodox"—and not without reason, for the scandalous lives of many of the spiritual leaders provided convincing arguments for the sectarians. Anticlericalism flared up in parts of France and northern Italy.

Many sectaries repudiated all the sacraments of the church[109]— the Donatist controversy again—while others instituted their own, often on the basis of dualistic doctrines that radically altered their character.[110] For example, the Bogomils (eleventh century), believing that water as a material element was a creation of the devil, replaced water baptism with the laying on of hands in initiation. They argued that since the apostle Paul received the Holy Spirit when hands were laid on him by Ananias (Acts 9:19), and since no mention is made of water in his baptism, then water baptism has been replaced by Spirit baptism. The dualists thus contended that when hands are placed on the heads of the converts, and the Lord's Prayer is recited, the candidates' sins are forgiven and they receive the Holy Spirit.[111] Among the Cathars, it was

108. *Ibid.*, p. 173.

109. Malcolm Lambert, *Medieval Heresy: Popular Movements from Bogomil to Hus* (London: Edward Arnold, 1977), pp. 50, 62, 90.

110. R. I. Moore, *The Birth of Popular Heresy: Documents of Medieval History*, vol. I (London: Edward Arnold, 1975), pp. 135ff.

111. Lambert, *Medieval Heresy*, pp. 20, 26, 62. A double initiation ceremony with the laying on of hands in the second stage was practiced by the Cathars, who were also dualists (twelfth-century Germany). Beliefs varied somewhat within the ranks of the Cathars. Some said that since the devil had also created the hand, only the recitation of the Lord's Prayer was efficacious in initiation. See Moore, *Birth of Popular Heresy*, pp. 132ff.

believed that the bishop conferred the Spirit in ordination by imposition of hands *and* by holding a copy of the New Testament
above the head of the candidate. Should the bishop be in a state
of sin when he confers orders, the act is nullified; to be effective,
the laying on of hands must be repeated by a worthy bishop.[112]
The church's response was scornful, since, they said, no man was
without sin; a wholly "worthy" bishop could not be found.[113]

Local bishops were given the task of suppressing heresy, but
their efforts were often halfhearted, especially if the secular authorities were sympathetic to the cause of dissent. Not until Pope
Innocent III took office (A.D. 1198) did the church flex its muscles
and prepare to take on these "heretics" (chiefly Waldenses), whose
increasing popularity and strength could no longer be ignored.

The church had adopted the world's pattern of leadership with
disastrous results, disastrous to "heretic" and "faithful" alike. Since
ordination was crucial to authority, evil practices tended to corrupt
the rite, and a great many of the clergy were involved in corrupt
practices. In response to this corruption, small groups broke away
from the church, themselves unfortunately falling prey to heretical
beliefs. The authority pattern the church had assumed invited such
sin.

SUMMARY

Several factors played a major part in the growth of ordination
rites in the early centuries. The church was young and vigorous
and was expanding rapidly geographically. The need for survival
as a distinctive entity with a simple, homogeneous message was
apparently the major factor leading to the centralization of authority in a rigid power structure. Born from Judaism, the church
had to struggle with its relationship to its Old Covenant parentage,
and find its identity as the community of the end times. The leadership pattern that evolved, and the ordination rites that were
formulated to define and protect that leadership, answered the
need for stability and permanence, but the church paid highly for
its security.

Reliance on Old Testament paradigms shaped organizational
forms in the early churches. In the writings of the Fathers, the
priests, Levites, elders, and prophets became the models for the
ministry. The function of leadership was to rule, judge, mediate
the revelation of God, and eventually to re-present the sacrifice of
Christ in the mass. Clement of Rome compares the ministry of the

112. Moore, *Birth of Popular Heresy*, p. 138.
113. *Ibid.*, p. 52.

apostles and their "successors" with the Jewish hierarchy. When in the context of the messianic kingdom Isaiah says, "I will make your overseers peace and your taskmasters righteousness" (Isa. 60:17 MT), Clement presents this text to the Corinthian church (which had just deposed its leaders) as "I will appoint their bishops in righteousness and their deacons in faith" (*To the Corinthians* 42:6)—a useful, if questionable, way of dealing with a threatening situation. Presbyters (very quickly termed ἱερεῖς, priests) were regarded in a certain sense as successors of the Mosaic Seventy (Num. 11:16–25),[114] although their authority derived from the apostles, not from Moses. They were also equated with the Levites, whose duty it was to serve the high priest; the presbyters (priests) were to serve the bishops as *their* assistants.

Along with the Old Testament leadership vocabulary derived from the cult came a mediatorial role for the Christian "priest-hood." The priests—the new Levites—stood (as Thomas Aquinas later expressed it) "in face of the community in the name of Christ."[115] Ordination imparted to them the spiritual authority to administer the sacraments, particularly the new sacrifice, the mass. Only through the offices of the priests could the laity be sanctified. By the time that the *Apostolic Constitutions* were being compiled the breach within the Christian community was permanently accomplished.

> Neither do we permit the laity to perform any of the offices belonging to the priesthood as for instance neither the sacrifice, nor baptism, nor the laying on of hands, nor the blessing whether the smaller or greater; for "No one taketh this honor to himself, but he that is called of God [Heb. 5:4]. For such sacred offices are conferred by the laying on of hands of the bishop. But a person to whom such an office is not committed but he seizes upon it for himself, he shall undergo the punishment of an Uzziah."[116]

The bishops were thus claiming for themselves all the public manifestations of the Christian religion, and were not hesitating to use Scripture to justify the prestige and power they assumed in the name of Christ.

114. Brightman, "The Sacramentary of Serapion," p. 256.
115. Fransen, "Orders and Ordination," p. 1146, quoting Thomas Aquinas.
116. *Apostolic Constitutions* III.10.6– 7. It is apparent from this statement that Old Testament designations for New Testament church officers served as vehicles for Old Testament concepts of office in the church. Later, though the Reformers looked with disapproval on terms such as "priest," they retained Old Testament models on which to base New Testament leadership roles. See Chapter 13, "Authority for Office."

The veneration of the early Fathers resulted in a quasi-canonical status being accorded their writings; thus, their interpretations of Scripture quite often became accepted in the church. Many of the Fathers treated the Old Testament Scriptures as normative for the ordering of the church, at least in certain selected aspects. Covenantal distinctives were subordinated to existential needs. As for the New Testament, the Fathers at first took the events of Acts 8 and Acts 19 as descriptive of the special manifestations of the Spirit at the inception of the new age. Such extraordinary occurrences had, however, apparently ceased. By the third century, the description of events was becoming confused with prescriptions for church practice.

> Tertullian and Cyprian felt compelled to attempt to force the puzzling narrative of Acts viii.1–17 into an uneasy synthesis with the received tradition that the gift of the Spirit was an essential aspect of the inward significance of water-baptism itself. These writers did not pause to enquire whether the conception of the Spirit in the mind of St. Luke was identical or not with that of St. Paul, and whether his accounts of the laying on of hands are to be accepted as typical of the general practice of Christian initiation in the apostolic age; they assumed that this was so, and were left with the task of harmonizing Scriptural evidence which was, on the face of it, self-contradictory.[117]

Thus the imposition of hands became intimately associated with the transmission of the Spirit in baptism. When the laying on of hands became a component of the rites accompanying installation into office, it was to be expected that a sacramental understanding of its significance would carry over to ordination.

Also receiving permanence through the writings of the Fathers and those who followed them was the impact of rabbinic succession theories on early church theology. Power could not be wielded effectively without a claim to antiquity. As the extreme "lionizing" of Moses characterized rabbinic Judaism, so Peter, "the prince of the apostles," was given unique authority and position in the church. The Moses-authority of the rabbis became the Peter-authority of the popes. Ordination set the clergy up and apart from the people of God. As Tertullian says, "It is the authority of the church and the honor which has acquired sanctity through the joint session of the Order, which has established the difference between the Order and the laity."[118] The authority of the church as

117. Lampe, *Seal of the Spirit*, p. 119.
118. Tertullian, *On Exhortation to Chastity* 7.

a whole was fast diminishing. The elevation of the "Order" enabled the clergy to impose uniformity within the church and to enforce an outward conformity that seemed to guarantee a secure and triumphant Christianity. In any case, the outcome was that in the west, the Roman Church and the Roman pope had the last word in all matters of faith and practice.

Hellenistic philosophies reinforced hierarchicalism in the church. Stoicism with its spiritual elitism, and neoplatonism with its immense hierarchies undoubtedly shaped early church ecclesiology. Pseudo-Dionysius the Aeropagite (sixth century) especially influenced Byzantine theology and practice, consolidating the mediatorial role of the hierarchs as those who dispensed the sacred mysteries.[119] That which was blatantly pagan was eliminated, but the sacraments became the "mysteries" of the church, and the Eucharist especially became the possession of the priesthood. In the Greco-Roman world, which regarded all innovations with suspicion, the suppression of diversity was deemed essential to Christianity's claim to be a valid religion distinct from Judaism.

With the institutionalizing of the church and the marriage of church and state under Constantine, the laying on of hands was completely shorn of its eschatological orientation. In context, it indicated the covenant faithfulness of God in empowering his new people to fulfill the commission of Acts 1:8. This motif now became a tool in the hands of the officers of the church to ensure the impregnability of their positions and to convince the skeptical that they held office by divine decree. Order became a key concept in the power structure of the church; only the ordained had the power of the keys (Matt. 18:18) and could baptize, confirm, and ordain. Only they, through the power they had received when hands were laid on them, were able to reenact the sacrifice of Christ in the mass. The ordinary believer, generally illiterate and ignorant, was at the mercy of the educated clergy. If the symbolism of the laying on of hands was not sufficiently explicit, the prayer that accompanied the rite made it very clear that the ordinand was indeed specially endowed by God and was, through this expressive rite, acknowledged to be one of the spiritual elite. The ordination rite was strengthened by pageantry and symbolic accoutrements, but the actual transmission of spiritual power occurred when the bishop laid his hands on the head of the kneeling candidate. This was the climax of the whole ordination ceremony.

119. Kelly, *Early Christian Doctrines*, p. 65.

Chapter 4

ORDINATION:
REFORMATION RUBRICS

By the time of Pope Eugene IV (fifteenth century) the sacraments of the church had achieved surpassing importance. They were the doorway to salvation; and the bishops, the stewards of the Spirit of God, held the keys. Ordination was one of the "Seven Sacraments" of the church, and was one of the three that were believed to imprint an indelible character on the soul, and hence be nonrepeatable. The laying on of hands played a crucial role in the rite. By the twelfth century

> the theory of the connexion of the rite [of imposition of hands] with the gift of the Holy Ghost was so firmly impressed upon Western Christendom that some ordinals put into the bishop's mouth at the time of imposition the words which have been retained in the English ordinal, "Receive the Holy Ghost."[1]

According to the Bull *Exultate Deo* issued by Eugene at the Florentine Council (A.D. 1439), the sacraments were a positive product of the work of Christ, and derived their efficacy from his passion. The purpose of the sacrament of ordination was to empower those who received it to lead the people.[2] Sacraments were effective only when administered with the intention of producing the effect for which they had been instituted. This *intentio* (purpose) was as much a part of the sacrament as the *materia* (in ordination, the laying on of hands), and the *forma* (the prayer of invocation, the *epiclesis*).[3] The grace conferred was certain because of the divine covenant with the church. For Augustine, the signs signified that

---

1. Edwin Hatch, "Ordination," *DCA*, p. 1508.
2. Seeburg II:125.
3. In the late nineteenth century, the Roman Catholic Church denied the legitimacy of Anglican ordination on the basis of a defective *intentio*.

which the accompanying grace effected in the recipient. Eugene IV, however, wrote that while the ancient sacraments did not cause grace, the church's sacraments both contained and conferred grace. The *charaeter spiritualis* received in those sacraments that were administered only once involved a participation in the priesthood of Christ, as well as supplying justifying grace.[4] The sacraments were effective *ex opere operato*; that is, the motive of the recipient did not affect the reception of grace, though the absence of an obstacle or mortal sin in the recipient made possible a further reception of grace.[5]

As ordination imparted the spiritual authority to administer all the other sacraments, and also gave the power of binding and loosing (Matt. 18:18), it embraced the whole sacramental system of the Roman Catholic Church. This, together with the decree of Pope Gregory the Great that the church *is* the kingdom, and that there is no salvation outside the church, ensured the supreme spiritual power of the Roman clergy. The abuse of this power, coupled with social and historical factors, paved the way for the Reformation crisis.

THE ORDERS AND DISSENT

Dissent within the Roman Church had, for the most part, been effectively and profitably channelled into the religious orders. These all professed a "Rule" made effective through a binding vow that, though not an ordination vow, nevertheless served to regulate and authenticate the religious status of the members of the Order.[6] When Gerhard Groote (A.D. 1380) attempted to establish a religious order with no "Rule," his innovation met with immediate hostility. If people were to form associations, read the Scripture

4. Seeburg II:128.
5. *Ibid.*, p. 129.
6. R. W. Southern (*Western Society and the Church in the Middle Ages*, pp. 340f.) says, "the need for a binding vow was one of the common assumptions that had bound together all the religious Orders in the Middle Ages. They were all based on one fundamental idea — that a life fully pleasing to God could not be lived in the secular world. . . . The forms that this life could take varied considerably . . . but whichever form was adopted, it had to be a lifelong commitment. Anything less than this was a practical denial of the announced intention of a total dedication to God. It was only this total dedication that gave religious Orders a claim to the privileges they enjoyed." Thus the Rule formed the crucial link between the Order and the authority structure of the church. Later religious orders (as, for example, the Society of Jesus) required ordination for full membership.

together in the common tongue, confess their sins to one another, and yet take no vow, surely there would be an end to all order in the church.[7] The problem was not new. Joshua had been troubled when Yahweh's Spirit rested on Eldad and Medad so that they prophesied in the camp (Num. 11:26). Though registered along with the rest of the seventy, they had not come to the tabernacle as the others had. "My lord Moses, forbid them," Joshua demanded. Moses' reply was prophetic: "Would that all the LORD's people were prophets," he said, "that the LORD would put his spirit upon them!" (Num. 11:29). The prophetic gift was sovereignly given.

> Joshua ... had to learn that a person cannot bind God with man-made rules. Joshua had a man-made rule: God really should not have placed his Spirit on the two men in the camp. This did not fit in with Joshua's concept of what was good and proper. God has bound himself with rules based on his own character, which he will never break, but men (including God's leaders) must never try to bind him with their own rules. He will not keep these rules.[8]

That the Spirit of God could not be fettered by even the most rigid of ecclesiastical structures was becoming increasingly evident in the nonconformist groups of the late Middle Ages.

The church considered this lack of conformity to be heresy. In twelfth-century France, the Waldenses, attempting to reinstitute what they believed to be New Testament norms, found themselves faced with a choice between submission to the hierarchy or the threat of extinction as heretics. When they appealed to the Third Lateran Council for permission to preach, one member of the Council is said to have replied:

> Shall the church give pearls to the swine, leave the Word to idiots whom we know to be incapable of receiving it? ... They now begin with extraordinary humility because they have not yet found a firm footing. But if we let them in, they will throw us out.[9]

The Waldenses responded by ordaining their own leaders. They generally chose young shepherds or husbandmen in whom the

7. *Ibid.*, p. 342. It is significant that the monastic option appeared with the institutionalization of a priestly hierarchy.

8. Francis Schaeffer, *Joshua and the Flow of Biblical History* (Downers Grove: InterVarsity Press, 1975), p. 17.

9. Donald F. Durnbaugh, *The Believers' Church* (New York: Macmillan, 1965), p. 44, quoted in Walter Nigg, *The Heretics* (E.T., New York: Alfred A. Knopf, 1962), p. 197.

church had recognized potential for leadership. The candidates were on probation for three or four years, during which time they were required to memorize the Gospels of Matthew and John and also some of the Epistles.[10] They were then ordained with the laying on of hands followed by the celebration of the Eucharist. This arrangement was not acceptable to the Roman Church, and years of persecution followed. The Waldenses lacked strong organization, and could not withstand the onslaught of the church, which of course meant that the civil authorities hounded them also. The church's stringent action was designed to keep the Bible out of the hands of the laity,[11] and above all to preserve its own authority. This it managed to do for some time, but the increasing corruption of the Roman priesthood was causing more and more unrest, and that not only among the uneducated and ignorant. The complaints of the Waldenses about the vices of the priests evoked a reply similar to the one that the Donatists had received centuries before when faced with the problem of unworthy priests. The Inquisitor, Peter von Pilichdorf (c. A.D. 1300), told them:

> ... What then? Are they on that account not priests? God forbid! For even as a man's goodness does not confer priesthood, so also doth his wickedness not take it away. ... Therefore, the worst man, if he be a priest, is more worthy than the holiest layman. ...[12]

Rumblings of dissatisfaction were to be heard inside the church, also. The writings of William of Occam and Marsilius of Padua heralded the beginnings of change, and along with the efforts of Wyclif and Hus paved the way for the coming schism.

Break with ancient tradition did not come easily. The *Unitas Fratrum* in Bohemia, finding themselves threatened by imminent persecution from the church, sought to establish their own ordination structures. Feeling a need for a legitimate succession from the primitive church, they sent delegates to Armenia, Greece, and even India, seeking bishops who would ordain their leaders. The mission failed, so in A.D. 1467 they set up their own ministerial order, thus breaking with both Rome and the Utraquist authorities. Their first ministers were chosen by lot,[13] and were then or-

10. G. H. Williams, *The Radical Reformation* (Philadelphia: Westminster Press, 1962), p. 527.

11. Council of Toulouse, A.D. 1229.

12. Quoted in G. C. Coulton, *The Inquisition and Liberty* (Boston: Beacon Press, 1959), p. 184.

13. Durnbaugh, *Believers' Church*, p. 59.

dained by a Waldensian bishop who, it was thought, could trace his ordination by succession back to the early church. Comenius was the last regularly ordained bishop of this group, but later Count Zinzendorf extended the chain of leadership into modern times as the Moravian Brethren.

Both the hierarchical structure of the church and the doctrines that undergirded the system unavoidably led to abuses of the "Order." Pope Gregory the Great had lamented:

> There are many who do not take money payments for ordination, but yet grant the ordination for human favour, and from this human praise, seek their sole reward. Thus the gift which they had freely received they do not freely give, because they expect in exchange for the granting of the holy office the payment of favour.[14]

Others also profited from the corruption that pervaded ordination. Hus, writing in A.D. 1413, tells us:

> In connection with the ordination of clergy it is the clerks who profit for they take a groschen and a con for the first ordination, and two groschens and two cons for the second ordination, while for the third and fourth they charge three groschen. ... Elsewhere they must pay even the barber and gatekeeper. ... Saint Gregory says "As it is not proper for the bishop to sell the laying on of hands, so a clerk or a notary should not sell his voice or pen at ordination.[15]

Such complaints, justified though they were, did not have the power to produce change. Still, the ferment was at work, and as Seeburg expresses it, "the new wine has not yet burst the old bottles."[16] The writers of late Scholasticism looked longingly to the authority of the Scriptures, but they nevertheless clung for the most part to the teachings of the church.

> When churchmen spoke of reformation they were almost always thinking of administrative, legal, or moral reformation; hardly ever of doctrinal reformation. They did not suppose the Pope's doctrine to be erroneous. ... They sometimes talked of a theology which should be less remote from human beings, more faithful to the Gospel. ... But to gain this end they had neither desire nor expectation of anything which could be called a change in doctrine.[17]

14. Matthew Spinka, *Advocates of Reform* (Philadelphia: Westminster Press, 1953), p. 202.

15. *Ibid.*, p. 228, quoting John Hus, *On Simony*.

16. Seeburg II:196.

17. Owen Chadwick, *The Reformation* (Grand Rapids: Eerdmans, 1965), p. 14.

Change of doctrine finally came with Martin Luther, and with the change came reformation in earnest.

THE MAGISTERIAL REFORMERS

Luther's teachings on ordination reflect two of the emphases he brought to reform: the Scriptures as the sole authority in the church, and the sinner's justification by grace through faith alone. For Luther, only baptism and the Lord's Supper were truly sacraments, for they alone were instituted by Christ. Ordination was a rite of the church and conferred no grace and no *character indelibilis*. Writing to certain of the spiritual descendents of John Hus, who were at this time in schism from Rome and yet were trying to maintain a priesthood based on the apostolic succession, he urged them, on the basis of 1 Cor. 14:30 and 1 Pet. 2:9, not to depend on furtive ordination by Italian bishops, but to select their own leaders and ordain them themselves.[18] He writes, "If we ask for such an example there is one in Acts 18 [vv. 24ff.] where we read of Apollos who came to Ephesus without call or ordination and taught fervently."[19] Tradition had a strong grip on the Bohemians; they refused Luther's advice.

Luther did believe, however, that ordination had a scriptural foundation:

Ordination indeed was instituted on the authority of Scripture, and according to the example and decrees of the Apostle in order to provide people with ministers of the Word. The public ministry of the Word, I hold, by which the mysteries of God are made known ought to be established by holy ordination as the highest and greatest of the functions of the church on which the whole power of the church depends, since the church is nothing without the Word, and everything in it exists by virtue of the Word alone.[20]

And he was quick to deny a sacramental aspect to the ordination rite. He continues, "When a pope or bishop anoints, grants tonsures, ordains, consecrates, dresses differently from laymen, he may make a hypocrite of a man, or an anointed image, but never

18. Luther, *Works* XL (St. Louis: Concordia, 1973), p. 40.

19. *Ibid.*, p. 37.

20. *Ibid.*, p. 11. By the "Word" Luther meant Christ in Scripture rather than the letter of Scripture itself. See Robert Paul, *The Church in Search of Itself* (Grand Rapids: Eerdmans, 1972), p. 135.

a Christian or a spiritually-minded man."[21] While maintaining the necessity of special ceremony in connection with pastoral duties, Luther nevertheless saw the implication of the doctrine of the priesthood of all believers.

> Everyone who has been baptized may claim that he already has been consecrated priest, bishop, or pope, even though it is not seemly for any particular person arbitrarily to exercise the office. . . . Only by the consent and command of the community should any individual person claim for himself what equally belongs to all. If it should happen that anyone abuses an office for which he has been chosen, and is dismissed for that reason, he would resume his former status. . . . Certainly a priest is no longer a priest after being unfrocked. Yet the Romanists have devised the claim to *characteres indelibilis*, and assert that a priest even if deposed, is different from a mere layman. They even hold the illusion that a priest can never be anything else than a priest, and therefore never a layman again. All these are human inventions and regulations.[22]

This was all well and good, but the institution of Luther's ideas was not so simple, if indeed he would have desired their consistent application. The princes of the realm were ready and waiting to step in if Rome could be ousted. The affairs of state and church were already enmeshed; both institutions were greedy for revenue from whatever source it could be obtained, and it was inconceivable that either priest or prince would willingly relinquish authority for the sake of a "new" truth. Nor were the common people ready for such responsibility as Luther envisaged as the ideal. Education had been the privilege of the monastic orders; the ordinary "Christian" was not only ignorant but superstitious, and perhaps unconverted. The excesses of the Münsterites called forth Luther's wrath and distrust. His confrontations with Carlstadt, who believed that those who ministered the Word should not be distinguished from other believers, strengthened his convictions that the ministry must be specially trained. In effect, he rejected any congregational type of church order.

The state-church alliance undoubtedly facilitated the spread of Protestantism in northern Europe and Britain, for civil rulers were more ready to institute reform than the clergy. They were

21. Luther, "An Appeal to the Ruling Class (1520)," quoted in Lewis W. Spitz, *The Protestant Reformation* (Englewood Cliffs: Prentice-Hall, 1966), p. 54.
22. *Ibid.*, pp. 54f.

not particularly interested in administrative reform, however, and without administrative reform, doctrinal reform was not possible. Practical considerations caused Luther to modify his earlier views on what constituted scriptural church government. Basing his rationale on Old Testament precedents, he relinquished church organizational matters to the state. The early Reformers, Bromiley says, "recalled the godly princes of the Old Testament and saw it as within the authority of Christian magistrates, and indeed as their duty, to take action for the spiritual welfare of their subjects."[23] Thus, by a hermeneutic that failed on certain critical issues to take into account the historical dimension of revelation, New Testament church organization retained many ties with Old Testament models. Samuel, for example, was often seen as the prototype of the church "minister."

Zwingli made a careful distinction between the doctrine of the priesthood of all believers and the office of the preacher, the latter being based on the twofold call of God and man.[24] Of rites not explicitly required by the Word he says, "As for consecrations, unctions, and other such rites which are destined to disappear, the wisest course is to have patience."[25]

Bucer was not primarily concerned with how ministers were chosen, whether by prince, bishop, or congregational choice, so long as they exhibited the qualifications set out in 1 Tim. and Titus.[26] Interested in reconciliation with Rome, Bucer was concerned with the "restoration of lawful ordination."[27] Consequently, he gave due weight to the candidate's "call" and the choice of the church; at the same time his model for an ordination prayer included the assertion ". . . by the laying on of hands with the word of the Lord and prayer, the gift of the Holy Spirit is by these means conferred."[28]

23. G. W. Bromiley, "Authority and Scripture," in *Scripture, Tradition, and Interpretation*, ed. W. Ward Gasque and William Sanford LaSor (Grand Rapids: Eerdmans, 1978), p. 23.

24. Jean Rilliet, *Zwingli* (E.T., Philadelphia: Westminster Press, 1964), p. 186. The concept of a special call to a holy life — a call for certain believers only — had originated in the monastic orders. "Vocation" set apart a spiritual elite. The Pauline doctrine of "call" as an integral part of every believer's conversion experience was undermined by the introduction of infant baptism as a routine church practice.

25. *Ibid.*, p. 127.

26. William Pauck, *Melanchthon and Bucer* (Philadelphia: Westminster Press, 1969), p. 239.

27. David Wright, *Martin Bucer* (Appleford: The Sutton Courtenay Press, 1972), p. 254.

28. *Ibid.*, p. 263.

Calvin's orderly frame of mind and legal training bear on his concept of church organization. He insisted on a "fixed form" and a "firm polity."[29] Even though he was a biblical restorationist, he conceded some leeway in forms. "We know that every church has liberty to frame for itself a form of government that is suitable and profitable for it," he said, "because the Lord has not provided anything definite."[30] He also laid great stress on "calling." Writing in the *Ecclesiastical Ordinances* he says:

> In order that nothing happen confusedly in the church, no one is to enter upon this office without a calling. In this it is necessary to consider three things, namely: the principal thing is the examination; then what belongs to the institution of the ministers; third, what ceremony or method of procedure it is good to observe in introducing them to office.[31]

The examination of the candidate involved his profession of the doctrine of the church, his agreement to maintain it, and an examination of his character and personal habits. Calvin based the institution and ceremony of induction on what he believed the ancient church did.

> The order is that ministers first elect such as ought to hold office; afterwards, that he be presented to the Council; and if he is found worthy, the Council receive and accept him, giving him certification to produce finally to the people when he preaches, in order that he be received by the common consent of the company of the faithful. If he be found to be unworthy, and show this after due probation, it is necessary to proceed to a new election for the choosing of another.
>
> As the matter of introducing him, it is good to use the [laying on] of hands, which ceremony was observed by the apostles and then in the ancient Church, providing that it takes place without superstition and without offence. But because there has been much superstition in the past and scandal might result, it is better to abstain from it because of the infirmity of the times.[32]

29. John Calvin, *Institutes* 4.10.27.

30. John Calvin, *Commentary on Paul the Apostle to the Corinthians*, 1 Cor. 11:3 (Edinburgh: Calvin Translation Society, 1847).

31. John Calvin, "Ecclesiastical Ordinances," in J. K. S. Reid, *Calvin: Theological Treatises, Translation, Introduction, and Notes*, Library of Christian Classics XXII (London: SCM, 1954), p. 58.

32. *Ibid.*, p. 59. According to John T. McNeill (*The History and Character of Calvinism* [London: Oxford Univ. Press, 1977 reprint], p. 161), the real reason for abrogating ordination temporarily was fear that the state might interfere in the selection of ministerial candidates. As it was, new ministers had to swear obedience to the civil authorities. Calvin's insistence on the importance of "call" may also reflect the struggle against the encroachment of state authority.

In an attempt to prevent abuse of ministerial authority Calvin spells out several safeguards. The minister must swear an oath in front of the Seigneury and must attend a weekly meeting to discuss the Scriptures. If differences of doctrine cannot be settled by the elders, the matter is to be taken to the magistrate.[33] "Intolerable crimes" in a minister are dealt with by the assembly of ministers and elders, and if necessary, the magistrate may depose the offender. Such "intolerable crimes" include heresy, schism, rebellion against ecclesiastical order, blasphemy, simony, dances, and "similar dissoluteness." Lesser faults, which may only require "fraternal admonition," included lying, slander, avarice, and "curiosity in investigating idle questions."[34] The guiding principle in Calvin's *Ordinances* is the keeping of good order. By rigid stricture Calvin built a sound ecclesiastical organization that was, for a hundred years, the most powerful force in Protestantism.

Ordinands were encouraged to obtain a university degree before ordination, but this standard was difficult to enforce. Sometimes country clergy were less stringently examined than those who were to preach in cities.[35] Candidates were examined in Latin and were required to know the differences between Protestant and Roman Catholic doctrine. Often, in order to fill vacant pulpits, poorly educated men were ordained to office. It was felt that it was better "for an ignorant man than no man to expound the Word of God, provided that ignorant man be a man of his Bible and of faith."[36] The Reformation emphasis on the primacy of the Word demanded that the clergy at least keep pace with the laity, some of whom now had the Bible in the vernacular. However, education in itself could not and did not produce a leadership all that superior to that which had called forth a desire for reformation in the first place. Certain abuses had been eliminated, and certain false doctrines refuted, but the implications of Reformation theology were not consistently carried through to their logical conclusions.

Ordination had lost its sacramental status, but continued to function as a means to regulate authority in the state-church coalition. The locus of succession of authority shifted from the person of the ordinand to the preaching of the Word, but only an ordained man was permitted to preach. The sacraments, two in number now

---

33. Calvin, "Ecclesiastical Ordinances," p. 60; McNeill, *History and Character*, pp. 161f. The "elders" were lay associates chosen by the magistrates in consultation with the ministers. Their duties related primarily to oversight and discipline.

34. Calvin, "Ecclesiastical Ordinances," pp. 60f.

35. Chadwick, *The Reformation*, p. 416.

36. *Ibid.*, p. 418.

instead of seven, had, at least in part, lost their sacramental character, but authority to administer them was still reserved for the ordained minister. In essence, the structure had changed but little; only because the number of the sacraments had been reduced and their significance been redefined were the clergy any less powerful than their Roman counterparts. Since ordination no longer conferred a *character indelibilis* on the ordinand, the power of the clergy centered less on him personally, and more on his function as an authority on the Word. Nevertheless, an aura of special divine favor continued to rest on the "minister," for he claimed a distinct and subsequent "call" from the Holy Spirit over and above the general call to ministry issued to all the elect of God at salvation. A sacramental standing might be denied to ordination, but there is no doubt that the idea of "character" had been retained. Many ministers believed "once ordained always ordained," and clergy and laity alike saw ordination as the *sine qua non* for the administration of the ordinances. In the new freedom and flowering of Renaissance culture, the ordained ministry, whether Catholic or Protestant, lost its monopolistic control of "church order." The pluriformity of the visible church could no longer be contained within the great hierarchical structures of the past.

THE RADICAL REFORMERS

The refusal to conform to the practices and doctrines of the "great Church" was nowhere more evident than in the so-called Radical Reformation movement. Unfortunately, some of the earlier manifestations of the new freedom took aberrant forms that brought suspicion and discredit to those who were seeking reform within and under New Testament norms. The followers of Socinus and Schweckenfeld, for example, rejected ordination to church office, seeing it as an attempt to restrict the working of the Spirit of God.[37] Excessive individualism, prophetism, and radical movements such as those of the Zwickau prophets and the *Spiritualisten* posed as great a threat to the orderliness and effectiveness of voluntary associations of believers as had that of the state-church Reformers and the civil authorities. Even though the Anabaptist movement was a lay movement, and the struggles with the magisterial Reformers tended to obscure the differences between the ordinary believers and their leaders, ordination was very quickly implemented as necessary to bring control and order into the ranks.

37. Williams, *Radical Reformation*, p. 159.

The *Schleitheim Confession* (A.D. 1527) is silent on the rite, but one of the tasks of the Martyrs' Synod in Augsburg (A.D. 1527) was the ordination of "apostles" to replenish the depleted leadership of the early Anabaptist movement.[38]

The tenacity of a tradition once incorporated into church structure is evidenced by the fact that in spite of the Anabaptist attitude to the established churches and their contempt for the pastors of these churches,[39] they continued to use the laying on of hands in ordination for their own church officers. Hounded into an underground movement and most cruelly persecuted by both the Roman Catholics and the magisterial Reformers, they nevertheless retained the rite of ordination—the power of which was due largely to the sacramentalism associated with the theory of apostolic succession from Peter. Several factors may have accounted for this anomaly. For the Anabaptists, the "fall" of the church had occurred with Constantinianism and the subsequent Augustinian justification of the doctrine of the "two swords."[40] It was from this time that they dated the evils that permeated the church. The early Donatists (fourth century) had practiced the laying on of hands in ordination; indeed, controversy over the theological implications of the imposition of hands had constituted a major part of the discussion at the Council of Arles (A.D. 316). When, therefore, the Reformers hurled the epithet *Donatisten!* at *them*,[41] they would have had little reason to question the rite, especially as it was a custom in pre-Constantinian times. The Anabaptists were biblical restitutionists; thus, the laying on of hands would no doubt seem to be an appropriate symbol accompanying the induction of church

38. *Ibid.*, p. 176.

39. Claus-Peter Clasen, *Anabaptism: A Social History 1525–1618* (Ithaca/London: Cornell Univ. Press, 1972), p. 77.

40. Franklin H. Littell, *The Origins of Sectarian Protestantism* (New York: Macmillan, 1964), p. 63. Menno Simons dated the "fall of the church" from the edict of Innocent I making infant baptism compulsory (A.D. 416). Ordination among the Anabaptists did not have the same focus as it had for the Reformers. For one thing, in the believers' churches, spiritual government functioned through the use of the ban, and only indirectly through the ordinances. Authority rested with the redeemed community led by the Spirit of God; acting on the principle of consensus, the church as a whole held the power of the keys and each chose its own spiritual leaders. The Anabaptists believed that the rise of the hierarchy was one sign of the "fall of the church" in the time of Constantine. Leadership must be community chosen leadership: "no special class of professionals was to be allowed to diminish the sovereignty of the community of believers in the matter of faith and order" (Littell, p. 93).

41. Leonard Verduin, *The Reformers and Their Stepchildren* (Grand Rapids: Eerdmans, 1964), p. 21.

officers. A people who in the early years of their existence (the 1520s) termed their itinerant evangelists "apostles" could hardly be accused of inconsistency in continuing to use this rite in their gatherings. Furthermore, they believed that they had "purified and disciplined" ordination in that their leaders were ordained upon election by the congregations. Menno Simons deemed the ordination of elders a safeguard against the excesses of the "enthusiasts."[42]

Article VIII of the *Augsburg Confession* (1530) throws an interesting sidelight on this state of affairs. While asserting that all ordinances in the church (except baptism and the Eucharist) were of "purely human origin and must prove their legitimacy by the gospel," it nevertheless "explicitly condemned the belief held by both the Donatists and the Anabaptists that the efficacy of the pastoral functions depended on the holiness and piety of the pastor."[43] Apparently, traces of a sacramental understanding of the rite still clung to the ordination to church office.

Throughout the various districts where Anabaptism flourished, divergent ordination practices were found, and various offices of church leadership existed. In the early years in the Netherlands, for example, offices often were not clearly distinguished. Preachers used to be chosen from among the deacons, and elders were selected from the preachers.[44] In the time of Menno Simons (who was himself reordained as an Anabaptist elder in 1539), the elders who conducted itinerant ministries formed a kind of council to discuss church matters, including ordination of new elders.[45] Laying on of hands also accompanied the ordination of deacons, but this practice was discontinued after A.D. 1650. With

42. The casting of lots and other random methods of selection were used also in the selection of leaders, even up to the present century in some communities. See also Littell, *Origins of Sectarian Protestantism*, pp. 15, 42.

43. Clasen, *Anabaptism*, p. 77. This principle was retained in Anglicanism. Article XXVI of the *Articles of Religion* (1562) of the Church of England states in part: "Although in the visible Church the evil be ever mingled with the good, and sometimes the evil have chief authority in the Ministration of the Word and Sacraments, yet forasmuch as they do not the same in their own name, but in Christ's, and do minister by his commission and authority, we may use their Ministry, both in hearing the Word of God, and in the receiving of the Sacraments. Neither is the effect of Christ's ordinance taken away by their wickedness, nor the grace of God's gifts diminished by from such as by faith and rightly do receive the Sacraments ministered unto them; which be effectual, because of Christ's institution and promise, although they be ministered by evil men."

44. N. van der Zijpp, "Ministry," *ME* III:699.

45. *Ibid.*

the proliferation of schisms among the Mennonites in the seventeenth century, practices varied from community to community. The Waterlanders, for example, abolished the laying on of hands for deacons in 1610 and for preachers in 1665, and by the nineteenth century all formal ordination among the Mennonites in Holland was discontinued.[46] Since Anabaptism was essentially a lay movement, preachers were chosen from the congregation and ordained. Generally, they received no formal theological training—nor any remuneration. The theological education of ministers was considered quite unnecessary, if not harmful, but by the late sixteenth century educated men, usually physicians, were being asked to assume leadership positions. In 1735 the Mennonite Theological Seminary was established in Amsterdam. Still, in the country churches, untrained and unsalaried lay preachers continued to outnumber trained men until the nineteenth century.[47]

Ordination among the Anabaptists was service oriented; preachers were called *Diener des Wortes* and stewards were *Diener des Notdurft*.[48] Especially in the early years of the movement, ordination was not tied primarily to the preaching ministry as it was with the magisterial Reformers. Ordained elders baptized, banned, administered communion, and ordained others; ordained preachers only preached or read the Scriptures.[49] The *Diaken-Dienaren*, whose job it was to care for the poor, and the deaconesses who also cared for the poor and sick, were considered a part of the "ministry."[50] Multiple ministerial leadership and shared ministries were common, and the authority vested in such leadership concerned the whole life of the community, not just the preaching and administration of the ordinances. Preaching was engaged in before ordination; often a probationary period was in fact deemed advisable.[51] Willingness to apply the ban was an essential duty of the ordained leader, acting on the advice of his council, and was all-important in maintaining the authority structure of the community. In the Hutterite ordination service, the candidate, even before being required to acknowledge the Confession of Faith, is asked, "Do you desire to exercise punishment and admonition with the right cour-

46. H. S. Bender, "Ordination," *ME* IV:73.
47. Van der Zijpp, *ME* III:701.
48. Littell, *Origins of Sectarian Protestantism*, p. 92.
49. Van der Zijpp, *ME* III:699.
50. *Ibid.*, p. 700.
51. C. Krahn, "Ministry," *ME* III:701.

age and diligence, so as to lead this congregation of the Lord that it might further be built and adorned in Him?"[52]

In Mennonite circles ordination was considered to confer a lifetime status:

> Ministers removed from office for causes such as heresy, or gross sin, or insubordination, or even for lesser causes, were not considered to have lost their ordination, but to have been "silenced," i.e. no longer allowed to preach, and could be restored to office without reordination.[53]

Mennonite ministers were accepted on transfer from other bodies, sometimes even from non-Mennonite denominations, without reordination.[54] The importance of ordination among the Mennonites apparently diminished when they no longer found themselves in the position of an embattled minority. Once tolerated, however, there was a loss of the brotherhood concept, so that there was a tendency to form power structures in the churches,[55] particularly in Russia, resulting eventually (1860) in the secession of those who became known as the Mennonite Brethren.[56]

ROMAN CATHOLIC REACTION

In reaction to the Reformation crises, the Roman Catholic stance on ordination was reaffirmed at Trent (A.D. 1546). Ordination, it was said, was instituted by Christ in connection with the Eucharist, and gave the clergy the sole authority to administer this sacrament for the remission or retention of sins. Ordination was reaffirmed as a sacrament of the church in which grace was conferred by the words and the signs of the rite, giving a permanent "character" to the ordinand. Eph. 4:11 and 1 Cor. 12:22ff. taught that not all have received the same spiritual power, and therefore hierarchichal church government was divinely ordained. The priesthood of all believers was rejected; the clergy became more than ever the "almoners of supernatural powers and the gatekeepers of the celestial world."[57] Ordination proved to be a bone of

52. John A. Hostetler, *Hutterite Society* (Baltimore: Johns Hopkins Univ. Press, 1974), p. 344. Hands were sometimes placed on the shoulders of the candidate at Hutterite ordination services.

53. Bender, "Ordination," *ME* IV:73.

54. *Ibid.*

55. J. A. Toews, *A History of the Mennonite Brethren Church* (Hillsboro, KS: Mennonite Brethren Publishing House, 1975), p. 21.

56. *Ibid.*, p. 302.

57. Seeburg II:449.

contention at Trent. Some of the bishops claimed that the power they received when hands were laid on them was directly from Christ, not delegated through the pope as the "vicar of Christ" who alone had the authority to dispense apostolic power. This question was decided later in favor of papal supremacy on the basis of the teachings of Thomas Aquinas.

Some minor reforms were made: the office of the sellers of indulgences was abolished and the training of the priesthood was improved. Now, anathemas were to be pronounced on any who dared to question the teachings of the church about its priestly caste. Rome recognized the importance of Holy Scripture, but also set up the traditions of the church "with equal feeling of reverence." The tension created by the existence of two equal authorities eventually moved in favor of tradition. In practice, Scripture was deprived of effective authority through subjection to the hermeneutical practices of the hierarchy of the church.[58] However, through the codifications of canon law the authoritative dicta of the clergy received permanence; eventually, the primacy and infallibility of the pope was enunciated at Vatican I in 1870.

As might have been expected, Rome's reaction to the Reformation was to strengthen ecclesiastical structures and to centralize its authority. The early church had employed similar methods in combatting Gnosticism. Ordination had retained its function as the key to power in the church. The Reformation focus on the centrality of preaching as the function of the ordained minister was influential in bringing a similar emphasis to the role of the priest. It had been the duty of the bishop to see that preaching was attended to, but actual permission to preach was granted through the provisions of canon law. It was now not enough that the priest officiate at the mass.

THE ANGLICAN ORDERS AND MORE DISSENT

The Reformation in England, at first more politically than religiously motivated, did not assume a fixed form until the *via media* between the Geneva Reformers and Rome became the doctrinal system of Anglicanism during the reign of Elizabeth I. After years of political and religious unrest, stability and order were the prime considerations for both church and state. The structuring of the Church of England reflects this desire for peace within the realm.

In his *Exhortation to Unity and Obedience* (1535), Thomas

58. Bromiley, "Authority and Scripture," p. 16.

Starkey had suggested that an appeal to "natural reason and natural law" would solve the problem of order. Many of the traditions
and ceremonies of the church, he said, were valuable for maintaining unity in the church, were not contrary to Scripture, and
ensured good order in the church.[59] Scriptural precedent, then, was
not to be the sole consideration in initiating customs in the church.
This could be seen as another assault on the authority of the Scriptures in the matter of church polity, or as a necessary stance in
view of the silence of Scripture on many of the issues faced by
those who were responsible for church government. The seeds of
dissent flourished in such soil. The details of church order could
now be wrestled out of the hands of the clergy, either on the basis
of "natural order," arguments from silence, or diverse interpretations of the text of Scripture. In any case, among the Anglicans
there was leeway for those ceremonies that did not violate scriptural principles as interpreted by the church hierarchy.

After Henry VIII declared himself "Supreme Head on Earth
of the English Church," Parliament, at his direction, acted to keep
religious order in the land. The *Ten Articles* (1536) mentioned only
three sacraments: baptism, the Eucharist, and penance. Bishops
were selected by the Crown, although official appointment came
through the dean of the cathedral of the diocese. Except for the
brief period when Mary sought to heal the schism with Rome,
Parliament passed several Acts of Uniformity (1549, 1552, 1559)
to ensure that religious affairs were conducted in an orderly manner, and that office-bearers in the church held acceptable views—
both political and religious. During the reign of Elizabeth I
(1558–1603), conformity to the *Thirty-Nine Articles* (which now
distinguished just two sacraments, baptism and the Eucharist)
had been a test of political loyalty.[60] During this period, the ordination of a priest did not automatically give him the right to
preach; only those who had been licensed for this purpose by the
bishop were permitted this privilege. Nor was the concept of the
apostolic succession considered to be of supreme importance at this

59. Lewis W. Spitz, *The Protestant Reformation* (Englewood Cliffs: Prentice-Hall, 1966), p. 157.

60. The Anglican use of the term "sacrament" with reference to ordination
is limited by the distinction drawn in the *Thirty-Nine Articles* (Article XXV),
between the two "sacraments of the Gospel" and the five "commonly called
sacraments." Article XXV differentiates between these five and the two sacraments "ordained by Christ" described in the Catechism as necessary to all men.
See also Johannes Feiner and Lukas Vischer, *The Common Catechism* (New
York: Seabury Press, 1975), p. 680.

time.[61] Later, however, conflict with Rome resulted in the assertion that the Anglicans *had* maintained the historic episcopate, if not through Archbishop Parker, then through Archbishop Laud. A strong and stable church was to be built by proper reverence for tradition, a tradition preserved and exemplified in episcopal ordination. Christ had ordained the episcopal form of church government to maintain the continuity and transmission of the faith,[62] and it was through the orderly succession of bishops appointed by the head of state (who was also the head of the church) that the faith could best be preserved.

Anglican ordination rites were a synthesis from various sources. The forms were based on pre-Reformation pontificals, and the interrogations and exhortations to the ordinands were largely derived from Bucer.[63] The three orders—bishop, priest, and deacon— were believed to be the biblical officers of church government, and all were ordained to office with the imposition of hands. Minor orders did not receive this rite. After at least one year's service as a deacon a man might qualify as a priest and be ordained to this office; a priest might later (though not before his thirtieth birthday) become a bishop. The office of deacon was based on Acts 6:1–6 and 1 Tim. 3:8–13. In addition to his general duties as the priest's assistant, he was expected to read the Scriptures and the homilies in the church, to baptize in the absence of the priest, and to preach if he had received permission from the bishop.[64] At the ordination of a priest, the bishop, after having said or sung the *Veni, Creator*

61. Even the great defender of Elizabethan Anglicanism, Richard Hooker, did not regard the apostolic succession as of divine origin. See "Anglicanism," *ODCC*, p. 57.

62. *The Book of Common Prayer*, 1966 ed. (1902), p. 305.

63. Unlike the medieval rites of Rome, most pre-Reformation English rites for the consecration of a bishop did not at first include the formula "receive the Holy Ghost" when hands were laid on him. Forms varied considerably; although there was a move toward simplification, much pomp and formality were deemed to be fitting to such an auspicious occasion. Hands often were placed on the candidate's head in silence, with the consecratory prayer either preceding the rite or following it later. Rituals were elaborated with various accoutrements and ceremonies. A bishop, for example, was given a staff, ring, and mitre, and various garments of office. In addition to imposing hands, the archbishop anointed the ordinand and later enthroned him at a separate rite. All such ceremonies were conducted in the context of the mass. See A. J. Maclean, "Ordination (Christian)," *HERE* 9:544f. On marriage and the ordination of the clergy in the Church of England see Derrick Sherwin Bailey, *The Man-Woman Relation in Christian Thought* (London: Longman's, Green, and Co. Ltd., 1959), pp. 190ff.

64. *The Book of Common Prayer*, p. 309.

Spiritus, laid his hands on the head of the ordinand (as did also any ordained priests who also happened to be present). Until 1662, the bishop had, in the *epiclesis*, prayed merely that the priest would receive the Holy Ghost. This now was made more specific, and perhaps in response to Roman Catholic criticism, the *intentio* of the rite became part of the consecratory prayer.

> Receive the Holy Ghost for the office and work of a Priest in the Church of God, now committed unto thee by the imposition of our hands. Whose sins thou dost forgive, they are forgiven; and whose sins thou dost retain, they are retained.[65]

As a result of the provisions of 1662, the priest now had authority both to administer the sacraments and to preach. The bishop's consecration included also the reading of the *Nicene Creed* and the King's (or Queen's) mandate for his consecration. He was also required to promise obedience to his archbishop. At the imposition of hands, the Spirit was again invoked, the archbishop adding, "And remember that thou stir up the grace of God which is given thee by this imposition of our hands. . . ."[66] The church may have denied full sacramental status to the rite of ordination, but it retained the language of sacrament. The reform element in the Anglican Church (the Puritans) objected to this phraseology, seeing it as a remnant of popery, but the liturgy was fixed by both law and custom.

In Scotland, in the meantime, a presbyterial form of church government based on Calvinistic principles had been established. At first, under the influence of John Knox (1560), the laying on of hands in ordination was abolished;[67] by 1572, however, the imposition of hands in ordination was reinstated, and has ever since been regarded as indispensable in the Church of Scotland. The power to ordain was in the hands of the presbytery. When the Westminster Assembly convened in England in 1643, the majority of the members, carefully chosen by the Parliament of the interregnum, and with the cooperation of their Scottish brethren, fa-

65. *Ibid.*, p. 315.
66. *Ibid.*, p. 319.
67. T. F. Torrance ("Consecration and Ordination," *SJT* 11 [1958], pp. 252f.) attributes this action to the view held by Knox that there was such a close relationship between the laying on of hands and the lifting up of hands in prayer, that the former is implied in the latter, and is, therefore, not an essential act in ordination. Torrance attributes the absence of the rite of the laying on of hands in ordination in early books of church order to a similar understanding by the earliest Fathers, that is, that the laying on of hands is implicit in the lifting up of hands in prayer.

vored the presbyterial system. With the concurrence of the General Assembly in Edinburgh, they issued a document entitled *Form of the Presbyterial Church Government and of the Ordination of Ministers* (1645) in which they plainly stated their belief that the order of church government is *de jure divino*, that is, divinely ordained; that the presbyterial system could be proved from Scripture, and that ordination was the function of the presbytery alone. No set form of words was stipulated for the rite, though God might be entreated on behalf of the ordinand to "fit him with his Holy Spirit," that he might fulfill his work of ministry, and that he might "both save himself and the people committed to his charge."[68] However, the Independents at the Assembly, even though they were biblical restorationists like the Calvinists, could not accept the implications of presbyterial ordination.[69]

Rigid church structures, whether Anglican or Calvinistic, could not contain the dynamic of the Spirit. In spite of restrictive measures, "laymen" who believed themselves called to preach the gospel by God exhorted whoever would listen to them. This greatly distressed the clerical establishment.

> Robert Baillie, a Scottish representative to the Westminster Assembly of Divines, looked with displeasure at the sight of lay preachers running "without any call, either from God or man into every shire of the Kingdome". . . . The enthusiasm generated by the lay preachers even made some impact at Cambridge, where undergraduates began preaching in their rooms and in the houses of the townfolk, causing concern that they might attempt to organize their own churches.[70]

As a result, Parliament forbade lay preaching in 1644, 1645, and again in 1646. The issue here was whether or not ordination hindered the freedom of the Spirit. Many believed that to insist on ordination as the *sine qua non* for preaching was to impose human restrictions on a sovereign Spirit who could work through whomever he wished.[71] It seems to have been accepted among many at this time that ordination *was* of human origin, for those who opposed lay preaching maintained that the Spirit worked through human means *including* ordination. The problem had far-reaching

68. Maclean, "Ordination (Christian)," p. 545.

69. The Presbyterians equated the offices of bishop and presbyter and so did not deny the validity of episcopal ordination.

70. Richard L. Greaves, "The Ordination Controversy and the Spirit of Reform in Puritan England," *JEH* XXI (1970), p. 225.

71. *Ibid.*

political and social overtones; theological argumentation by itself was not likely to convince either side to change its mind. Fear that if the ordination requirement was dropped fanatics would have free rein in the pulpits brought this answer from Oliver Cromwell:

> Approbation [i.e., ordination] is an act of conveniency in respect of order; not of necessity, to give faculty to preach the gospel. Your pretended fear lest error should step in, is like the man who will keep all the wine out of the country lest men should be drunk. It will be found an unjust and unwise jealousy, to deny a man the liberty he has by nature upon a supposition he may abuse it.[72]

Under Cromwell ordination was neither condemned nor made mandatory; regulation was achieved by a Committee of Triers who had the sole power of examining the fitness of candidates for pastoral office. In this way, the freedom of the Spirit was felt to be safeguarded. George Fox, the Quaker, had this to say on the subject:

> Let there be no outward Law to hinder or restrain any People from hearing any whom they believe is a minister of the Gospel, nor yet to compel any to hear any one they believe is not a minister of the Gospel; for an outward Law can but restrain or compel to the Good, but the Law and Power of God only in the heart: therefore let there be a free Liberty for all people to meet concerning their worship.[73]

Among the Independents and Separatists, primitivistic leanings contributed to anticlericalism.[74] The professional clergy represented an authoritarianism equally repressive, whether coming from Anglicans or Presbyterians.[75] Ordination was associated with the privileged classes of society, those who had a vested interest in maintaining the *status quo*. The clergy were accused of hiding behind the sanctity of divine ordination, an accusation not without plausibility, since they were excused from paying taxes and from military service. The ordinary believer received no such prefer-

72. Quoted from *The Letters and Speeches of Oliver Cromwell* in Greaves, "The Ordination Controversy," p. 228.

73. Quoted from *A Collection of the Sacred Books and Writings . . . by George Fox*, and cited in Greaves, "The Ordination Controversy," p. 228.

74. The Calvinists were also biblical restorationists, but their position *vis à vis* the state influenced their point of view on ordination. See note 32 above.

75. The alliance of church and state meant that any threat to religious authority was also a threat to political authority, for ordained ministers were the pillars of government. Thomas Hall, the Presbyterian, asserted that in both church and state superiors must govern and inferiors obey. The masses were to be subservient to the ruling classes, for such had God ordained.

ential treatment; he not only paid taxes, but if not impressed for military service was subject to a special tithe as well.

The right of women to preach had also become an issue at this time, paralleling a humanist-oriented movement in society to improve the status of women. Some of the Independents, including the Quakers and Fifth Monarchy people, and also some of the Anabaptists, did permit obviously gifted women to preach. The clergy fiercely opposed this. Greaves remarks:

> Their opponents were legion and were fortified by both Scripture and tradition. Robert Baillie, one of the Presbyterian divines of Westminster Assembly fame, conjured up images of the Münster fiasco when he uttered a dire warning that the Anabaptists had given women liberty to preach.[76]

The comparatively uneducated women did not stand a chance since they were given to understand that not only the clergy but God himself was offended by such activity. Thus, this particular threat by the clergy was of short duration.

The activities of Thomas Munzer and his followers were not typical of Anabaptists in general, yet the bogey of Münsterism was employed frequently by those whose overriding concern was the preservation of state-church concord. Lay preaching was seen as leading to social disintegration, the result being an orderly England racked with Münster-like rebellions.[77] The clergy could retain control only by relying on the arm of the state—and this they did to the fullest possible extent.

In 1643 Parliament had ordered the publication of *The Form of Church Government to be Used in the Church of England and Ireland*, in which the "Lords and Commons assembled in Parliament" declared that the terms "elder," "presbyter," and "bishop" signified the same function and that therefore ordination performed by a bishop was valid and was "not to be disclaimed by any that have received it."[78] When the episcopate finally was restored by Charles II, another Act of Uniformity was passed (1662), the result of which was that 2,400 ministers who had been presbyterially ordained, and who refused to be reordained by a bishop of the Church of England, were prohibited from holding office. This was

76. Greaves, "The Ordination Controversy," p. 236.
77. Cf. "Preface," *The Book of Common Prayer*. See also A. C. Underwood, *A History of the English Baptists* (Baptist Union of Great Britain and Ireland, 1947), pp. 58, 89.
78. Quoted in "Ordination, Nonconformity and Separation," *CQR* 19 (1884), p. 41.

a reversal of previous practice, for during the reigns of James I and Charles I, those with Puritan leanings in the church could seek a license to preach from a sympathetic bishop.[79] Now it was either conform or separate. Those who chose the latter course found themselves very often without a living; equally painful was the fact that they were now relegated to the camp of the socially inferior Independents and Baptists. Temporary relief came in 1672 with the issuance of the *Declaration of Indulgence*, which permitted Separatists to apply for a license to teach or preach. The various "Nonconformists" made the most of their opportunities to consolidate their positions. John Bunyan and his co-laborers were particularly effective in developing organizational cohesiveness. The *Act of Toleration* (1869) "was in part an implicit recognition that his organizational response had been successful."[80] The Separatist Presbyterians started ordaining their own ministers, though they still looked longingly to the state church. Of these, the Puritan Richard Baxter remarked:

> Those of them who do administer the sacraments and do that which is like the Separatists' way (e.g. call or ordain ministers), yet *do it not on their own principles* but *pro tempore*, until God shall give them opportunity to serve Him in the established way, it being reformed and well-ordered parish churches that are most agreeable to their desires.[81]

This attitude was reflected in the formula of ordination that was set down at the Westminster Assembly and used for many years by the English Presbyterians. The ordinand was asked, "Do you promise you will be zealous and faithful in the defense of the truth and unity against error and schism?"[82] Believing that God assigned specific gifts for ministry in each local covenanted congregation, a man who left his work in effect negated his ordination; reordination might be required if he moved to another charge.[83] Then too, for sufficient cause a man might be deprived of his status as an ordained minister.[84] In America, with the growth of univer-

79. W. Haller, *The Rise of Puritanism* (New York: Harper & Bros., 1957), p. 53.

80. Richard L. Greaves, "The Organizational Response of Nonconformity to Repression and Indulgence: The Case of Bedfordshire," *Church History* XLIV (1975), p. 484.

81. "The Nonconformists' Plea," quoted in "Ordination, Nonconformity and Separation," pp. 42f.

82. "Ordination, Nonconformity and Separation," p. 43.

83. Robert Paul, *Ministry* (Grand Rapids: Eerdmans, 1965), p. 160.

84. Durnbaugh, *Believers' Church*, p. 148.

sities such as Yale and Harvard, which had been founded primarily for the training of clergy, it became the practice to confer ordination automatically on the successful completion of a formal examination.

In the "established" churches, there was not only a sharp division between clergy and laity, but also a clear division between higher and lower clergy. The yeoman's son, even though a graduate of Cambridge or Oxford, might remain an ordained deacon for years; the son of "good family" was frequently ordained deacon and priest the same day.[85] Such practices were tied to financial benefits; much of the wrangling in the British Parliament over state-church affairs in the nineteenth century had to do with financial matters concerning the ordained clergy.[86] Dissenters and Catholics as well as Anglicans were obliged to contribute to the financial support of the clergy of the Church of England. Understandably, anticlerical feeling was rife and dissent thrived, both inside and outside the church. Changes came slowly, more often than not reflecting cultural changes in society. The effect of the Enlightenment can be seen in the *Clerical Subscription Act* of 1869. This act changed the formulae of ordination in the Anglican Church. The oath of allegiance to the sovereign was retained, but acknowledgment of royal supremacy was no longer imposed, nor was the ordinand required to "acknowledge all and every article of the *Thirty-Nine Articles* to be agreeable to the Word of God." "General Assent" was sufficient.[87]

Early in the Methodist movement John Wesley struggled with the problem of ordination. He was himself an ordained Anglican priest, and a believer in the apostolic succession.[88] Once he became convinced that "bishop" and "presbyter" were synonymous terms, he claimed as much right to ordain as a bishop. Faced with a shortage of preachers as his movement grew, he had to resort to "laymen," though reluctantly. Yet in time he could say:

> Give me one hundred preachers who fear nothing but sin, and
> desire nothing but God, and I care not a straw whether they

85. Urban T. Holmes, *The Future Shape of the Ministry* (New York: Seabury Press, 1971), pp. 80, 83.
86. Owen Chadwick, *The Victorian Church*, Part I (Oxford: Oxford Univ. Press, 1966), pp. 81ff.
87. "The Clerical Subscription Act," *ODCC*, p. 305.
88. Durnbaugh, *Believers' Church*, p. 132.

are clergymen or laymen; such alone will shake the gates of Hell, and set up the kingdom of heaven upon earth.[89]

Wesley was torn between a desire not to break with the Church of England and the conviction that the gospel must be preached at all costs. Both the parish system and the requirement that preachers were to be episcopally ordained so hindered his work that he could see no alternative but schism. "If we cannot stop a separation without stopping lay preachers," he remarked in a letter to Samuel Walker, "the case is clear—we cannot stop it at all. . . ."[90] One alternative was to do his own ordaining. Pressed by the need for evangelism in America, Wesley ordained Thomas Coke, who was already an ordained priest, as "superintendent" for America. Coke and Wesley then ordained other presbyters, some of whom were sent to Scotland. Wesley justified this action by arguing that administration of the sacraments requires ordination; the ultimate result was a break with the parent church.

Inconsistencies in the functions of lay and ordained preachers eventually led to a split within the ranks of the Methodists. The New Connection seceded in 1797 over clergy-laity distinctions, as did the Free Methodists in 1836.[91] The reaction of the Wesleyan Methodists was to tighten up their structures.

In 1818 the usage of the Conference was conformed to what has long been the ordinary unofficial custom, and the preachers began to be styled in the Wesleyan Methodist Magazine and in other official publications "Reverend," a fact which may seem trivial, but which in reality was of important significance.[92]

One important outcome was, no doubt, the secession of 1836, though the growing insistence on theological training for ministers may have been a contributing factor. The rite of the laying on of hands in connection with ordination was given official sanction in 1836.[93]

89. Quoted in Horton Davies, *The English Free Churches* (Oxford: Oxford Univ. Press, 1952), p. 133.

90. Robert W. Burtner and Robert E. Chiles, *A Compend of Wesley's Theology* (New York: Abingdon, 1954), p. 256.

91. The Wesleyan party would not accept that the minister "was to be essentially little if anything more than the hired preacher and officer of the Society, pecuniarly dependent on the one hand, and, on the other, denuded of all pastoral authority or prerogative whatever" (James H. Rigg, *A Comparative View of Church Organizations: Primitive and Protestant*, 3rd ed. [London: Charles H. Kelly, 1893], pp. 307ff.).

92. *Ibid.*, p. 309.

93. *Ibid.*

However, unordained men implemented Methodism in America for the most part, and Wesley himself had no illusions about the role of ordination in the spread of the gospel. "Was Mr. Calvin ordained?" he asked. "Was he either Priest or Deacon? And were not most of those whom it pleased God to employ in promoting the Reformation abroad, laymen also? Could that great work have been promoted at all in many places, if laymen had not preached?"[94] The answers were apparent.

The Plymouth Brethren also had their roots in Anglicanism. Again the original intent of the group was not secession. Anthony Groves (1795–1853), who was preparing for the priesthood in the Church of England, gave up the thought of ordination when he realized that by subscribing to the Thirty-Nine Articles he would be endorsing military service. When informed by the Church Missionary Society that he would have to be ordained if he wished to work under their auspices, he concluded that ordination was not necessary for true ministry.[95] J. N. Darby, who was later influential in the movement, had been ordained a deacon in the Church of England in 1825 and a priest in 1826, but resigned his curacy in 1828. He declared that elders and deacons were quite unnecessary, and that believers need only meet together to await the return of Christ. This group soon separated and lapsed into extreme authoritarianism. Another group, the "Open" or Independent Brethren,[96] perceived the need for a "recognized eldership and for ordered government within the church."[97] They also believed, however, that the ministry of the Word was not to be restricted to formal leadership, for God gives such gifts of ministry to whom he wills. Regulation was possible through the exercise of self-discipline by the speaker, and through the vigilance of the church as a whole.[98] The lack of formal organization among the Brethren invited diversity, which, unfortunately, often took the form of dissension and strife. Yet even without the stability provided by cen-

94. Burtner and Chiles, *Compend of Wesley's Theology*, p. 262, quoting from Wesley's *Works*, "A Farther Appeal to Men of Reason and Religion," III:10, 12.

95. Ordination was necessary that he might administer the sacraments. See also Harold H. Rowden, *The Origins of the Brethren: 1825–1850* (London: Pickering & Inglis, 1967).

96. The seventeenth-century "Plymouth Brethren" who were led by John Robinson and others had believed that ministers — and even sermons — were not absolutely necessary. See Durnbaugh, *Believers' Church*, p. 287.

97. F. Roy Coad, *A History of the Brethren Movement* (Grand Rapids: Eerdmans, 1968), p. 124.

98. *Ibid.*, p. 269.

tralized governmental structures the movement grew and became very influential.

The Quakers did not ordain leaders, either. Robert Barclay (1678) believed that those who preached should so do without "human commission or literature,"[99] that the Spirit might minister through whom he chose, unhindered by human regulations. In practice it was found necessary to appoint elders whose duty it was to counsel those who spoke in the meetings;[100] "ministers" were either "approved," "recommended," or "recorded."[101] Overseers, whose duties included home visitation and oversight of the lives of the people, provided a pastoral aspect of ministry. Women as well as men were permitted to preach the gospel. This movement grew rapidly not only in Britain but in America and throughout the world. Later, a similar phenomenon occurred in the Salvation Army with its pseudo-military structure.

History would seem to indicate, therefore, that "success" in carrying out the gospel mandate was not tied to any one pattern of church government. The deposit of faith was fixed; its mode of dissemination, however, could not be bound by rites and forms, not even those which, their proponents claimed, were dictated by Scripture. When the hierarchy of the Church of England undertook to force conformity to their organizational structure they had a measure of success; when, by means of ordination, they sought to silence those who were burdened to tell others the good news of Jesus Christ, they in effect forced the schism they so greatly deplored. Restraints, of which ordination was one, may at times have been deemed advisable. It was quite evident that the Holy Spirit overruled such restrictions when it pleased him to do so.

THE BAPTISTS

John Smyth, "the first English Baptist,"[102] was a graduate of Cambridge and an ordained Anglican priest who had adopted Puritan ideas during his student days. In 1606 he separated from the Church of England and was again ordained, this time as pastor of a Sep-

99. Robert Barclay, "Apology for the Quakers," in *Documents of the Christian Church*, ed. H. Bettenson, 2nd ed. (Oxford: Oxford Univ. Press, 1963), p. 358.

100. Howard H. Brinton, *Friends for 300 Years* (Pendle Hill Publications and the Philadelphia Yearly Meeting of the Religious Society of Friends, 1964), p. 92.

101. *Ibid.*

102. Underwood, *History of the English Baptists*, p. 33.

aratist congregation at Gainsborough. Smyth taught that church officers should be elected from the congregation by majority vote, and upon approval of their stand be ordained with fasting, prayer, and the imposition of hands. The laying on of hands served to point out the man for whom prayer had been made, and to assure the ordinand that "the Lord by the Church giveth him power to administer."[103] While in Amsterdam, where his group had fled to escape persecution, Smyth's congregation adopted believers' baptism as the basis for church membership. Before long there was division over the administration of the ordinances. Smyth had sought out the Waterlander Mennonites, hoping for union with them so that baptism could be performed by ordained elders.[104] Thomas Helwys and others took exception to this. They believed that God had not reserved the ministry of the Word and the administration of the ordinances for a particular class of men. Furthermore, if only elders could baptize "it was tantamount to going back to the idea of apostolic succession."[105] Smyth replied:

> I deny all succession except in the truth: and I hold that we are not to violate the order of the primitive church . . . it is not lawful for everyone that seeth the truth to baptize, for then these might be as many churches as couples in the world.[106]

Helwys' group returned to England in 1612 and established a church at Spitalfields, a church led and officered by laymen. Further division occurred in Smyth's congregation over the necessity for the ordination of church officers,[107] and the Waterlander Mennonites were again approached, but they declined any kind of organic union with the Baptists.

Until this time "ministry" had been conceived of as a local church function, but the urge for evangelism was producing the need for associational ties. The connection was made by the ordination of itinerant evangelists, on whom hands were laid by ministers representing the churches.[108] Thus in 1655 a Thomas Collier

103. *Ibid.*, p. 36.

104. John Christian, *A History of the Baptists* (Nashville: Broadman Press, 1922), pp. 227, 232.

105. Underwood, *History of the English Baptists*, p. 39.

106. *Ibid.*, p. 43, quoting Smyth's *Works*, p. 578.

107. Evidently the issue was the administration of the sacraments by unordained elders. Underwood, *History of the English Baptists*, p. 50, and Torbet, *History of the Baptists*, p. 39, do not agree on the details. It seems that Elias Tookey was excluded by the church in Spitalfields because he saw nothing amiss in an unordained man presiding at the Lord's Supper.

108. Torbet, *History of the Baptists*, p. 56.

was ordained as "General Superintendent and Messenger to all the Associated Churches." But during the early years of the Restoration ordination was not possible in either the General or Particular Baptist churches. The first recorded ordination of a dissenting minister after 1660 seems to have been that of Benjamin Keach in 1668.[109]

The position of the Baptists on ordination can be detected in their creedal statements, which proliferated in the troubled years of the seventeenth century. Between 1644 and 1656 the Particular Baptists, in answer to accusations that they were fomenting Pelagianism and anarchy,[110] drew up a series of confessions of faith. The first, the *London Confession of 1644*, was in many areas similar to the *True Confession* (1596) of the Baptists who had gone to Amsterdam to seek union with the Mennonites. This document permitted lay preaching by appointment of the congregation, stipulating, however, that no sacraments were to be administered until "the Pastors or Teachers bee chosen and ordeyned into their Office."[111] The Confession of 1644, unlike Smyth's *Short Confession* of 1610 (which called for ordination of church officers by the laying on of hands by the elders of the church),[112] does not mention ordination to church office, and deliberately stipulates that baptism may be administered by a "preaching Disciple, it being no where tyed to a particular Church, Officer, or person extraordinarily sent."[113] Underwood remarks: "Perhaps no Confession of Faith has had so formative an influence on Baptist life as this one."[114] With the Restoration, however, came renewed persecution. The need for a united front among the dissenters influenced the formularies of the *Second London Confession* (1677), especially those articles which had to do with church government. The *Westminster Confession* was used as the base, with suitable alterations reflecting Particular Baptist policy in a time of stress. On the authority of 1 Tim. 4:14 and Acts 6:3, 5, 6, ordination became the norm for church office.

109. Underwood, *History of the English Baptists*, pp. 109f.
110. William J. Lumpkin, *Baptist Confessions of Faith*, rev. ed. (Valley Forge: Judson Press, 1969), p. 144.
111. *A True Confession*, Article 34, quoted in Lumpkin, *Baptist Confessions*, p. 93.
112. *A Short Confession*, Article 26 in Lumpkin, *Baptist Confessions*, p. 109.
113. *The London Confession*, Articles 44, 41, in Lumpkin, *Baptist Confessions*, pp. 168, 167.
114. Underwood, *History of the English Baptists*, p. 152.

> The way appointed by Christ for the Calling of any person, fitted, and gifted by the Holy Spirit, unto the office of Bishop, or Elder, in a Church, is, that he be chosen thereunto by the common suffrage of the Church it self; and Solemnly set apart by Fasting and Prayer, with imposition of hands of the Eldership of the Church, if there be any before Constituted therein; And of a Deacon that he be chosen by the like suffrage, and set apart by Prayer, and the like Imposition of hands.[115]

In addition to the preaching ministry, these officers were set apart "for the peculiar administration of Ordinances, and Execution of Power, or Duty."[116] There was also a provision for "lay" preachers.

> Although it be incumbent upon the Bishops or Pastors of the Churches to be instant in Preaching the Word, by way of Office; yet the work of Preaching the Word, is not so peculiarly confined to them; but that others also gifted, and fitted by the Holy Spirit for it, and approved, and called by the Church, may and ought to perform it.[117]

Acts 11:19–21 and 1 Pet. 4:10, 11 were quoted in support of this practice.

The stance of the General Baptists is evident from their confession (1651) entitled *Thirty Congregations Gathered According to the Primitive Pattern*:

> Fasting and Prayer ought to be used, and laying on of hands, for the Ordaining of servants or Officers to attend about the service of God; Acts 13:3.[118]

Their response to the explosive growth of Quakerism took the form of attack by pamphlet and the formulation of confessions.

> Many religious groups looked frantically about for some defense against the almost irresistible enthusiasm of the new movement. Some General Baptist Leaders . . . decided to publish a thorough criticism of the Quaker positions, and to issue a confession of their own faith.[119]

These confessions, as might be expected, reacted to the Quakers'

---

115. *The Second London Confession*, Chapter XXVI, Section 8, in Lumpkin, *Baptist Confessions*, p. 287.

116. *Ibid.*

117. *The Second London Confession*, Chapter XXVI, Section 11, in Lumpkin, *Baptist Confessions*, p. 288.

118. *The Faith and Practice of Thirty Congregations Gathered According to the Primitive Pattern*, Article 73, in Lumpkin, *Baptist Confessions*, p. 187.

119. Lumpkin, *Baptist Confessions*, p. 189.

denial of the need for an ordained ministry by stipulating fasting, prayer, and the laying on of hands in induction to church office.[120] The *Standard Confession* (1660), although not speaking for all General Baptists,[121] illustrates the shift in practice that had occurred in some Baptist churches; the laying on of hands now took place at baptism. A severe censure of the Baptists by the Puritans could have influenced the shift, although the Baptists claimed scriptural warrant, citing the teaching of Heb. 6:1, 2; Acts 8:12, 15, 17; and Acts 19:6. Even 2 Tim. 1:6 (where Paul lays hands on Timothy) was cited in connection with baptism.[122] Ordination to church office was now to follow the pattern of Acts 14:23, with no mention made of the laying on of hands.[123] Later, with the return of more stable conditions and the need for unity among the dissenters, the *Orthodox Creed* (1679) was drawn up by a group of General Baptists to "unite and confirm all true Protestants."[124] This creed called for the imposition of hands at *both* baptism and ordination.[125] Article XXXII states the purpose of the laying on of hands in baptism:

> Prayer, with imposition of hands by the bishop, or elder, on baptized believers, as such, for the reception of the holy promised spirit of Christ, we believe is a principle of Christ's doctrine, and ought to be practised and submitted to by every baptized believer in order to receive the promised spirit of the father and son.[126]

At a time when the Church of England was asserting its power as the state church, there was a tendency among the General Baptists to "elevate the ministry and centralize authority."[127] It is also evident that there was an inclination to attach a sacramental understanding to the rite of the laying on of hands.

Among the Calvinistic Baptists in America, Elias Keach in-

120. *The True Gospel Faith Declared According to the Scriptures* (1654), Article 23, in Lumpkin, *Baptist Confessions*, p. 194; *The Somerset Confession* (1656), Article XXXI, in Lumpkin, p. 212. Texts cited were Acts 6:6; 13:3; and 14:23.

121. Lumpkin, *Baptist Confessions*, p. 221.

122. *The Standard Confession*, Article XXII, in Lumpkin, *Baptist Confessions*, p. 229.

123. *Ibid.*, Article XV.

124. Lumpkin, *Baptist Confessions*, p. 295.

125. *The Orthodox Creed*, Articles XXXI and XXXII, in Lumpkin, *Baptist Confessions*, pp. 319ff.

126. *Ibid.*, Article XXXII, in Lumpkin, *Baptist Confessions*, pp. 320f.

127. Lumpkin, *Baptist Confessions*, p. 296.

troduced the practice of the laying on of hands in baptism in 1670. The *Philadelphia Confession* (1742) devotes Chapter XXXI to the laying on of hands (with prayer) on baptized believers, calling it an "ordinance of Christ."[128] After citing Heb. 5:12; Acts 6:1, 2; 8:17, 18; 19:6 it is stated that

> The end of this ordinance is not for the extraordinary gift of the Spirit but for (Eph. 1:13, 14) a farther reception of the Holy Spirit of promise, or for the addition of the graces of the Spirit, and the influences thereof; to confirm, strengthen, and comfort them in Christ Jesus; it being ratified and established by the (Acts 8 and 19:6) extraordinary gifts of the Spirit in primitive times.[129]

The resemblance to the doctrine of confirmation as taught in the Episcopal Church is remarkable. The *New Hampshire Confession* (1833) omits mention of the imposition of hands entirely.

Decline set in among the Baptists (and other dissenters) during the reign of William and Mary (1869–1702). They turned their attention to the formation of creeds and the definition of organizational structures.[130] The General Baptists declared a threefold order of ministers: messengers, elders, and deacons, all of whom were now ordained to office.[131] The elder was the pastor of the local congregation and was expected to stay with his flock for life.[132] There were also preachers who were ordained, but they did not generally administer the sacraments.[133] The role of "messenger" gained in importance as evangelistic fervor declined; in time, the ordaining function came to be assigned to these messengers.[134]

The relationship between ordination and the ordinances continued to cause problems for the Particular Baptists. In 1693 the Bristol Assembly declared that only elders could administer baptism and the Lord's Supper, except for those "called to the office by the suffrage of the church, who had not yet been ordained by the laying on of hands."[135] The truth was that a requirement such

---

128. *The Philadelphia Confession*, Article XXXI, in Lumpkin, *Baptist Confessions*, p. 351.

129. *Ibid.*

130. Torbet, *History of the Baptists*, pp. 63ff.

131. Underwood, *History of the English Baptists*, p. 119.

132. *Ibid.*

133. *Ibid.*

134. *Ibid.*, p. 121.

135. *Ibid.*, p. 130.

as ordination could not be enforced until an educated ministry was available for leadership in the churches. Armitage points out that

> they knew nothing of our modern Councils for Ordination, but commonly, as a mere matter of courtesy, invited neighboring pastors, not as representatives of other Churches, but on their personal kindness, to take part in the public recognition services.[136]

So busy were the Baptists with disputes over hymn-singing, the question of open or close communion, and the Calvinism-Arminianism controversy, that we hear of no real disputes over ordination for many years.

On the other hand, John Gill, the acerbic hyper-Calvinist, was outspoken in his views on ordination. He did not oppose a public induction service; he did, however, see that the laying on of hands could not be divorced from sacramental modes of thought. On the imposition of hands in the New Testament he says: "Though there was χειροτονία a *stretching out of hands*, yet there was no χειροθεσία the *imposition of hands* used at . . . ordination."[137] Of the appointment of church officers in Acts 14:23 and Titus 1:5 he notes that Paul gave

> no orders and instructions to lay hands on them; which he would not have omitted had it been material, and so essential to ordination as some would make it to be. . . . The hands of ministers now being empty and they having no gifts to convey through the use of this rite, of course it ought to cease.[138]

Gill argued from the Scriptures, but the voices of tradition were strong. To remove the laying on of hands from the rite of ordination would be virtually to destroy the solemnity of the ceremony. Of all the variations in ordination to church office, the laying on of hands and the *epiclesis* were the "irreducible minimum."[139] Practical considerations took priority over theological arguments.

SUMMARY

Ordination with the laying on of hands survived the Reformation but in the process lost both form and content. Romish embellish-

---

136. Thomas Armitage, *A History of the Baptists*, vol. I (Minneapolis: James and Klock Christian Publishing House, 1977 reprint), p. 567.

137. John Gill, *Body of Divinity* (Atlanta: Turner Lassiter, 1965, reprint), p. 868.

138. *Ibid.*, p. 869.

139. Maclean, "Ordination," *HERE* 9:551.

ments were removed; content was re-formed in keeping with the theological positions of the various groups and their need to preserve their organizational integrity. Six facts stand out:

1) Ordination with prayer and the imposition of hands continued to be the norm in the induction of church officers. Even those who discontinued the rite tended later to restore it to use.

2) Although in Protestantism ordination was not one of the "seven sacraments of the church," it did retain a sacramental or semisacramental character in some denominations (notably the Anglican). Even among the Baptists, a sacramental understanding of the act of the laying on of hands tended to reassert itself in times of stress.

3) In the rejection of sacramentalism the rite became representative; certain duties were delegated by the church to the ordinand. The candidate was ordained on the basis of all or some of several factors: a subjective "call," educational attainment, experience (as in an internship situation), or the objective evidence of gifts for leadership and/or preaching.

4) Even among those who denied a person-to-person apostolic succession from Peter, the idea of succession through personal agency persisted. For example, the early Baptists in Britain looked for their leaders through the direction of the Holy Spirit in the church, but when the time came to ordain a man they stipulated that he be set apart by "fasting and prayer with the imposition of hands by the eldership of the church."[140]

5) Ordination was an integral part of the doctrine of ministry. Changes in the function of the "minister" brought changes to the doctrine and practice of ordination. With the denial that ordination was a sacrament of the church, and that the ordained priest had the power to reenact the sacrifice of Christ at the mass, emphasis shifted from the Eucharist as the central rite of the church to preaching as the central rite. Ordination now set apart the preacher instead of the priest. Since the imposition of hands continued to be the highlight of the ceremony, many of the ideas formerly associated with ordination under the old regime were carried over into Protestantism. Especially persistent were the ideas of "character" and succession. Ordination was still also the *sine qua non* for the administration of baptism and the Lord's Supper.

6) Following the Reformation, the increased flexibility of the

140. *The Second London Confession*, Article IX, in Lumpkin, *Baptist Confessions*, p. 287.

organizational structures of the church, of which ordination was
a part, meant that political and religious pressures tended to alter
both the meaning of ordination and the use to which it was put.
Among Baptists there was overlap and selectivity in the use of
proof-texts to support the laying on of hands in baptism and ordination. A study of the Baptist confessions suggests that ordination practices were not so much based on Scripture as that Scripture
was employed to justify practices that were deemed necessary to
preserve denominational identity.

As a result of the Reformation, ordination with the laying on
of hands lost authority. There were both theological and historical reasons for this. The decline in the sacramental understanding of the rite and the altered view of the nature of apostolic
succession led to a shift in the basis on which the authority of the
clergy rested. A sense of special "call" over and above the general
call of all believers to ministry, a sort of ecclesiastical "divine
right," became the chief argument for right to church office. Historically, it had become apparent that whether or not ordination
had preceded the preaching of the Word made no difference to its
effectiveness. Whatever ordination might do for church structures,
the gospel could be preached successfully without it.

Chapter 5

ORDINATION: SUBSEQUENT DEVELOPMENTS

E. C. Nelson says of some of the early German and Swedish settlers in America, "Lutheran colonists would probably have found it difficult to explain just what ordination was, but it was part of their churchly heritage from Europe to expect a minister to be ordained."[1] This statement is representative of the attitudes of many Protestants to the ordination of their leaders. With the New World gaining its inhabitants from diverse religious backgrounds, ordination was undoubtedly a major factor in retaining denominational identities and distinctives in times of great social and political upheaval. Many groups, no longer upheld by state support, found themselves thrown upon their own resources. Whether or not the theological rationale for ordination was understood, it was no time to question it as a valid rite of the church.

EXPANSION IN AMERICA

Anglicans in the American colonies found themselves in serious difficulties in trying to adapt the English system to their new situation. For one thing, they had no bishop who could confirm and ordain. Commissaries sent by the bishop of London did not have this power; nor did they have the aura of authority and tradition that came through the laying on of hands in consecration. Anglican graduates from Harvard could be sent to England for ordination to the diaconate or priesthood, but this was both time-consuming and costly. In spite of the efforts of the bishop of London, and

1. E. Clifford Nelson, ed., *The Lutherans in North America* (Philadelphia: Fortress Press, 1975), section 47.

repeated appeals to the reigning monarchs,[2] the Church of England in America was deprived of episcopal leadership for 177 years.[3]

Political factors were, of course, involved. The colonists had brought their religious differences with them when they crossed the ocean; the Puritans particularly were not enamored of religious toleration, especially if it took the form of encouraging episcopacy in their midst. Some Anglican clerics frankly looked upon the episcopal system as a means of binding the Empire together,[4] hardly a popular view in a time of rising anti-imperialism. Pamphlet battles raged between the clerics of Anglican and Congregationalist factions. Charles Chauncy, a leading minister of the First Church (Congregational), Boston, even went to the trouble of tracing the historical development of episcopacy to the end of the second century, and remarked that "no one had ever anywhere seen bishops like those the Church of England proposed to introduce to America."[5]

The American Revolution almost destroyed the Anglican Church in America. Since the need for episcopal leadership was essential to its survival, the clergy in Connecticut finally sent Samuel Seabury to England for ordination. Because he could not sign an oath of allegiance to the Crown, however, he could not be consecrated in England. He went, therefore, to Scotland, and in 1784 received the laying on of hands for the office of a bishop.[6] Two years later, new legislation was enacted in Parliament "to make it possible for the Apostolic Succession to be established in America."[7] After the Revolution, American Anglicanism gained new citizenship as the Protestant Episcopal Church, which made minor revisions in the *Book of Common Prayer* and formulated a constitution.[8] Unique to the American structure was the requirement that in approving candidates for ordination, the bishop must act

2. Raymond W. Albright, *A History of the Protestant Episcopal Church* (New York: Macmillan, 1964), pp. 97ff. The appeal to Queen Anne (1709) came to nought due to her death; an appeal to George I also failed. He distrusted the clergy and was not interested in sending bishops to America.

3. *Ibid.*, p. 96.

4. *Ibid.*, p. 106. Thomas Chandler, a prominent New Jersey Anglican clergyman from 1746–1766, championed this cause.

5. *Ibid.*, p. 107. He entitled this pamphlet "A Compleat View of Episcopacy."

6. William B. Williamson, *A Handbook for Episcopalians* (New York: Morehouse-Barlow Co., 1961), pp. 26f.

7. *Ibid.*

8. Albright, *History of the Protestant Episcopal Church*, pp. 135ff. In 1792 a somewhat revised "Form of Making, Ordaining, and Consecrating Bishops, Priests, and Deacons" was incorporated into the constitution. The Thirty-Nine Articles were introduced in 1801, but subscription by the clergy and laity was not required.

with the approval of the standing committee of the convention.[9] With the establishment of episcopal government, the Protestant Episcopal Church at last found itself on firm ground.

In the beginning years of many denominations in America lay preaching was accepted. Early preachers in the Methodist movement were not ordained but they did not have the right to administer the sacraments, either.[10] After the Revolution, when the Methodist Episcopal Church formed in Baltimore (1784), it called for more formalized structures and instituted ordination. But it was not long before concern for the preservation of lay rights resulted in the formation of a separate body, the Methodist Protestant Church (1828).[11] In the early years of Lutheranism in America lay preaching was also a common phenomenon. Henry Muhlenberg, a leading German Lutheran minister in Pennsylvania in the 1740s, not only approved of unordained preachers but had no theological objections to their administering Holy Communion.[12] In general, however, ordination was considered the norm in Lutheranism. Lay preaching among Baptists and other groups was also characteristic of the American frontier and was instrumental in carrying the gospel to the most remote communities. However, once churches were organized along denominational lines, an ordained ministry was in most cases regarded as desirable.

The swing to "high-churchism" among some of the Southern Baptists demonstrates the persistent recurrence of succession theories often tied directly to the laying on of hands in ordination. In the search for a locus of authority in the organizational church, four succession theories were current in Southern Baptist circles in the first half of the nineteenth century,[13] one of which claimed

> a succession of validly ordained ministers from the apostles, who were ordained by Jesus, to the present. Under this theory, the validity of the "orders" (ordination), and not the form of church organization, furnishes the channel through which the stream of history flows and assures the apostolicity of the church. Only ordained ministers may be members of the pres-

9. *Ibid.*, p. 142. It seems that Samuel Seabury was not one to brook curbs to his authority.

10. Nolan B. Harmon, *Understanding the United Methodist Church*, 2nd rev. ed. (Nashville: Abingdon, 1974), p. 17.

11. *Ibid.*, pp. 19f.

12. Nelson, *Lutherans in North America*, section 47 (Journals of Muhlenberg 3:255, 256).

13. William Wright Barnes, *The Southern Baptist Convention 1845 – 1953* (Nashville: Broadman Press, 1954), pp. 101f.

bytery to ordain a minister, and each ordaining presbytery
must have at least three members.[14]

This "Landmarkism" view always interpreted "church" in the New
Testament as a reference to the local church, and since only Baptist
churches were churches in the New Testament sense, only Baptist
ministers were validly ordained ministers.[15] Most Baptists would
not concur with these extreme views. Even so, the remark of a
Lutheran writer is *a propos*: "Protestantism has in practice embraced the doctrine of orders it attributes to Roman Catholicism,
that the ministry is an order rather than a particular function."[16]
Many of those in the "free" churches in early America had come
from denominations in which the clergy played the dominant role;
they now valued their freedom from hierarchical control. Under
such circumstances, clericalism was watched with a wary eye.

A study of the "Christians" (Disciples) in postrevolutionary
America reveals the tenacity of ordination traditions in church
organizational patterns. The original leaders of this movement,
who came from diverse backgrounds—Methodist, Baptist, and
Presbyterian—all had become disenchanted with what they saw
as oppressive clericalism in their denominations. With the collapse
of confidence in the hierarchical ordering of Christianity, they
turned to a radical individualism that maintained that each believer was entitled to his own interpretation of the Bible. Provided
that he was guided by the Spirit of God, he could dispense with
those insights from Scripture found in the historical reflections of
God's people in the past, especially as articulated in the creeds.[17]
The "Christians" believed that inflexible ecclesiastical structures
were hindering the work of the Spirit of God in the churches. Yet
though they insistently repudiated the use of the title "Reverend,"[18] they continued to lay hands on their candidates in ordination.[19] Ministers needed only to "obtain license from God to
preach the simple Gospel *with the Holy Ghost sent down from
heaven*," though the church also tried them for the soundness of

14. *Ibid.*

15. *Ibid.*, pp. 104f.

16. Eric W. Gritsch and Robert W. Jenson, *Lutheranism* (Philadelphia:
Fortress Press, 1976), p. 122.

17. Nathan O. Hatch, "The Christian Movement and the Demand for a
Theology of the People," *The Journal of American History*, vol. 67, no. 3 (Dec.
1980), p. 560.

18. Winfred Ernest Garrison and Alfred T. De Groot, *The Disciples of
Christ, A History*, rev. ed. (St. Louis: Bethany Press, 1958), pp. 92, 109, 342.

19. *Ibid.*, pp. 342, 441. Ordination was not, however, mandatory (see p. 116).

their faith.[20] Since only those who had been ordained could administer the ordinances,[21] it is no surprise that ordination became the rule.[22]

Early in the history of these "Christians" it became evident that the individualization of the doctrine of the priesthood of all believers was undermining the stability and cohesiveness of the churches.[23] Growing factionalism in their ranks necessitated the tightening of organizational structures.[24] As a result, the "Christians" found themselves reverting to the very "mediating elitism"[25] they had so bitterly attacked in the first place.

ROME SINCE VATICAN II

The twentieth century brought little alteration in the ordination rites in Rome. Nevertheless, facing pressure from sociological ferment, the Roman Catholics have had to find a way of coping with change without endangering their claims to catholicity. According to Vatican II, the church is not a static reality but a "continuous creation," and although a hierarchy, it is a hierarchy of "service and ministry."[26] There is a new emphasis on the church as the "people of God," with a recognition that the laity also have gifts of ministry. This does not mean, however, that clergy-laity distinctions are decreasing. The laity must function outside of church institutions, as auxiliaries of the clergy and in specific subordination to them.[27] There is, insists the church, an essential difference between the common priesthood of the laity and the special priesthood of those ordained to be ministers or servants of the people of God. The church, as an institution, possesses the charism of Christ's sacerdotal power, which is bestowed upon the priest in ordination. Thus, the priesthood of the laity differs in essence from that of those who have received holy orders.[28]

20. *Ibid.*, p. 109.

21. *Ibid.*, p. 215.

22. *Ibid.*, p. 441.

23. The crisis of authority that precipitated the birth of the American nation undoubtedly modified postrevolutionary ecclesiology in America. See Hatch, "The Christian Movement...."

24. Hatch, "The Christian Movement...," p. 565, n. 70.

25. *Ibid.*, p. 551.

26. Holmes, *Future Shape of the Ministry*, p. 142.

27. Gary McEoin, *What Happened at Rome: Vatican II* (New York: Holt, Rinehart, & Winston, 1966), p. 61.

28. Karl Rahner, *A Theology of Pastoral Action* (Montreal: Palm Publishers, 1968), p. 73.

Ecumenical pressures, however, have forced a reappraisal of certain historic pronouncements of the church.

> Vatican II threw new light on the decisive role of sacramental ordination . . . its role had been obscured by a too individualistic notion of the sacraments as a privileged means of grace, and by the predominance of a juridical notion of the Church, as though the kingly powers of Christ were delegated to bishops, priests and faithful through the agency of the Vicar of Christ, the Pope. In this way, the Church seemed to be established primarily on the primacy of jurisdiction of the Roman Pontiff, a doctrine completely foreign to the gospel and Christian antiquity.[29]

Trent is to be considered in context: it was concerned above all with defending the reality of the ministry against certain reformers who wished to suppress the distinction between the community and the minister.[30] Because the traditions of the church have arisen in the course of history, papal pronouncements, it is said, must be subject to the process of historical criticism for their true significance to be revealed. Dogma is developed and nurtured in the womb of the church: as long as the church exists such dogma will continue to evolve. Thus the Augustinian doctrine of the *character* received at ordination may well be modified with the passage of time.

> If some theologians are hesitant when sociologists and pastoral needs suggest the institution of part-time priests, it is primarily the scholastic doctrine of the character which causes difficulty. But a scholastic tradition, adopted without critical study of its content and its historical evolution, should not be allowed to break the pastoral reform of the priesthood.[31]

The church must adapt to survive.

Some of the insights of the Reformation are modifying the position of Rome. According to Berkouwer, Roman Catholics since Vatican II have been seeking to combine succession of witness to the faith with personal succession resting on legitimate ordination, "with the historical ties created by the physical laying on of hands by proper bishops being given content by the spiritual tie with the apostolic word."[32]

29. Piet Fransen, "Orders and Ordination," *SacraM*, pp. 1145f.

30. The "reformers" are not specified; this is not, apparently, a reference to the magisterial Reformers, for they also held ecclesiastical offices in high regard.

31. Fransen, "Orders and Ordination," p. 1147.

32. G. C. Berkouwer, *The Second Vatican Council and the New Catholicism* (Grand Rapids: Eerdmans, 1965), pp. 169f.

Recently, there have been some voices in the church speaking rather plainly about the priesthood of believers. According to Hans Küng,

> this priesthood of all believers by no means excludes a particular pastoral ministry. ... Those who are empowered to exercise a particular pastoral ministry in the Church are not, at least as far as the New Testament tells us, a separate caste of consecrated priests, as they often are in primitive religions. They do not act as mediators between God and the people by means of ritual actions which they alone can perform, representing the people before God in sacrifice, and representing God to the people through oracular statements and lawgiving. In the Church of Jesus Christ, who is the only high priest and mediator, all the faithful are priests and clergy.[33]

From the tone of recent papal pronouncements, however, it may reasonably be inferred that these views are not acceptable to John Paul II and the College of Cardinals. When we read on the accession of Pope John Paul I, "He is the Most Eminent and Most Reverend Lord Cardinal Albini Luciano who has taken the name of John Paul I,"[34] we realize that change in the church is a slow process.

EPISCOPAL ORDINATION AND ECUMENICISM

In spite of the *via media* the Anglicans are only now learning to encompass change without forcing schism. The Church of England has had some painful experiences with Rome, particularly over ordination. A commission appointed by Pope Leo XIII had this judgment to make on the Anglican priesthood:

> ... In the rite of the accomplishment and administration of any sacrament we rightly distinguish between the ceremonial part and the essential part, which are usually called the matter and the form. And all are aware that the sacraments of the new law, being sensible signs and signs efficacious of invisible grace, ought both to signify the grace which they effect and to

---

33. Hans Küng, *The Church*, p. 438. The concern that the laity assume a more active role in the eucharistic worship of the church has been voiced since the time of Pope Pius XII. Nevertheless, there is always the fear that such a trend might eventually threaten the office of the ordained priest. See H. Shelton Smith, Robert T. Handy, and Lefferts A. Loetscher, eds., *American Christianity: Interpretation and Documents 1820–1960*, vol. II (New York: Charles Scribner's Sons, 1963), pp. 496f.

34. *Time*, Sept. 4, 1978, p. 64.

effect the grace they signify. . . . Now the words which up to
the last generation were universally held by Anglicans to be
the proper form of ordination to the priesthood, viz. *Receive
the Holy Ghost*, are surely far from the precise signification of
the order of the priesthood, or its grace and power, which is
especially the power of consecrating and offering the true body
and blood of the Lord in that sacrifice which is no mere com-
memoration of the sacrifice accomplished on the cross. This
form was indeed afterwards augmented by the words *for the
office and work of a priest*, but this rather proves that Anglicans saw that the first form was defective and inadequate.
And the addition, even if it were able to give the necessary
significance to the form, was brought in too late, for a century
had elapsed after the acceptance of the Edwardian Ordinal:
the hierarchy had died out and there remained no power to
ordain.[35]

The ordination of bishops received the same verdict. Since, according to Leo, the *intentio* was defective, ordination performed according to the Anglican formula was "utterly invalid and altogether
void."[36] As might be expected, this brought quick rebuttals from
the archbishops of Canterbury and York. It was some consolation
that Anglican Orders had been recognized by the Old Catholics
and many parts of the Eastern Orthodox Church. The fact remains,
however, that except for those in the Tractarian movement, Anglicans do not consider their ordained men priests in the Roman
Catholic sense, because the mass is not considered a sacrifice.

It simply cannot be denied that at the Reformation the notion
of a sacrificial priesthood was firmly repudiated. Indeed, at the
ordination of a priest, the medieval habit of giving the man
a patten and chalice as the emblem of his priestly office was
significantly altered. From now on, he was given a Bible. It is
hardly surprising, therefore, that Anglican orders are condemned by Rome because they lack the intention to make a
man a priest in the sacrificial sense. The old priest has become
the new presbyter. That is the position of the Church of England. Whatever the views of some of her members, a church's
doctrine must be judged by her formularies. There is no doubt
that the formularies of the Church of England, the Bible, the
Book of Common Prayer, and the Articles of Religion, do not

35. From the Epistle *Apostolical Curial* 1896, quoted in H. Bettenson, ed.,
Documents of the Christian Church, 2nd ed. (Oxford: Oxford Univ. Press,
1963), pp. 385f.
36. *Ibid.*

favour the interpretation of priesthood and sacrifice advocated by "Catholic" Christendom.[37]

It is this very issue that is hindering ecumenical concord. In *A Statement of the Ministry Agreed by the Anglican-Roman Catholic International Commission* (1973) it is indicated that certain areas of agreement have been reached: the goal of the ordained ministry is to serve the priesthood of all the faithful; the Holy Spirit provides the ordained ministry; bishops and presbyters at their ordination are given the authority to pronounce God's forgiveness of sins; ordination is a sacramental act; the laying on of hands is an "outward sign of the gifts bestowed," etc.[38] Two crucial areas that are intimately associated with the doctrine of ordination have not yet been resolved: the problems of authority and primacy.[39] These are none other than those confronting Luther in the sixteenth century.

Ordination has been the stumbling block in other ecumenical discussions. In Canada in the 1920s, when the Presbyterian, Methodist, and Congregationalist churches were exploring the possibility of organic union, they approached the Anglicans to invite their participation in the proposed talks. The latter replied that they would only do so if the negotiating churches would accept the *Lambeth Quadrilateral of 1888*, which meant accepting the doctrine of apostolic succession as the basis for valid ordination.[40] The implication here seemed to be that the ministers of the Free churches would be placed in an inferior position before joint discussion would be in order. This wasn't the only problem, though. Even before contemplating union, the Presbyterians had been having doctrinal problems that focused on the ordination rite. As Chown explains,

> it was well known, and a fact publicly stated by leading ministers of the Presbyterian Church in Canada, that at the ordination and induction of ministers of that Communion they were privileged to accept the [Westminster] Confession with silent mental reservations. This practice was so well understood that to conform to it was not regarded as moral dishonesty or verbal deceit, whatever delicate compunctions may

37. Michael Green, "Called to Serve," in *Christian Foundations*, vol. I, ed. Philip Edgcumbe Hughes (Philadelphia: Westminster Press, 1964), pp. 86f.
38. Johannes Feiner and Lukas Vischer, eds., *The Common Catechism* (New York: Seabury Press, 1975), pp. 677ff.
39. *Ibid.*
40. S. D. Chown, *The Story of Church Union in Canada* (Toronto: Ryerson Press, 1930), p. 31.

have been inwardly felt about making a vow which did not explicitly carry with it their real convictions.[41]

With union, the *Westminster Confession* was put "reverently on the shelf as one of the historic battles of the Reformed Church."[42] Most of the Methodists were flexible on this point, and the Congregationalists were in the minority. The new "Creed" was broad enough that ordinands could accept office without compromising their beliefs.

The Protestant Episcopal Church in the United States took a different tack in approaching the Congregationalists on the subject of union. *The Joint Commission on Unity* (1922) proposed a Concordat in which Congregational ministers might receive Episcopal ordination without becoming members of the Episcopal Church and without ceasing to be pastors of their congregations. An additional clause stated that a congregation whose minister was to be ordained not only should be agreeable to such ordination, but should also declare "its purpose to receive in the future the ministrations and the Sacraments of one who shall have been ordained to the Priesthood by a Bishop."[43] Such a move would have made Episcopalians of Congregationalists. The motion was tabled.

PRESENT PRACTICES

In keeping with the Reformation emphasis on the preaching of the Word as the primary function of the ordained minister, ordination in those communities that claim Puritan or Methodist roots has tended to become closely associated with academic preparation for the ministry. In most Protestant denominations, lay preaching is looked upon as a stopgap measure at best. Under certain circumstances, licensed lay preaching is permitted in both the United Methodist Churches in the U.S.A.[44] and in the United Church of Canada,[45] though the ideal is still a seminary-educated ministry. However, the United Methodist Church also ordains "deacons" and "elders" with the laying on of hands. On the authority of Acts 6

41. *Ibid.*, pp. 69f.
42. *Ibid.*, pp. 74f.
43. Albright, *History of the Protestant Episcopal Church*, p. 353.
44. Harmon, *Understanding the United Methodist Church*, p. 17.
45. *Manual of the United Church of Canada: Constitution and Government* (Toronto: The United Church Publishing House, 1928), pp. 25f. Licensing to preach was a local church function and was subject to yearly renewal.

and the ministries of Stephen and Philip, a deacon may perform all ministerial functions in his own charge, including assisting at Holy Communion. He may advance to the rank of elder, in which case both elders and the bishop lay their hands on him, praying for him to be imbued with the Spirit "for the work of an elder in the Church of God."[46] The bishop is "consecrated" for administrative duties, not "ordained."[47] Ordination is a denominational, not a local church function, confers permanent office, and is conducted at the annual conference.

Until recently the majority of Southern Baptist ministers were "tent-makers"; that is, they depended on secular employment for their incomes. The emergence of a full-time, paid professional ministry has been a comparatively recent development,[48] a trend that has been paralleled in the Mennonite churches.

In merger discussions with United Presbyterians, the "Southern" Presbyterians (Presbyterian Church in the United States) found that ordination vows required of ministers was a touchy subject. They eventually (1977) approved a change in their own vows that permitted ordinands a little more leeway in their understanding of their church's creedal affirmations.[49] Implicit in all the contention over ordination is the assumption that ordination will preserve denominational identity, an identity that is seen to represent the "orthodox" position. In an increasingly pluralistic Christianity, ordination as a basis for guaranteeing orthodoxy becomes less and less effective.

The Roman Catholic and Anglican understandings of ordina-

46. Harmon, *Understanding the United Methodist Church*, p. 115.

47. *Ibid.*, p. 118.

48. Albert McClellan, "Southern Baptist Roots in Practice and Polity," *Review and Expositor*, vol. LXXV, no. 2 (Spring 1978), p. 289.

49. Arthur C. Piepkorn, *Profiles in Belief*, vol. II (New York: Harper & Row, 1978), p. 316. The old vow read "Do you sincerely receive and adopt the Confession of Faith and the Catechisms of this Church as containing the system of doctrine taught in the Holy Scriptures?"; the new vow reads "Do you sincerely receive and adopt the Confessions of this Church as, in their essentials, authentic and reliable expositions of what Scripture leads us to believe and do, and will you be instructed and led by them as you lead the people of God?" Piepkorn notes that the Symbolical Books (i.e., the catechisms and creeds) "operate explicitly with the concept of a de facto succession of ordained ministers" (p. 87). Thus the pastor is regarded as a successor of the apostles, even though the upheaval of the Reformation prevented the continuation of the historic episcopate through apostolic succession.

tion as a sacrament and a "minor sacrament"[50] have been carefully defined and refined in the fires of controversy. The Church of England now requires the ordinand to undergo the scrutiny of a selection committee,[51] meet the conditions stipulated in the *Book of Common Prayer*, and present three letters of testimonial from beneficed clergymen as to his suitability for office.[52] Two opportunities are given to the laity to object publicly to his ordination. The bishop, however, makes the final decision, and may reject a recommendation if he sees fit.[53] The newly ordained man is expected to continue his studies.

Other denominations have stated their views on ordination. The Lutheran position holds that "The appointment and the existence of the ordained ministry . . . is a 'visible word' . . . a sacrament performed not on the one ordained but on the community."[54] The United Methodists assert a representative position. "In ordination, the Church affirms and continues the apostolic ministry which it authorizes and authenticates through persons empowered by the Holy Spirit. As such, those who are ordained are committed to becoming conscious representatives of the whole gospel and are responsible for the transmission of that gospel. . . ."[55] The literature on ordination coming from various Baptists, Pentecostals, and others of "evangelical" stance testifies to the influence of their theological forbears. Ordination has been accepted in most of these bodies with few questions asked, and is assumed to be based on reliable scriptural norms. Generally, one text in which the laying

50. Article XXV of the *Thirty-Nine Articles* states "There are two Sacraments ordained of Christ our Lord in the Gospel, that is to say, Baptism, and the Supper of the Lord. Those five commonly called Sacraments, that is to say, Confirmation, Penance, Orders, Matrimony, and extreme Unction, are not to be counted for Sacraments of the Gospel, being such as have grown partly of the corrupt following of the Apostles, partly are states of life allowed in the Scriptures; but yet have not like nature of Sacraments with Baptism, and the Lord's Supper, for that they have not any visible sign or ceremony ordained of God" (*The Book of Common Prayer*, 1662 revision).

51. The selection board consists of a panel of clergy and laity selected by the bishop. Guy Mayfield, *The Church of England: Its Members and Its Business*, 2nd ed. (London: Oxford Univ. Press, 1963), pp. 73ff.

52. *Ibid.*, p. 79.

53. *Ibid.*, p. 73.

54. Gritsch and Jensen, *Lutheranism*, p. 120.

55. *The Book of Discipline of the United Methodist Church* (1976), p. 446. A slightly different position is taken by T. F. Torrance, "Consecration and Ordination," *SJT* 11 (1958), pp. 242ff., and by Robert Paul in *Ministry*, pp. 13ff.

on of hands occurs is accepted as sufficient evidence for the rite,[56] and so long as it is understood that the imposition of hands does not confer "grace," further theological elaboration is seldom attempted. Great emphasis is placed on "call" understood in the monastic and Reformation sense rather than the Pauline (and Petrine) identification of "call" with the process of salvation:[57] "call" has replaced the doctrine of the apostolic succession as the source of the divine legitimization of the rite. Traditions die hard. Frequently, representative concepts[58] and vestiges of sacramentalism creep in,[59] even though Strong's definition of ordination as "a recognition of powers previously conferred by God, and a consequent formal authorization, on the part of the church, to exercise gifts already bestowed"[60] would fairly accurately express the position of most "evangelicals." Nevertheless, such definitions are often belied in the actual church situation of ordination.

In spite of insistence in most Baptist groups that ordination is a function of the local church, the actual ceremony quickly takes on a denominational significance, usually justified by an appeal to Acts 15.[61] The main purpose of the rite often seems to be a test of denominational conformity rather than any evaluation of "call" or gifts for preaching. A candidate may be isolated or quarantined if he deviates from the group's doctrinal position[62]—whether or not he believes himself called to the ministry, and whether or not he

56. Acts 13:3 is commonly used; sometimes also 1 Tim. 4:14, but 2 Tim. 1:6 with its implication of sacramentalism is generally avoided.

57. K. L. Schmidt, "καλέω," *TDNT* III:488f. Luther's translation of "call" as *Beruf* (vocation, occupation) rather than *Berufung* (summons, nomination) resulted in a semantic shift in the meaning of "call" that has been perpetuated in Articles XVI, XXVI, and XXVII of the Augsburg Confession. The use of "call" in the non-Pauline sense has been carried over into English. See also L. Coenen, "Calling," *NIDNTT* II:271ff.

58. For example, Strong, *Systematic Theology*, p. 918; Kenneth Hamilton, *To Turn From Idols* (Grand Rapids: Eerdmans, 1973), p. 208.

59. The very title "Reverend" accorded the ordained minister implies that grace has been conferred in the laying on of hands. Sacramentalism is also implicit in the widely held idea "once ordained, always ordained," common among those who deny the transference of grace in the imposition of hands.

60. Strong, *Systematic Theology*, p. 918.

61. This in spite of the fact that the Jerusalem Council was not dealing with church office: see Hiscox, p. 370, on this subject. Typical of denominational literature on this and related topics is R. L. Matthews, *The Ordination of Men Called of God to the Ministry of the Word* (Des Plaines: Regular Baptist Press, 1973).

62. Arnold T. Olson, *This We Believe* (Minneapolis: Free Church Publications, 1973), p. 50.

demonstrates gifts for preaching. The right of a church or an association of churches to exclude an unsuitable candidate is not in
question. What *is* dubious is the use of the rite of ordination for
this purpose.[63]

The insistence among some that only the ordained may administer baptism and conduct the Lord's Supper demonstrates the
persistence of the sacramental view of ordination. With reference
to Swedish Lutherans who had broken away from the state church
(c. 1880), Olson notes that

> the fact that only ordained Lutherans could fill the Lutheran
> pulpit, only ordained Lutherans could serve communion and
> then only to Lutherans, was deeply ingrained in the people.
> Old traditions are hard to drop. The thought that there was
> a special virtue in who officiated at the communion service
> lingered on even after the open break.[64]

When Strong says that the imposition of hands is a natural
symbol of the communication "not of grace but of authority"[65] he
comes very close to contradicting his own definition of ordination.
Inconsistencies also emerge in the early Baptist confessions. The
True Confession (1596) had restricted the administration of the
sacraments to the ordained[66] and frequently the laying on of hands
was, and still is, reserved for those who had themselves received
the imposition of hands.[67] The early American Congregationalists
found this a troublesome issue. According to the *Cambridge Plat-
form* (1648), when no ordained elders were available it was per-
missible for brethren nominated by the church to impose hands in
ordination.[68] One might also wonder why, if there is no thought

63. 1 Tim. 5:22 is sometimes used to justify the use of ordination as a test
of orthodoxy. On the enigmatic character of this text see Chapter 7. Olson
(*This We Believe*) cites an example: "There was a time when the question of
the eternal security of the believer was such an issue that pastors sitting in on
ordaining councils sat in the pew at the time of the public ordination service
refusing to participate in the 'laying on of hands' because the candidate leaned
to the Calvinistic view on some of the doctrines" (p. 48).

64. Olson, *This We Believe*, p. 274.

65. Strong, *Systematic Theology*, p. 924.

66. *A True Confession*, Article 34, quoted in Lumpkin, *Baptist Confessions*, p. 93.

67. For example, *The Second London Confession* (1677), Chapter XXVI ,
Section 8, quoted in Lumpkin, *Baptist Confessions*, p. 287.

68. See Hiscox, p. 372. Inconsistencies in Baptist doctrines of ordination
can be detected in the stance of the New Connexion (General) Baptists in
Britain in the late seventeenth and early eighteenth centuries. For example,
they considered that "it may not be improper for a minister of the Gospel, who
administers the ordinance of baptism, to administer the Lord's Supper, though

of the transmission of "grace," hands are not just placed but are *pressed* on the head of the ordinand. The Baptist writer Hiscox recognizes that reordination presents no problems if grace is not conferred. "Reordination, or recognition, whichever the Church and candidate may prefer, is equally effective, and a matter of indifference. The purpose and effect of both are the same."[69]

Both "classic" Pentecostalism and the charismatic renewal movement of the 1960s and 1970s have seen the reapplication of Acts 19:1–11 to a latter day "new Pentecost" in which the laying on of hands is again practiced for the reception of supernatural gifts, particularly tongues.[70] The writings of those concerned leave no doubt that they consider the physical imposition of hands to be an important factor in the reception of the gifts of the Spirit.[71] As might be expected, in those confessions in which the imposition of hands has been the prerogative of the bishops, the emergence of the rite among the laity has caused no little disturbance. Thus when glossolalia appeared among Episcopalians in the 1960s, the practice was discouraged and tongues-speaking was looked upon with suspicion.[72] The concern was not all on the side of the clergy, though; for many neopentecostals there was an inherent antithesis between the clerical institutions of the church and the free operation of the Spirit in the new charismatic communities. Roman Catholic interpretation, therefore, shies away from attributing any sacramental efficacy to the rite; it is "prayer in action," a gesture that any person may make; therefore, imposition of hands is not

---

unordained . . . but ordination to the deacon's office gives no such right" (Underwood, *History of the English Baptists*, p. 158). Yet later (1920), when the Baptist Union of Great Britain and Ireland rejected the appeal of the Lambeth Conference for unity with the Anglicans, but also declared that "any full descriptions of the ministerial functions exercised among us must also take account of other believers who, at the call of the church, may preside at the Lord's Supper, or fulfil any other duties which the church assign to them" (Underwood, pp. 261– 263, reply to the Lambeth *Appeal to All Christian People*).

69. Hiscox, p. 384. He comments "Whether ordination be supposed to represent the verity of a divine call, or the validity of ministerial acts, in either case recognition and ordination stand on the same ground. The one is as effectual in ascertaining his call, and declaring his authority, as the other, . . . since ordination is not to empower but to approve" (p. 385).

70. See Chapter 9.

71. This was certainly so in the case of Agnes Ozman and in many others who have since requested the laying on of hands in the mainstream Pentecostal movement.

72. Edward D. O'Connor, *The Pentecostal Movement in the Catholic Church*, rev. ed. (Notre Dame: Ave Maria Press, 1971), p. 24.

essential to baptism in the Spirit.[73] This interpretation minimizes the threat to hierarchical authority, and opens the way for integration of the charismatic communities within existing authority structures. Pastoral supervision will suffice to counteract aberrations that may develop,[74] and fruits of the movement will contribute positively to the life of the church. Among some separatist Fundamentalists, however, opposition to glossolalia lies in part not in their use of the laying on of hands, but in a fear that the transdenominational character of the charismatic renewal movement will fortify the base for ecumenical accord.

The representative view of ordination presents equally difficult problems of confusion and inconsistency. For one thing, it assumes a single church leadership pattern, a situation that did not hold in apostolic times and does not hold now. Any person who would claim to represent the church as a community must indeed claim a broad range of spiritual gifts if he or she is to represent adequately. The representative view posits an elitism quite contrary to the spirit of the New Testament. There is the ever-present threat that representation will slip over into mediation and remove the believer further away from his God.

Practical problems in either view of ordination abound. Once committed to "the ministry," is an individual never to be permitted changes in his or her beliefs or life-style, regardless of what honesty dictates? Is ordination a device to maintain the *status quo* at all costs? What about parachurch organizations? How do the tax concessions of the state fit into a theology of ordination? We could go on, but perhaps it is enough at this time to suggest that the doctrines of ordination stand in need of reassessment if the church is to retain any credibility in a rapidly changing society.

73. *Ibid.*, p. 136.
74. *Ibid.*, pp. 175, 223.

Chapter 6

IN RETROSPECT

The laying on of hands in induction to office originated in the time of Moses when the congregation of Israel laid hands on the Levites as the representatives of their firstborn (Num. 8:10), and when Moses commissioned Joshua by laying his hands on him (Num. 27:23; Deut. 34:9). In these pericopes, the foundations for understanding the New Testament rite are laid down.

The imposition of hands on Joshua by Moses was a sacramental act; that is, there was a transference of an objective entity, whether this be thought of as *hôḏ*, majesty (Num. 27:20 MT), δόξα, glory (Num. 27:20 LXX), or the spirit of wisdom (רוּחַ חָכְמָה, *rûaḥ ḥokmāh* MT, πνεύματος συνέσεως LXX, Deut. 34:9). The rite was performed in conjunction with a significant crisis in the advance of the plan of redemption of the people of God: the Israelites are now to move into the land promised to them by Yahweh, the God of the Covenant. His promise to them is about to be fulfilled, and Joshua, empowered by God through the hands of Moses, plays an instrumental role in this fulfillment.

When the Israelites lay their hands on the Levites, the latter accept responsibility, as far as the cult is concerned, for God's Covenant people. The Levites are God's special possession; they have replaced the firstborn in the stream of redemptive history. It is after they have been sanctified and are acceptable to God (a "wave-offering," Num. 8:13) that they become representatives. Their service has a dual character: they serve God through Aaron the high priest, and they serve the congregation by becoming "a wave-offering from the people of Israel" (Num. 8:11). It is through the Levites that the revelation of God is made known to the scattered tribes. Thus the Old Testament portrays the imposition of hands as both a sacramental and a representative rite.

The significance and scope of the laying on of hands in rabbinic Judaism is difficult to assess. There is no doubt that this act was

103

associated primarily with Temple sacrifice; allusions to the practice in other contexts is infrequent. It is possible that even before A.D. 70 hands were being laid on rabbinic scholars on the basis of their intellectual attainments, and as an indication of their stewardship of the wisdom of Moses, though some scholars would argue that this was a later custom. In its rabbinic application to the professional scholar, the imposition of hands lost its eschatological orientation. It became a badge of office, a credential. This came about largely through the midrashic exegesis of Num. 27:16–23; Deut. 34:9; and Num. 11:24–30. By establishing a succession from Moses, the mediator of the Old Covenant, a mediatorial element was introduced into the role of the ordained rabbi. In view of the Hellenistic climate of the times, it is not surprising that an elitist class, those who were the custodians of the "mysteries" of God, emerged.

The earliest postapostolic evidence for the imposition of hands in induction to church office comes from late second- or early third-century writings. These manuscripts exhibit textual problems that make dating difficult. However, there is no doubt that ordination was an established custom by the fourth century, and that it was by then an integral part of the doctrine of apostolic succession. As the belief grew that "character" was bestowed on the candidate in ordination, and that the bishop had the power to mediate the Spirit for office, the rite became restricted to the higher orders of the clergy. Ceremonial induction to office was embellished with symbolic garments and solemn ritual; the essence of the rite was expressed in the laying on of hands and the accompanying prayer invoking the Spirit. Thus endowed with apostolic authority, the bishop played a key role in mediating the salvation of God to the masses. Power struggles, both within the church and between the church and state, resulted in the establishment of a rigid hierarchical system in which tradition, sanctified by the authority of the pope, played the dominant role. Scriptural endorsement for ordination was not necessary; the teachings of the church sufficed and were final. An ecclesiastical caste, ensconced behind their ordination vows, had usurped the priesthood of the people of God, and in so doing had also encroached on the prerogatives of the Lord whom they professed to serve.

The rumblings of dissent, which had been heard through the centuries, erupted into a clamor with Luther. Doctrinal reformation shook the theory of apostolic succession, but the ordination tradition, though transformed theologically, survived as a guarantor of authority in a period of instability. The rationale for ordination was now sought in the preaching of the gospel rather than in the administration of the ordinances. Still, for the most part, ordination was considered a *sine qua non* for baptizing and conducting the Lord's Supper. Most Protestants held to this tradition very tenaciously; those who did not, found themselves in the minority.

With the focus on preaching as the central rite of the church, and the loss (in some confessions) of a sacramental understanding of the laying on of hands, the representative aspect of the rite came to the fore. Instead of being a priest to the people of God—as had formerly been the case—the minister assumed the role of the Levite. He became *the* representative of the church, the one whose duty it was to convey the revelation of God to the people. The congregation adopted a passive role. Since the ordained man was paid to perform the ministerial functions of the church, he tended to take on a mediatorial role, interpreting the Word and will of God to the church. As the "man of God" or the "man of the cloth" he also epitomized the church to the world. Mutual discernment of gifts among believers became unnecessary, with a consequent loss of a sense of community. Protestantism became individualistic. Attention was focused on the great pulpiteer and the charismatic evangelist, and salvation became strictly an individual matter. Discernment of ministerial gifts was now largely the responsibility of the man who believed he had been "called," rather than the outcome of a consensus among the believing community. The church's leaders were there chiefly through personal initiative and choice.

The gifts for the functioning of the body of Christ, the church, were, it would seem, concentrated in this one person, the ordained minister. Instead of admonishing and teaching one another (Rom. 15:14; Col. 3:16), believers took their problems to their "ministers." In addition to being a preacher, evangelist, administrator of the ordinances, marryer, buryer, and the overseer of a "team," he now became a counselor as well. Which of these gifts did ordination recognize when hands were imposed? Was one Christian really "called" to all these roles in the church? Twentieth-century doctrines of ordination among Protestants not only conflict with each other, but exhibit numerous internal inconsistencies. Since all claim their doctrines are based on the Scriptures, we must now try to determine what the New Testament actually teaches about the laying on of hands for induction to office in the church.

Part II

THE LAYING ON
OF HANDS

Chapter 7

GOD'S MIGHTY HAND

Christianity has been described as an incarnational religion. We read that "the Word became flesh and dwelt among us, full of grace and truth; we have beheld his glory, glory as of the only Son from the Father" (John 1:14). Again we meet the glory of God, now incarnate in the Christ. Since the revelation of God in Christ took human form, it should not surprise us when the written revelation communicates in human terms. Such anthropomorphisms express the activity of God among people, illustrating the rich diversity of God's actions. Our concern here is with the references to the "hand" of God.

God's "hand" is said to accomplish great and mighty deeds. We are dealing with metaphor, to be sure. But when Christ, during his earthly ministry, laid hands on the sick and healed them (Luke 4:40) we are out of the realm of metaphor and into reality. Then too, when "God did extraordinary miracles by the hands of Paul" (Acts 19:11), the plain sense of Scripture does not permit us to relegate these physical acts to the sphere of symbolic language. The fact is that God chose to perform signs and wonders through the physical contact of an intermediary. There was nothing improbable about this to first-century Jews (Mark 5:23; 7:32; cf. Acts 8:18). Throughout their history, God had privileged his servants to act on his behalf. While prayer is sometimes mentioned in conjunction with the laying on of hands, the emphasis is on the act itself. When Paul healed the father of Publius (Acts 28:7, 8), he "visited him and prayed, and putting his hands on him healed him." The healing cannot be attributed to the prayer only, nor is the laying on of hands a form of prayer. The imposition of hands cannot be discounted as mere anagogue. Ultimately, of course, God was the source of the miracle, but in this case both the prayer and the imposition of hands were part of the mechanism of healing. God used both the prayers and the hands of Paul to accomplish his will. Paul's hands were not merely a symbol of God's act; they were literally laid on and shared in the event. Thus there is a mediatorial aspect to the laying on of hands. No act of the believer is autonomous; especially is this so of what he does with his hands, for they express his will. When hands are laid on a person in an ecclesiastical setting they express the will of God through human agency. The imposition of hands makes a very serious statement indeed about the activity of God.

When Paul says to Timothy, "I remind you to rekindle the gift of God that is within you through the laying on of my hands" (2 Tim. 1:6), the exegete must beware lest distaste for the abuses that have attended a sacramental understanding of the rite of the laying on of hands pushes him into a docetic interpretation that sees only the divine source of Timothy's charisma. The fact remains that Paul plainly asserts that it is not just a matter of the imposition of hands in general, but it is *his* hands that are the agents. The use of the possessive personal pronoun with "hands" emphasizes the personal agency of Paul: this is τῶν χειρῶν μου, *my* hands (2 Tim. 1:6). Similarly, the Samaritans received the Spirit of God through (διά) the hands of the apostles (Acts 8:18). Even if we choose to think of the apostles, or Paul, as little more than channels for the reception of the gifts, there is no way that the laying on of hands in these and other contexts can be taken as mere symbolic gestures. The reality of the results has to be taken with the reality of the means, and due weight must be given to both the divine Source who graciously provides the gifts and to the human agents through whom they are actually given. If, as has been said, selectivity leads to heresy, we must endeavor to conform our emphases to those of the texts we confront, lest in a misplaced zeal for the sovereignty of God we remove the human features from his revelation, and "in that moment remove ourselves from God."[1] The fact that man is made in the image of God presupposes communication in anthropomorphic terms. The fact that the incarnate Christ is portrayed as the Second Adam gives dignity and content to the actions of the man in Christ. The laying on of hands must be seen in this light.

"Hand" is used in the Scriptures in both a literal and a metaphorical sense. In the works of our Lord the two senses tend to merge (e.g., Mark 6:2). Blendiger notes that

in Biblical usage particular importance is attached to the use

1. W. Vischer, "Words and the Word: The Anthropomorphisms of the Biblical Revelation," *Int* III (1949), p. 7.

of *cheir* as part for the whole, as a substitute for the person and his activity and dealings. Thus the hand of God stands for his majesty and supreme power in the affairs of men.[2]

The hand of God is that through which his will is performed; God's hand created the heaven and the earth (Isa. 48:13), and guides the movement of redemptive history (Exod. 7:4; cf. Heb. 8:9). The hand is the instrument of man's will also, so that when Moses lays his hand on Joshua (Num. 27:20) Moses is mediating that Godly principle, that authority of God, necessary for the progression of God's plan of redemption. Joshua receives some of the "majesty" Moses had himself received from God.

Ἐπιτιθεῖν τὰς χεῖρας (to lay hands on) occurs twenty times in the New Testament;[3] ἐπίθεσις τῶν χειρῶν (the laying on of hands) four.[4] Most often these expressions are used in connection with miracles of healing, signs that the messianic age has already dawned,[5] though they are also found in the context of blessing, baptism, and mission.

The Old Testament distinguishes the placing and the pressing of hands, the former being used in the context of blessing,[6] and the latter in the cultic rites and in Moses' ordination of Joshua.

> Where an offering or a consecration is concerned, the texts invariably employ *samakh*, "to lean one's hands upon somebody or something"; but where a blessing is concerned, the verbs used are *śîm* and *shîth*, "to place one's hands."[7]

The distinction between *sāmak* and םיש, *śîm*, is lost in the LXX, both being translated by ἐπιτιθεῖν or a cognate. Daube attempts to distinguish between the placing and the pressing of hands in the New Testament use of ἐπίθεσις τῶν χειρῶν (the laying on of hands) according to context,[8] but it is difficult to categorize some references. Matt. 19:13 presents no problem, though, as Jesus blesses the children by placing his hands on them. But when the Seven are set before the apostles (Acts 6:6) and Scripture says "they

---

2. C. Blendiger, "δεξιά," *NIDNTT* II:146.

3. Matt. 9:18; 19:13, 15; Mark 5:23; 6:5; 7:32; 8:23, 25; 10:16; [16:18]; Luke 4:40; 13:13; Acts 6:6; 8:17, 19; 9:17; 13:3; 19:6; 18:8; 1 Tim. 5:22.

4. Acts 8:18; Heb. 6:2; 1 Tim. 4:14; 2 Tim. 1:6.

5. H.-G. Schütz, "ἐπιτίθημι," *NIDNTT* II:151.

6. Eduard Lohse, "χείρ," *TDNT* IX:428. Neither in the Old Testament nor in the rabbinic tradition is the laying on of hands associated with miraculous healing.

7. Daube, *New Testament and Rabbinic Judaism*, p. 224.

8. *Ibid.*, pp. 225ff.

prayed and laid their hands upon them," the intent of the verb is more difficult to assess, if indeed the two meanings can be distinguished at all in this case. Grammatically, "they" could refer either to the apostles or to the whole multitude. A corporate act of blessing is possible but hardly likely to be the principal intent of the laying on of hands here. When we eliminate the texts that clearly refer to healing and blessing, we are left with nine references to the laying on of hands: five in Acts (6:6; 8:17; 9:12ff.; 13:3; 19:6), one in Heb. (6:2), two in 1 Tim. (4:14; 5:22), and one in 2 Tim. (1:6).

Before we discuss these remaining texts, we should look at those texts in which healing or blessing occurs. In the New Testament Gospels Jesus heals by the laying on of hands (Mark 6:5; Luke 4:40; 13:13); by touch (ἅπτομαι, Matt. 8:3, 15; 20:34); and by a combination of the two (Mark 8:22ff.). Sometimes he healed by word alone (Matt. 8:5–13; 9:1ff.; 15:28; 17:18). The sick were also healed when they touched the garment of Jesus (Matt. 9:21; 14:36). The casting out of demons was accomplished without resort to physical contact (Mark 9:29; cf. Acts 19:14); yet Jesus touched the body of Jairus' daughter when he revived her (Mark 5:41), although he could have simply spoken a word; instead, he deliberately touched her. When a laying on of hands was requested for a deaf-mute (Mark 7:32), Jesus chose to heal by a different method. It is evident, then, that Jesus' healing power was not restricted by any mode of transfer. He might, or again he might not, lay hands on when healing the sick. In spite of the fact that physical contact often accompanied the miracles of our Lord, the Scriptures make it abundantly clear that the power to heal rested in the person of Jesus—and not even his physical presence was necessary (Luke 7:7ff.). The "signs and wonders" done by the hands of the apostles followed a strikingly similar pattern (Acts 14:3). Simon the Sorcerer thought that the power to confer the Holy Spirit was dependent on the laying on of hands of the apostles Peter and John (Acts 8:18). Peter hastens to correct him: "Your silver perish with you, because you thought you could obtain the gift of God with money!" (Acts 8:20). The imposition of hands was a sign, and a significant one, but the "wonder" was not dependent on the sign; its manifestation was subject to the sovereign will of the Spirit.

Matthew records that Jesus blessed little children by laying hands on them (Matt. 19:15). Jesus acted just as a Jewish father would;[9] to the Jewish parents this was more than a symbolic act. In Old Testament usage the act of blessing involved a word in-

9. H.-G. Link, "Blessing, Blessed, Happy," *NIDNTT* I:213.

vested with power and an action ratifying it.[10] בָּרַךְ, *bārak*, bless,
means basically to endow with beneficial power.[11] The actions that
accompany a blessing indicate a transference of the benefits of God
by the laying on of hands or even by the raising of hands.[12] Thus
Hebrew modes of thought do not permit us to isolate the laying on
of hands from the accompanying word or the results of the act
itself. The richness of meaning that has developed in the Old Testament usage of "hand," a richness that has been carried over into
the New Testament, is best preserved in the context of the accompanying word and the evident results.

Eduard Lohse notes that the expressions about the hand of
God in the New Testament occur mainly in the writings of Luke,
particularly in connection with Old Testament allusions.[13] The laying-on-of-hands motif is most frequent in Luke's writings also. If,
as Filson suggests, Luke sees the church as the "divinely given
continuation of the life of Israel,"[14] then it might be profitable to
see just what role the hand of God played in the history of the
Israel of the Old Covenant. Does the hand of God function similarly
in the history of the New Israel?

By metonymy, the hands of God may actually represent his
person. Jacob blesses his son Joseph, but the benefit comes

> by the hands of the Mighty One of Jacob
> (by the name of Shepherd, the Rock of Israel),
> by the God of your father who will help you,
> by God Almighty who will bless you. . . . (Gen. 49:24, 25)

God's right hand is God's power (Exod. 15:6). It is his hand that
accomplishes the redemption of his people: "I will lay my hand
upon Egypt and bring forth my hosts, my people, the sons of Israel"
(Exod. 7:4). At the institution of the feast of the Passover, Moses
repeatedly reminds the people that "with a strong hand the LORD
has brought you out of Egypt" (Exod. 13:9; cf. 13:3, 14, 16). Israelite
fathers are to teach their sons their history: "We were Pharaoh's
slaves in Egypt; and the LORD brought us out of Egypt with a
mighty hand" (Deut. 6:21). When Moses instructs the Israelites

10. *Ibid.*, p. 207.

11. *Ibid.*

12. *Ibid.* Cf. Luke 24:50 where Jesus blesses the disciples in this way
before his departure.

13. E. Lohse, "χείρ," *TDNT* IX:431.

14. Floyd V. Filson, "The Journey Motif in Luke-Acts," in *Apostolic History
and the Gospel*, ed. W. Ward Gasque and Ralph P. Martin (Exeter: Paternoster
Press, 1970), p. 75.

who are about to enter the Promised Land, he reminds them that their redemption was an act of the hand of God: ". . . the LORD has brought you out with a mighty hand and redeemed you . . ." (Deut. 7:8; see also 9:16; 11:2–4; 26:8; Josh. 4:24; Neh. 1:10; Ps. 136:12).

The mighty hand of God redeemed his people, and he committed the Promised Land to the Israelites, giving the nations one after another "into their hands" (Deut. 7:24; Josh. 2:24; and *passim* in Judges). "Not one of all their enemies had withstood them, for the LORD had given all their enemies into their hands" (Josh. 21:44). God had commissioned his people to take the land; it was their responsibility as a whole (Josh. 1:2), although he enabled them to do so. However, this was not marked by a ritual of any kind; rather, the transaction was consummated through the revelation of God "spoken by Moses" (Deut. 7:17ff.). This revelation is often said to have come "by the hand of Moses" (Lev. 8:36; 10:11; 26:46; Num. 4:45, 49; 27:23; 2 Chron. 35:6, etc.; the RSV translates this phrase merely "by Moses"). The hand of Moses underscores his role as the mediator of the Sinaitic Covenant. Thus, even in these metaphoric expressions ("commanded by the hand of Moses" and "spoken by the hand of Moses"), "hand" very plainly connotes mediation or transference, just as it does in the ritual of sacrifice.

It comes as no surprise, therefore, when Luke says that the "hand of the Lord" was with John the Baptist, the herald of the messianic age (Luke 1:66), or when the Baptist remarks that the Father has given all things into the "hand" of Jesus (John 3:35). After Pentecost, when the chief priests and elders tried to hinder the disciples in spreading the gospel, it was the "hand and the will" of the Lord (Acts 4:28) that had foreordained this; and when the men of Cyprus and Cyrene brought the gospel to Antioch, "the hand of the Lord was with them" and many believed and turned to the Lord (Acts 11:21). For Luke, the events of the new age are in continuity with those of the old. The "hand" of the Lord, whether immediately, or mediately through the hands of his servants, is intimately bound up with the advance of the gospel. Thus, in the New Testament as in the Old, the mighty hand of God is at work, redeeming a people for himself. The plan of redemption is in the hand of God.

Chapter 8

"AN ELEMENTARY DOCTRINE"

> Therefore let us leave the elementary doctrine of Christ and
> go on to maturity, not laying again a foundation of repentance
> from dead works and faith toward God, with instructions about
> ablutions, the laying on of hands, the resurrection of the dead,
> and eternal judgment. (Heb. 6:1, 2)

Whether we take the "elementary teachings about Christ" (Heb.
6:1 NIV) as a reference to the incarnate Christ, or as alluding to
the eternal Christ, there is no doubt that the laying on of hands
in Heb. 6:2 is not speaking of ordination to office in the church,
nor has this text been cited in support of any such claim. We could,
therefore, legitimately dispense with a discussion of Heb. 6:1, 2
were it not for the fact that this text has been used to argue that
imposition of hands was customary in the churches of the first
century, though, it is claimed, in the context of baptism.[1] Since it
has also been associated with the laying on of hands in Acts 8 and
Acts 19 to teach the need for confirmation,[2] we will discuss it briefly
before considering more pertinent texts.

The letter to the Hebrews is addressed to Christians who are
still clinging to Jewish cultic practices. They are having difficulties
relating the old ways to the new, in knowing what is to be laid

---

1. William L. Lumpkin, *Baptist Confessions*, p. 222. Heb. 6:1, 2 was accepted by some Baptists (c. 1660) as a creedal standard in connection with
baptism. This text is also cited in the *Philadelphia Confession* (1742) as a
scriptural norm for the laying on of hands in baptism; Lumpkin, p. 351. See
also G. R. Beasley-Murray, *Baptism in the New Testament* (Grand Rapids:
Eerdmans, 1962), pp. 242ff.

2. James D. G. Dunn, *Baptism in the Holy Spirit* (London: SCM, 1970),
pp. 205f.; Brooke Foss Westcott, *An Exposition of Hebrews* (Grand Rapids:
Eerdmans [1892]), p. 146.

aside and what is to be retained.[3] The author of this book is not
simply enumerating the merits of the New Covenant in contrast
to the Old, nor is he setting the testaments against each other.
The stalwarts of Israel testify to the faithful acts of God in the
past; the same faith that empowered the people of the Old Covenant encompasses those of the New. Jesus Christ is not only the
present perfecter, but he pioneered the faith of all of God's people,
from the "men of old" to the present (Heb. 11:2; 12:1, 2; cf. Rev.
22:13). There is continuity here: the acts of God in Jesus Christ
did not start at Bethlehem. So also the struggle with sin and the
"race" for the goal of salvation is one with the old way (Heb. 12:1).
The writer, in contrasting the Old and New Covenants, does not
imply that the Old is worthless, but insists that in it lay the kernel
of the New; the Old was good, but the New is better. His theme is
the completion, the perfection, of the Old in the New.[4] Thus, he
starts with the revelation of Christ at creation (Heb. 1:2, 10) and
carries his argument through to the One in whom the process is
completed, Jesus Christ. His point of reference is not the earthly
life of Christ as the center of history, but the Christ who has come
at the "end of the age" (Heb. 9:26), the same Christ who laid the
foundations in the beginning (Heb. 1:10).

What, then, are these "elementary doctrines of Christ" of Heb.
6:1 that are not again to be laid? The phrase is τὸν τῆς ἀρχῆς τοῦ
Χριστοῦ λόγον, the beginning of the word of Christ, that is, about
Christ[5]—the Christ of the Old Testament as well as of the New.
The translation of λόγος as "doctrine" is misleading to the modern
reader. This is not a reference to theological formulations about
the incarnate Christ, but to the revelatory events of the past that
prefigured the messianic events of the present. Mt. Sinai must be

3. Perhaps these "Hebrews" were of the same faction that opposed the
Hellenists of Acts 6:1. See E. Earle Ellis, *Prophecy and Hermeneutic in Early
Christianity* (Grand Rapids: Eerdmans, 1978), p. 128. See also Philip Edgcumbe
Hughes, *A Commentary on the Epistle to the Hebrews* (Grand Rapids: Eerd-
mans, 1977), pp. 12ff.; F. F. Bruce, *The Epistle to the Hebrews*, New International
Commentary on the New Testament (Grand Rapids: Eerdmans, 1964), pp. xxivff.

4. Hebrews is replete with the idea of fulfillment, consummation, and goal,
as expressed by τελειόω, τέλος, τέλειος, and τελειωτής, always in the context
of the contrast and progression between the Old and the New Covenants. Care
must be taken not to extract any of these words and apply them independently
of their covenantal milieu. Thus, to make τελείων in Heb. 5:14 and τελειότητα
in Heb. 6:1 references to a stage in the growth of a Christian to spiritual ma-
turity (as though such a goal were attainable in this life) is to violate the
purpose and plan of the epistle.

5. Jean Héring, *The Epistle to the Hebrews* (E.T., London: Epworth Press,
1970), p. 43. On this as an objective genitive see Hughes, p. 195, n. 3.

left, for the "Hebrews" have now come to Mt. Zion (Heb. 12:18–24). The foundational teachings[6] about Christ were not coincident with his advent and ministry. The readers of this letter, as instructed Jews, would know that God deals with his people after the pattern of the Exodus. Thus salvation is a journey with a new Promised Land as the goal, and the writer to the Hebrews is the guide.[7] We must not impose a crisis-experience way of thinking of salvation on an author who pictures salvation as a pilgrimage.[8] Just as the Israelites journeyed through the desert (Heb. 3:16–42) but never arrived at their goal, falling (Heb. 3:17, ἔπεσεν) in the desert, so too the "Hebrews" may fall by the way (παραπεσόντας, Heb. 6:6), never reaching *their* goal.

Several expressions used in Heb. 6:1, 2 require our attention. First, what does the author mean by his reference to the laying on of hands. Is he talking about the "old" or the "new" here? Since questions over observance of the Mosaic law motivate much of the writing in our New Testament, it should occasion no surprise when the laying on of hands is mentioned in a casual way.

The "dead works" are mentioned again in Heb. 9:14: ". . . how much more shall the blood of Christ . . . purify your conscience from dead works to serve the living God." Surely "dead works" here refers to the sacrifices of the Levitical system; is there any reason to believe that the reference in Heb. 6:1 is any different? As for "faith," this is "faith toward God," not faith *in* Christ. Faith in Christ is not mentioned, but faith toward God was as much a mark of Old Covenant believers as it is of those of the New. The Jews were well aware that ritual without repentance and faith was worthless. Perhaps the writer of this letter had the words of the prophet Isaiah in mind:

"What to me is the multitude of your sacrifices? says the Lord; I have had enough of burnt offerings of rams and the fat of fed beasts; I do not delight in the blood of bulls, or of lambs, or of

---

6. It does not seem likely that a writer who was comparing the Old and New Covenants would consider foundations as having been laid (θεμέλιον καταβαλλόμενοι, Heb. 6:1; cf. Heb. 5:12) in the time of Christ; if he did, it would be *new* foundations. Furthermore, both καταβάλλω and καταβολή are terms used in the creation of the world, as is also θεμελιόω (Heb. 1:10; 4:3; 9:26). The translations of ἀρχή as "elementary" and λόγος as "doctrine" are unfortunate, for this tends to set the reader's reference point at the earthly ministry of Christ rather than at the Old Testament prefigurations of Christ. See also Arthur W. Pink, *An Exposition of Hebrews* (Grand Rapids: Eerdmans, 1954), p. 278.

7. Héring, *Epistle to the Hebrews*, p. 43.

8. William B. Johnsson, "The Pilgrimage Motif in the Book of Hebrews," *JBL* 97, no. 2 (June 1978), pp. 249f.

he-goats. . . . Wash yourselves; make yourselves clean; remove the evils of your doings from before my eyes; cease to do evil" (Isa. 1:11, 16).

"Baptism" (βαπτισμός, Heb. 6:2) means the washing of lustrations, ablutions; it is a word associated with ritual purification (Mark 7:4; Heb. 9:10). This is not John's baptism or Christian baptism, for which the word used is βάπτισμα. Furthermore, this is the plural, washings (βαπτισμῶν), and is intimately coupled with the laying on of hands by the use of the particle τε. Numerous attempts have been made to reconcile the use of this word with what is assumed to be its Christian reference. The results are not convincing. Since ritual washings were an important feature of first-century Judaism, both rabbinic and sectarian,[9] and since the relationship between the Old and the New are at issue in this letter, there is no reason for avoiding the plain meaning given to the imposition of hands by the context in which it is found. Nor is there historical evidence that the laying on of hands was a part of Christian baptism at this time. The imposition of hands in Acts 8:19 and Acts 19:6 had kairotic significance (see Chapter 9). The use of τε instead of καί as the connective relating βαπτισμῶν διδαχῆς and ἐπιθέσεώς . . . χειρῶν in Heb. 6:2 indicates a single ceremony is in mind.[10] That what we have here is a reference to the Levitical rites of lustrations and the laying on of hands in the daily Temple ritual of sacrifice is in harmony with both the context and what we know of early Christian baptism.[11]

The "resurrection of the dead and eternal judgment" (Heb. 6:2) were not solely Christian doctrines, either. Though there are only vague hints of a belief in the resurrection in the preexilic parts of the Old Testament, the same does not hold for Pharisaic Judaism of the intertestamental period. Even our Lord becomes embroiled in a discussion on this subject with the Sadducees (Luke 20:27–38).

9. See, for example, the *Manual of Discipline* iii.4f.; iv.21; iii.9. T. H. Gaster, *The Dead Sea Scriptures* (Garden City: Anchor Press, 1976), pp. 47ff.

10. Dunn, *Baptism in the Holy Spirit*, p. 207.

11. Thomas Hewitt, *The Epistle to the Hebrews*, Tyndale New Testament Commentary (Grand Rapids: Eerdmans, 1960), p. 105, remarks that the evidence here does not favor a reference to Christian baptism. The "Six Principle" Baptists (Providence, Rhode Island, 1639), basing their practices on Heb. 6:1, 2 and the incidents in Acts 8 and Acts 19, believed that the laying on of hands was an apostolic rite required for the reception of the Holy Spirit and necessary for interchurch fellowship.

Both resurrection and judgment were salient themes in apocalyptic Judaism, also.[12]

The writer to the Hebrews has thus maintained a consistent approach, contrasting (but not opposing) the Old with the New, the good with the better, the "child" with the adult (Heb. 5:13, 14). The imposition of hands in Heb. 6:2 is not a reference to baptismal practice, but to the failure of converts from Judaism to realize that Temple sacrifice is now obsolete as a way of dealing with sin. Christ has provided a new and better way. He has "entered once for all into the Holy Place, taking not the blood of goats and calves but his own blood, thus securing an eternal redemption" (Heb. 9:12).

12. Hewitt, *Epistle to the Hebrews*, p. 105; Adin Steinsaltz, *Essential Talmud*, pp. 21, 102; Leon Morris, *Apocalyptic* (Grand Rapids: Eerdmans, 1972), pp. 46, 67; cf. Dan. 7:9, 10; 12:2; 2 Macc. 7; Acts 23:8.

Chapter 9

THE LAYING ON OF
HANDS IN ACTS

Ἐπιτιθεῖν τὰς χεῖρας, to lay hands on, occurs five times in Acts in constructions that might be construed as indicating induction into ecclesiastical office through the laying on of hands: 6:1–6 (the Seven); 8:14–25 (the Samaritans); 9:10–18 (the conversion of Saul); 13:1–3 (Paul and Barnabas); and 19:1–7 (the Ephesian Twelve). These texts have been subject to conflicting interpretations over the centuries. When taken as proof-texts for formulating theological positions on baptism, confirmation, ordination, or the reception of spiritual gifts, they have proved to be manageable only if treated selectively, that is, only if some are ignored completely or are dismissed as not pertinent to the doctrine in question.

Confusion over the teaching of Acts 19:1–7 is evident in the writings of Tertullian.[1] By the third century, baptism and confirmation were becoming separate rites based on the interpretation of Acts 8:14–25; 9:10–18; and 19:1–7, as teaching two phases to Christian initiation.[2] Acts 8:17ff. and 19:1–7 are still cited in support of confirmation,[3] ordination,[4] and the "second blessing" doc-

---

1. J. N. D. Kelly, *Early Christian Doctrines*, p. 209.
2. *Ibid.*, p. 210.
3. These texts are used to support the doctrine of a second work of "grace," whether in the form of confirmation or the "second blessing" doctrine of Pentecostalism. They also serve for those who understand ordination with the laying on of hands as a sacrament of the church. See P. T. Camelot, "Confirmation," *NCE* IV:147f.; Philip Schaff, *History of the Christian Church* II:157; R. E. O. White, *The Biblical Doctrine of Initiation* (London: Hodder & Stoughton, 1960), pp. 352ff.; G. W. H. Lampe, *Seal of the Spirit, passim*. The more recent revisions of the *Book of Common Prayer* (e.g., the Canadian revisions of 1918 and 1959) have added parts of Acts 8 and 19 to their "Order of Confirmation"; the 1959 edition has added that this is an "Apostolic rite."
4. C. W. Carter and R. Earle (*The Acts of the Apostles* [Grand Rapids: Zondervan, 1973], p. 115) state that "most authorities seem to agree that the

trine of Pentecostalism.[5] If all three[6] of these conflicting positions can be defended by scholars, one may be forgiven for suspecting that theological presuppositions have been permitted to influence the interpretations of the texts. Scripture itself must be allowed to interpret Scripture. Let us credit the writer of Luke-Acts with consistency in his use of the laying-on-of-hands motif, and then give every text an opportunity to contribute its evidence to our understanding.

Selectivity in the choice of texts inevitably leads to eisegesis. If the imposition of hands is an essential part of the ordination service (and historical evidence would confirm this), then none of these texts can be neglected or explained away as not relevant to the topic. As anyone who has witnessed an ordination ceremony will testify, the laying on of hands is a very important part of the rite; even those who affirm that no grace is imparted treat the imposition of hands as the climax of the whole affair. In defending or explaining their ordination rites, manuals and handbooks intended for denominational use generally quote one or two texts at the most. Baptist denominational literature generally cites Acts 13:1–3, ignoring other texts in which the laying on of hands occurs.[7] Those who favor a presbyterial form of church government stress 1 Tim. 4:14; they may acknowledge Acts 6:6; 13:3; and 1 Tim. 5:22, but usually either ignore 1 Tim. 1:6 or conflate it with 1 Tim. 4:14.[8] The Roman Catholic position is somewhat different. Since

---

mission of Peter and John to Samaria was to consecrate or ordain." This statement is apparently taken *verbatim* from *The Wesleyan Bible Commentary*, IV:535, ed. R. Earle, Harvey J. S. Blaney, and C. W. Carter (Grand Rapids: Eerdmans, 1964). This writer found no other commentators who suggested that these texts refer to ordination.

5. See Dunn, *Baptism in the Holy Spirit*, p. 55; Michael Green, *I Believe in the Holy Spirit* (Grand Rapids: Eerdmans, 1975), p. 136; W. J. Hollenweger, *The Pentecostals* (Minneapolis: Augsburg, 1972), pp. 317, 513; Robert G. Gromacki, *The Modern Tongues Movement* (Nutley, NJ: Presbyterian and Reformed, 1974), pp. 87ff., 92ff.

6. These texts are also cited in support of the practice of the laying on of hands in baptism. See G. R. Beasley-Murray, *Baptism in the New Testament*, p. 125; E. A. Payne, *The Baptist Union: A Short History* (London: The Carey Kingsgate Press, 1958), p. 135; Frederick Dale Bruner, *A Theology of the Holy Spirit* (Grand Rapids: Eerdmans, 1970), p. 20.

7. A. H. Strong, *Systematic Theology*, p. 919, omits Acts 8:14–25; 19:1–7; and 2 Tim. 1:6 in discussing ordination. The *Handbook of Regular Baptist Churches of British Columbia* (Vancouver, B.C., 1976), p. 32, is typical of much denominational literature in that it quotes only Acts 13:1–3 in connection with ordination.

8. L. Berkhof, *Systematic Theology* (Grand Rapids: Eerdmans, 1938), p. 588; Lawrence R. Eyres, *The Elders of the Church* (Philadelphia: Presbyterian & Reformed, 1977 reprint), pp. 45ff.; T. F. Torrance, "Consecration and Ordination,"

the authoritative teaching of Christ is still to be heard through the hierarchy of the church, there is not the pressure to bring conformity to the scriptural texts. Piet Fransen comments:

> It is still debated whether Acts 13:1–3; 6:1–6; 14:22, 20, deal with true priestly ordinations. The texts are too short to allow of a definitive conclusion. There is hardly room for debate about 1 Tim. 4:14 and 2 Tim. 1:6 when taken together; and 1 Tim. 5:22 and Tit. 1:5 may refer to an ordination. . . . It may . . . be presumed that the laying on of hands is not a "substantive" element of the sacramental rite, but a rite instituted by the church.[9]

Some admit that the doctrine of ordination occasions a good deal of misunderstanding and that the subject is complex, but they nevertheless encourage the ordination of their ministerial candidates.[10] Fair exegetical practice demands that all texts that bear on what may appear to be induction to church office with the imposition of hands be given due weight and thorough consideration.

Most commentators believe that the Gospel of Luke and the Book of Acts were originally a two-volume work that became separated when the canon of the New Testament was arranged.[11] The preface to Luke (Luke 1:1–4) may be taken as an indication of his methodology in both works, Acts being a continuation of Luke (Acts 1:1). Luke says that he availed himself of sources, chose those that suited his purposes, and assembled them with a view to accuracy, orderly arrangement, and reliability (Luke 1:2–4). He saw that about which he wrote as fulfillment of the promises of God.[12]

SJT 11 (1958), pp. 235ff. takes all the pertinent texts into consideration, but says the imposition of hands in Acts 6:6 is "lay ordination," and Acts 13:1–3 is authorization for a special limited mission, not ordination "in the proper sense." On combining the texts from 1 and 2 Tim., he says ". . . it is clear that the Presbytery is the medium of ordination although Paul has a special part in it, and Timothy afterwards takes a similar place in the ordination of others" (p. 239). The last statement is based on 1 Tim. 5:22, a text which has caused exegetes much trouble. There is not sufficient evidence to infer that Timothy laid hands on others in the presence of a body of elders.

9. Fransen, "Ordination," p. 1130.

10. See, for example, the *Handbook of the Regular Baptist Churches of British Columbia*, p. 31.

11. Johannes Munck, *The Acts of the Apostles* (Garden City: Doubleday & Co., 1967), p. xv; I. Howard Marshall, *Luke: Historian and Theologian* (Grand Rapids: Zondervan, 1970), p. 40; *contra*, E. Haenchen, *The Acts of the Apostles, A Commentary* (Oxford: Basil Blackwell, 1971), p. 99, n. 1.

12. Luke 21:24, πληρωθῶσιν; cf. Luke 1:23, 57; 2:6, 21f., πίμπλημι; Acts 7:23, 30; 9:23; 19:21; 24:27, πληρόω; Luke 9:51; Acts 2:1, συμπληρόω.

This fulfillment is accomplished by the "hand" of God. As in the LXX, Luke and Acts abound in expressions using χείρ, hand, and its compounds.[13] The hand expresses the will, whether of man or of God. The betrayal and death of our Lord was predestined by the hand (χείρ) and the will (ἡ βουλή) of God (Acts 4:28). Thus, God's hand and his will are synonymous.

In compiling and arranging his material, Luke is aware that God has both a temporal and a geographical framework according to which his plan is unfolded. Before his ascension, Jesus' disciples questioned him: "Lord, will you at this time restore the kingdom to Israel?" (Acts 1:6). Jesus replies that God alone knows the times and the seasons, that is, the temporal framework (Acts 1:7). He does, however, prophetically proclaim the pattern for geographical expansion in Acts 1:8: "But you shall receive power when the Holy Spirit has come upon you; and you shall be my witnesses in Jerusalem and in all Judea and Samaria and to the end of the earth." Luke depicts the "hand" of God fulfilling this prophecy, the hand of God through his servants on whom hands are laid.

Throughout his narrative, the author of Luke-Acts associates "hand" with pivotal milestones in the lives of those about whom he writes.[14] The "hand of the Lord" was with John the Baptist (Luke 1:66). Our Lord was betrayed by the hands of men (διὰ χειρὸς ἀνόμων, Luke 20:19; 21:12; 22:21, 25). At his ascension, the Lord blessed his disciples by raising his hands (Luke 24:50). When Stephen recounts the history of the people of God, Luke chooses to include Moses' untimely attempt to deliver his brethren "through his hand" (διὰ χειρὸς αὐτοῦ, Acts 7:25), that is, through the agency of his hand. Perhaps Luke has included this incident to show that it must be the hand of God that sets the temporal aspects of the plan of redemption, not the hands of men. At the proper time, Moses is summoned to his appointed task "by the hand of an angel" (σὺν χειρὶ ἀγγέλλου, Acts 7:35).[15] When the men of Cyprus and Cyrene preached at Antioch, the "hand of the Lord" was with them and many believed (Acts 11:21).

It follows, then, that those texts in which Luke speaks of the

13. For example, Luke 1:1, ἐπιχειρέω; Acts 9:8; 22:11, χειραγωγέω; Acts 13:11, χειραγωγός; Acts 27:19, αὐτόχειρ; Acts 7:48; 17:24, χειροποίητος; Acts 14:23, χειροτονέω; Acts 22:14, προχειρίζομαι.

14. The sending of the Spirit at Pentecost is a notable exception.

15. Moses attempted to deliver his people through (διά) his hand (Acts 7:25), that is, he actually murdered with his hands. Luke consistently uses διά, through, to express real agency (cf. Acts 5:12; 8:18; 11:30; 14:3; 19:11, 26). When he is avoiding direct agency he employs σύν, as in Acts 7:35.

laying on of hands must be interpreted in the context of his pen-
chant for using "hand" to express the will or plan of God as he
moves among his people to establish his kingdom (Acts 1:6). To
isolate these texts from each other or from their function in the
whole of Luke-Acts is to invite distortion of their meaning. For
Luke, the events he narrates in the interval during which the
Spirit carries on the ministry of Jesus are events ordained by the
hand of God. Just as God gave the tribes of Canaan into the "hands"
of the Israelites (see Josh. 2:24; 4:24; 6:2; 8:1, 7; 10:8, 19, 30, 32;
etc.), he will now do the same for the New Israel. The laying-on-
of-hands episodes occur as milestones in the fulfillment theme of
Luke, events foreordained by God and fulfilled by the Spirit of
Jesus (Acts 16:7).

Luke's dependence on Old Testament sources is evident in
Luke-Acts, but the extent of this dependence is not often realized.
For example, he frequently uses Old Testament literary genres; in
fact, one writer terms the central section of his Gospel a "Christian
Deuteronomy."[16] He also employs the vocabulary of the LXX for
purposes of recall and association of ideas. In addition to the use
of catchwords, verbal analogy, and familiar motif (as in the laying
on of hands) we detect more subtle allusions, faint to the modern
Christian, but unmistakably intentional. To the Israelites, the Exodus events and the occupation of Canaan were the foundation on
which all further redemptive activity of God was built; when he
said he would build his church it was no exception. So the life of
the New Israel is patterned on the Old and the language and
thought forms of the Old interpret the New. Unfortunately, the
massive theological formularies of the two thousand years that
stand between our thought-world and that of the first century often
serve as effective barriers to *our* understanding of these texts. So
when Luke narrates the expansion of the church and Paul's "missionary journeys" as the conquest of the new Promised Land, it is
essential to *our* understanding that we also link the first-century
texts to the ones in which they have their roots. We may then be
able to view the situation as did the early church, with this provision: twentieth-century suppositions about church office, sacrament, and evangelism must be suspended—at least until the ancient

16. C. F. Evans, "The Central Section of St. Luke's Gospel," in *Studies in
the Gospels*, ed. D. E. Nineham (Oxford: Basil Blackwell, 1967), pp. 42–50. See
also John Drury, *Tradition and Design in Luke's Gospel* (London: Darton,
Longman, and Todd, 1976), pp. 50ff., 138ff., 163f., 187f.

texts have first been permitted to speak their message loudly and clearly.

God had promised Israel (Jacob) that he would make of him a great nation in Egypt (Gen. 46:3), an extension of the promise originally given to Abraham (Gen. 15:5). As Luke expresses it, when the "time of promise" drew near (Acts 7:17), Moses led the people out of Egypt to the borders of the Promised Land. According to Luke, it is again a "time of promise"; this time, the promise of the Spirit (Acts 1:4; cf. Luke 24:49; Acts 2:16ff.) to the disciples and to those who are "far off" (Acts 2:39). The time is ripe for the new Exodus, with new wilderness experiences to be faced, and new territories to be taken for the gospel of Jesus Christ: Judea, Samaria, and the "end of the earth" (Acts 1:8). Not only does Luke interpret the victories in the new Promised Land in terms of those of the Old, but he also draws analogies between the lives of those who now lead the people of God to those who led in olden times. For example, as Joshua was a man who would "go out before them and come in before them" (Num. 27:17), and as Moses draws near to the end of his life and is no longer able to "go out and come in" (Deut. 31:2), so also Peter remarks that Jesus "went in and out" among them during his earthly ministry (Acts 1:21), and Paul "went in and out among them" at Jerusalem (Acts 9:28). This is more than mere Hebrew idiom for leadership, as the context clearly indicates.[17] Jesus is the prophet like Moses (Acts 3:23), but Paul too has the Moses-wisdom, for he has been divinely chosen to carry on the ministry of our Lord. The devout Jew, whether or not now a Christian, would not fail to get the message.

The speeches of Stephen, Peter, and Paul, as recorded in Acts, demonstrate the midrashic use of Scripture common in the rabbinic circles of Luke's day.[18] Paul and Barnabas, for example, in speaking to the Jews at Antioch, quote Isa. 49:6 in explanation of their mission to the Gentiles, applying the servant theme to their contribution in bringing salvation to the "uttermost parts of the

17. Luke draws the analogies between Moses and Paul with a deft touch; steeped in the history of their faith, this would be quite adequate for his readers. The experiences of Paul echo those of Moses: as happened to Moses, attempts are made on the life of Paul (Acts 9:23, 29; cf. Exod. 1:22; 2:15); both have a vision of the glory of God and hear the bat $qôl$ (Acts 9:4f.; 22:9–11; cf. Exod. 3:2–6); as Moses has Aaron to speak for him, so Paul has Barnabas (Acts 9:27; cf. Exod. 4:15f.). There is, therefore, a significant loss when, as in the NASB, "he went in and out among them in Jerusalem" (Acts 9:28) is translated as "he ... moving about freely in Jerusalem." This attempt to interpret the idiom has resulted in the loss of the Old Testament connotation.

18. Richard Longenecker, *Biblical Exegesis*, pp. 97f.

earth" (Acts 13:47). Luke also employs midrash in interpreting his sources.[19] According to Longenecker,

> Midrashic interpretation, in effect, ostensibly takes its point of departure from the biblical text itself . . . and seeks to explicate the hidden meanings contained therein by means of agreed upon hermeneutical rules in order to contemporize the revelation of God for the people of God. It may be briefly characterized by the maxim: "That has relevance to This. . . ."[20]

This is precisely what Luke does with the laying-on-of-hands motif of the Old Testament Scriptures; he uses it as a hermeneutical tool in interpreting the fulfillment of promise in the new Israel. Because this motif includes the term "hand," representing the will and plan of God, it is eminently suitable for this purpose. We may now ask what meaning Luke attaches to the imposition of hands in the Book of Acts.

It becomes apparent before long that attempts to construct doctrinal formulas from these texts result in bewildering contradictions. Let's ask, for example, whether the laying on of hands is the function of those who hold apostolic office.[21] For the Samaritans (Acts 8:14–25) and the Ephesian Twelve (Acts 19:1–7) the answer is "yes"; for Paul (Acts 9:10–18), it is "no"; for Paul and Barnabas (Acts 13:1–3)[22] and the Seven (Acts 6:1–6)[23] the evidence is grammatically inconclusive. Do the texts explicitly state that the Holy Spirit or spiritual gifts were given through the laying on of hands? For the Samaritans and Ephesians the answer is "yes," and for the Seven and Paul and Barnabas "no"; as for Paul, his sight was restored and he was filled with the Spirit, but the imposition of hands seems to be primarily concerned with his healing

19. Acts 2:37; cf. Ps. 18:16 (LXX); Acts 5:2; cf. Josh. 7:1 (LXX); Acts 6:6; cf. Num. 17:16ff. (LXX); Acts 8:26; cf. 2 Kgs. 17:2 (LXX); etc.

20. Longenecker, *Biblical Exegesis*, p. 37.

21. Much depends on one's definition of "apostle." G. W. H. Lampe, "The Holy Spirit in the Writings of St. Luke," in *Studies in the Gospels*, ed. D. E. Nineham, p. 199, suggests that Ananias may have received a "special apostolic commission" for this task. F. F. Bruce in *The Book of the Acts* (London: Marshall, Morgan, & Scott, 1954), p. 200, concurs.

22. The text is not clear as to who laid hands on Paul and Barnabas.

23. Carter and Earle, *Acts of the Apostles*, p. 88; J. B. Lightfoot, *Saint Paul's Epistle to the Philippians* (London: Macmillan & Co., 1888), p. 187; Bruce, *Book of Acts*, p. 154 all interpret this as the laying on of hands by the twelve apostles. Schweizer, *Church Order*, p. 208, and Leon Morris, *Ministers of God*, p. 88, admit that the text is ambiguous. David Daube, *New Testament and Rabbinic Judaism*, p. 237, says that the "entire brotherhood" laid hands on them.

(cf. v. 12).[24] Did those on whom hands were laid receive this rite *because* they were displaying qualifications for church leadership? For the Samaritans, the Ephesian Twelve, and Paul, the answer is "no." In the case of Paul and Barnabas leadership qualities had been evident for some time; the rite was not performed *because* they were prophets and teachers. As for the Seven, the mediate initiative for the laying on of hands came from the apostles, and only then did the question of spiritual qualifications arise; furthermore, at this time the emphasis would appear to be on practical duties, not prophetic ones (Acts 6:1–4). Finally, were hands imposed for induction to church office? There is no evidence that the Samaritans or Ephesians who received this rite became office-bearers, nor did Paul receive his apostleship in this manner (cf. Gal. 1:1). The Seven had a temporary function to fulfill; almost immediately Stephen and Philip are seen to be itinerant evangelists (cf. Acts 21:8).[25] The commissioning of Paul and Barnabas was likewise for temporary mission. They were already serving as prophets or teachers, and they later went separate ways in their missionary activity.

We might pose other questions, but we have already demonstrated the theological diversity of these texts. Could it be that we are asking the *wrong* questions? The grammatical ambiguities we encounter might suggest as much. Perhaps Luke was *not* concerned with the niceties of church office. Surely, as a careful and intelligent author, if he had intended to legislate such matters he would have expressed himself with precision so that the church of Christ would know how to install its officers. The fact remains that he is either imprecise or silent on "orders." We can expect unsatisfactory answers if we try to force Luke to answer questions he is not even addressing in Acts. The Spirit of God has some instruction for his people through Luke. Let's listen carefully enough to ask the right questions.

THE HELLENISTS

The key to understanding the laying-on-of-hands motif in Luke's writings is to be found in his abundant recourse to Old Testament

24. Bruce, *Book of Acts*, p. 201, and Haenchen, *Acts of the Apostles*, p. 325, say that Paul received both recovery of sight and the Spirit through the imposition of hands.

25. Schweizer, *Church Order*, p. 30. Morris, *Ministers of God*, pp. 82ff., gives a detailed discussion of the pros and cons of this as the office of deacon.

allusion. Luke explains the choice and mission of the Seven in Acts 6 by analogy with the events of the Exodus and the entry into the Promised Land. Like all great teachers, Luke starts with the familiar; Septuagint terminology and rabbinic tradition are both called into service.

In Acts 6:1 Luke tells us the disciples were increasing (πληθυνόντων), that is, they were "multiplying." This has happened before when the power of God has come upon his people, and is an indication that fulfillment of the covenant promise given initially to Abraham is imminent: "I will indeed bless you, and I will multiply your descendants as the stars of heaven and as the sand which is on the seashore. And your descendants shall possess the gate of their enemies" (Gen. 22:17). Just as a crisis developed among the Israelites in Egypt when they were "multiplying" (Exod. 1:7, 10, 20) prior to the Exodus, the Hellenists were also facing a crisis, one involving the worship of God. This is not immediately apparent in Acts 6:1. Only when Stephen subsequently addresses the council can we detect the real contentions between the Hebraic and Hellenistic Christians, though we have a hint as to the nature of the problem in Acts 6:7: "and a great many of the priests were obedient to the faith." Evidently the Hellenists were being accused of laxity in observance of the Law, an issue that surfaces constantly in the early church. As happened with the Israelites in Egypt, obedience to God resulted in persecution. And just as surely as the Israelites were driven out of Egypt, so the Hellenists are driven out of Jerusalem. Note how skillfully Luke presents his case. God raised up Moses who did "signs and wonders" before Pharaoh (Exod. 7:3), signs and wonders performed by his "hand" (Exod. 4:17). In the same way Stephen, on whom hands have been laid, performs signs and wonders (Acts 6:8). God is about to take for himself a new people; as he had separated a people for himself in Egypt, so again severance is necessary that the gospel might flourish among the Gentiles, a gospel detached from Jewish traditions.

The disciples are not only "multiplying"; they are also "murmuring" (ἐγένετο γογγυσμός, Acts 6:1). That is, they were dissatisfied with the provision being made for their widows. The Israelites also murmured over the way God provided for *them* when they set out for the Promised Land. They complained (διεγόγγυζε, Exod. 16:2 LXX), and God heard their murmuring (γογγυσμόν, Exod. 16:7 LXX). As Moses summoned the Israelites to come before God (Exod. 16:9), so too the twelve apostles summon the disciples (Acts 6:2). Murmuring has other connotations. When Joshua and the others were sent to spy out Canaan, the Israelites murmured against Moses (διεγόγγυζον, Num. 14:2 LXX), complaining that "our wives and our little ones will become a prey" (Num. 14:3; cf. v. 31). It now becomes clear why Luke writes about the incident of the widow's support; his readers will recall the challenge facing the Israelites as they were to cross into the new land. Luke, under the inspiration of the Spirit of God, now brings a traditional element into the picture. When the Israelites in the desert murmur (γογγύζων, Num. 11:1 LXX), Moses finds the burden of administration more than he can handle. God tells him to select seventy of the elders of the people, "and I will take some of the spirit which is upon you and put it upon them; and they shall bear the burden of the people with you, that you may not bear it yourself alone" (Num. 11:17). The Twelve of Acts 6:1, 2 likewise feel overburdened with administrative duties, and so select seven who are "of good repute, full of the Spirit and of wisdom" (Acts 6:3). Thus, the wisdom of Moses is seen to be viable in the new community. Luke, we see, is moving in the area of rabbinic tradition. He proceeds to combine the commissioning of the Seventy with the Moses-Joshua ordination, not to demonstrate succession through the laying on of hands as had the rabbis, but to alert his readers to the New Covenant conquest in which they are participating.

As Moses had picked out Joshua (ἐπισκέψασθω, Num. 27:16 LXX), set him before Eleazar the priest and all the congregation, and "laid his hands on him" (ἐπέθηκε τὰς χεῖρας αὐτοῦ ἐπ' αὐτόν, Num. 27:23 LXX), so too the brethren of Acts 6 pick out (ἐπισκέψασθε) seven men full of the Spirit and set them before the apostles; then "they prayed and laid their hands upon them" (προσευξάμενοι ἐπέθηκεν αὐτοῖς τὰς χεῖρας, Acts 6:6).[26] By using midrashic principles such as *gezerah shawah* (verbal analogy), *kayoze bo bemaqom 'aḥer* (exposition by means of another similar passage), and *dabar halamed me'inyano* (a meaning established by its context),[27] Luke has interpreted the selection and commissioning of the Seven as fulfillment of a covenant promise. The church is now launched on the first phase (after Pentecost) of its charge to be witnesses in "Jerusalem and in all Judea and Samaria and to the end of the earth" (Acts 1:8).

The power of the Spirit, evidenced by signs and wonders, had

26. Neither the LXX nor the Greek text of the New Testament clearly designates the subjects of the verbs ἐπέθηκε or ἐπέθηκαν.

27. Longenecker, *Biblical Exegesis*, pp. 34f.; Hermann L. Strack, *Introduction to the Talmud and Midrash* (New York: Athenaeum, 1976), p. 94.

given the initial impetus in Jerusalem. Now the church must move out into "all Judea." Through the preaching of Philip in Samaria, Peter and John are drawn there also; and after the martyrdom of Stephen the church is dispersed through persecution. Thus, Acts 6:1–6 is not concerned with church office. The events related have covenantal and temporal significance; their prior function is analogical.

On the basis of the presence of διαχονία, service, which occurs twice in this pericope, and because the laying on of hands is also mentioned here, church office has been read into this passage. "Service," however, is the daily ministry to the needy; the reference is not personal. Nor, after hands were laid on them, did the Seven settle into administration; they moved on to wider roles. Those who would liken this incident to the laying on of hands on the Levites (Num. 8:10) as assistants to the priests, may note that Luke avoids verbal parallels with the imposition of hands in the cult.[28] He draws his analogy from the commissioning of Joshua, *not* the consecration of the Levites. As the laying on of hands on Joshua marked the initial stage in the entry into Canaan, so the imposition of hands on the Seven marks the entry of the new Israel into the lands designated in Acts 1:8. God is delivering a new land into the hands of his people (cf. Josh. 2:24; 6:2; 8:1, 18; 10:8, 19, 30, 32; 21:44, etc.).

THE SAMARITANS AND EPHESIANS

Since the imposition of hands on the Samaritans (Acts 8:14–25) and on the disciples at Ephesus (Acts 19:1–7) appears in connection with baptism, these passages will be considered together.

Most commentators concede that these texts are of an unusual character.[29] It is difficult indeed to fit them into any consistent doctrine of Christian initiation. The Samaritans had become believers through the preaching of Philip. They were "full of joy" (Acts 8:8) and were already manifesting the life of the Spirit,[30] yet when the apostles Peter and John were sent to them from

---

28. T. F. Torrance, "Consecration and Ordination," *SJT* 11 (1958), p. 237, and many others. Henry Chadwick, *Early Church*, p. 48, points out that Irenaeus was the first to identify the Seven as deacons.

29. Lampe, *Seal of the Spirit*, p. xx; see also Michael Green, *I Believe*, pp. 134, 137; Bruner, *Theology of the Holy Spirit*, p. 20; Marshall, *Luke: Historian and Theologian*, p. 213.

30. J. E. L. Oulton, "The Holy Spirit Baptism and the Laying on of Hands in Acts," *ExposT* LXVI (1954–1955), p. 238.

Jerusalem, prayed for them (Acts 8:14), and laid hands on them (Acts 8:17), they received (ἐλάμβανον, were receiving) the Spirit.[31] Pentecost has come to Samaria,[32] and another milestone has been set in the advance of the gospel. When Paul preached in Ephesus he found disciples who, though they had received John's baptism, were apparently unaware of the Spirit.[33] However, Luke does not appear to be concerned about either the mechanics of church leadership or baptismal rites. Believers are baptized and leaders lead throughout Acts without mention of any rite of the imposition of hands. Thus, when Luke employs this motif we need to seek elsewhere for his reasons. They are to be found in the fulfillment theme presented in Acts 1:8; through the hands of the apostles the coming of the Spirit in pentecostal power is authoritatively linked to his coming on the day of Pentecost (Acts 2). This happened first with the Hellenists,[34] then with the Samaritans and the Ephesians. During his ministry, Jesus had expressly forbidden his twelve disciples to go to these territories. "Go nowhere among the Gentiles, and enter no town of the Samaritans" (Matt. 10:5). Now, however, the time to advance had come, and since the prohibition had been given to those of apostolic office, the withdrawal of the prohibition must come through those holding apostolic office also. The Ephesian Twelve now have the Spirit of God; the gospel has reached the "end of the earth."

It should be noted that when Luke records other advances of the gospel (as, for example, when the men of Cyprus and Cyrene speak the gospel to the Greeks in Antioch, Acts 11:20f.) he specifically mentions that the "hand" of the Lord is with them. The "hand" of God moves his church.

Although the laying-on-of-hands motif is prominent in these texts, Luke makes no allusion to the Moses-Joshua commissioning. In the Samaritan incident, however, he clearly alludes to the Song of Moses. Moses' final words to the Israelites who are about to enter Canaan include the Gentiles in the future plans of God: "Rejoice, ye Gentiles, with his people" (Deut. 32:43 LXX; cf. Rom. 15:10). This, too, was a critical time in the history of Israel. Moses had finished writing "all the words of the law" (Deut. 31:24) and

31. Green, *I Believe*, p. 138, interprets the use of the imperfect here as signifying repeated manifestations of the Spirit.

32. Lampe, "Holy Spirit . . . ," p. 72.

33. Green, *I Believe*, p. 135, suggests that the disciples may not have heard of the availability of the Spirit.

34. The analogy of Acts 6:1–6 with the ordination of Joshua suggests that it was the apostles who laid hands on the Seven.

had committed the covenant document to the Levites for safe-keep-
ing (Deut. 31:25, 26). He had reminded Joshua and the congregation of the saving acts of God, and had recalled God's promise
to Joshua: "You shall bring the children of Israel into the land
which I swore to give them" (Deut. 31:23). He had also cautioned
them: "Take heed [προσέχετε LXX] with all your heart to all these
words which I testify [διαμαρτύρομαι LXX] to you this day" (Deut.
31:23). Similarly, the Samaritans had taken heed (προσεῖχον, Acts
8:10) to the words of Philip, and had taken heed (again προσεῖχον,
Acts 8:10) also to Simon Magus. Peter and John, having testified
(διαμαρτυράμενοι) and spoken the Word of the Lord, return to Jerusalem (Acts 8:25). Luke clearly sees these new advances—to the
Samaritans and to the Ephesians—as fulfillment of the promise
of Acts 1:8. He uses Old Testament allusions and the Old Testament motif of the laying on of hands to show the significance of
the arrival of the witness at Samaria and Ephesus.

PAUL AND BARNABAS

Only the first of the three accounts of Paul's conversion (Acts 9:1–19;
22:4–16; 26:9–18) mentions the laying on of hands. A comparison
of the texts does nothing to pinpoint what actually happened when
Ananias laid hands on Paul; whether the act is to be associated
with the healing only,[35] or with both the healing and the reception
of the Spirit,[36] or with Paul's baptism and commissioning,[37] is a
matter of conjecture. Certainly Paul did not differentiate the various aspects of his conversion experience,[38] nor can we extricate
the imposition of hands on Paul and apply it to any one facet of
his Damascus Road experience. Paul is emphatic that his apostleship is "by the will of God" (2 Cor. 1:1) and is not "from men nor
through (διά) man" (Gal. 1:1; cf. Gal. 1:12–17). He needs no laying
on of hands to commission him for his task, either at this time or
later; neither does Luke allude in Acts 9:1–19 to either the ordination of Joshua or the consecration of the Levites. Is Luke using
this motif because the appearance of the great apostle to the Gentiles is such a momentous event, or has he other associations in

35. Cf. Acts 7:35; White, *Biblical Doctrine*, p. 196, n. 3.

36. Bruce, *Book of Acts*, p. 202.

37. Dunn, *Baptism in the Holy Spirit*, pp. 74ff.; Oulton, "The Holy Spirit
Baptism," p. 239; H.-G. Schütz, "ἐπιτίθημι," *NIDNTT* II:152.

38. Walter Schmithals, *The Office of Apostle in the Early Church* (E.T.,
Nashville: Abingdon, 1969), p. 31; Richard Longenecker, *The Ministry and Message of Paul* (Grand Rapids: Zondervan, 1971), p. 33.

mind? Lampe concludes that because Paul immediately preaches with power (Acts 9:20, 22, 27), he was thus launched upon his specific mission.[39] He was, however, still preaching to Jews in the synagogue (v. 20) and in Jerusalem (v. 27). Later, Paul ministers for a year at Antioch, apparently as a teacher (Acts 11:26; 15:35). This year seems to have been preparatory in nature; Paul had not yet started in earnest his itinerant mission to the Gentiles.

The imposition of hands on Paul for the recovery of his sight and the filling of the Spirit should perhaps be seen in a more personal light. Paul often asserts his apostolic authority (e.g., 2 Cor. 10:8; 13:16; Gal. 1:15–17; etc.); Luke does the same by giving Paul's apostleship priestly overtones.[40] Again Luke alludes to the Old Testament Scriptures, this time to the Temple ritual. Paul depicts his own life as a drink-offering poured out for the Gentiles. Writing from prison he says, "Even if I am to be poured out as a libation upon the sacrificial offering of your faith, I am glad and rejoice with you all" (Phil. 2:17), and again, "For I am already on the point of being sacrificed; the time of my departure has come" (2 Tim. 4:6).[41] When, after three days of blindness, Paul receives the laying on of hands from Ananias, he is pictured as the sacrificial offering for the sake of the Gentiles, that they too may be sanctified and made acceptable to God.

Fowler draws attention to the similarities between the ministry of Moses and the apostles' ministries.[42] Luke does not hesitate to draw on events in the Moses-Aaron association to clarify the Paul-Barnabas mission. As Moses had Aaron to bring him to the elders (Exod. 4:27), so Paul has Barnabas the Levite to do the same for him (Acts 9:27); as Aaron went with Moses to Pharaoh (Exod. 5:1), so Barnabas is Paul's companion as he sets off on his first missionary journey. Later, Moses' and Aaron's relationship is marked by sharp contention (Exod. 32:21ff.), as is that of Paul and Barnabas (Acts 15:37ff.).

When hands are laid on Paul and Barnabas (Acts 13:1–3), Luke clearly alludes to the consecration of the Levites (Num. 8:5ff.).

39. Lampe, "Holy Spirit . . . ," p. 72.

40. Paul, for example, is a "chosen vessel," σκεῦος; cf. Exod. 30:27– 30 LXX.

41. Paul also sees himself as having been given priestly authority. He is a priest of the gospel who presides at the offering up of the Gentiles (cf. Isa. 66:20) who have been purified by the Holy Spirit (Rom. 15:16). The vocabulary here is also reminiscent of the sacrificial system.

42. Stuart Fowler, "The Continuance of the Charismata," *EvanQ* XLV, no. 3 (July– Sept. 1973), p. 180.

The prophets and teachers are worshiping (λειτουργούντων) the Lord and fasting (Acts 13:3). Λειτουργεῖν, worship, is used in the LXX of the cultic service of priest and Levite. Its use in the New Testament is rare, and so is not to be passed over lightly. The usual word here would be διακονία, service, but Luke avoids it. Fasting played a part in cultic purification rites and also was practiced in preparation for receiving special revelation from God; for example, Moses fasted before receiving the "words of the covenant" from God at Sinai (Exod. 34:28). In Acts 13:2, also when prophets and teachers were fasting, the Holy Spirit directed that Paul and Barnabas be set apart (ἀφορίσατε) for their work (ἔργον), and hands were laid on them (ἐπιθέντες τὰς χεῖρας αὐτοῖς, v. 3).[43] Similarly, Aaron was to separate (ἀφοριεῖ, Num. 8:11 LXX) the Levites so that they might "work the works" (ἐργάζεσθαι τὰ ἔργα, Num. 8:11 LXX) of the Lord. The sons of Israel laid hands on the Levites (Num. 8:10), who thus assumed a mediatorial role. Later, the care of the Word of the Lord, the covenant document, was entrusted to the Levites of Israel (Deut. 31:25f.). The implications of these allusions to the Levites for the mission of Paul and Barnabas are indeed illuminating. The laying on of hands on these two was neither to recognize gifts for leadership nor to commission them for service; such was not necessary. Paul and Barnabas were setting out to mediate the New Covenant to the peoples, both Jew and Gentile. They had the priestly authority to do so.

Thus Luke employs pesher-type midrashic exposition to properly root the infant church in its traditions and heritage. His use of the laying-on-of-hands motif contextualizes the New Covenant events, thereby illuminating them for his readers. The importance of context in interpretation is universally acknowledged. Luke's Old Testament context is not always apparent in English translation, but it is vitally important even so. These texts should not be expected to yield data for present-day church rites. The events recorded are temporally conditioned—and it is this aspect that gives them their significance. Under the guidance of the Spirit of God, Luke uses the laying on of hands as an interpretative tool to highlight occurrences of critical importance and the roles of the people involved. He uses images and forms creatively, so that the new Israel may know who they are and where they are going. The

---

43. Longenecker, *Ministry and Message of Paul*, p. 42, basing his argument on grammatical considerations, believes that the body of believers as a whole laid hands on Barnabas and Paul. The allusions to the laying on of hands on the Levites in Acts 13:1–3 lend force to his argument.

new redemption in Christ Jesus is molded on the Exodus prototype. Like Yahweh of old, the risen Christ is leading and upholding his chosen people that they may one day fully attain the new Promised Land.

Chapter 10

THE LAYING ON OF HANDS IN 1 AND 2 TIMOTHY

In 1 and 2 Tim., the laying-on-of-hands motif occurs in 1 Tim. 4:14; 5:22; and 2 Tim. 1:6. Most commentators believe that 1 Tim. 4:14 and 2 Tim. 1:6 refer to the same event.[1] This assumption can be neither proved nor disproved by exegetical methods. A decision to treat these two texts as referring to two separate occasions, or to conflate them to one, is necessary only if the exegete is trying to formulate a theology of ordination.

Paul refers only once in his epistles[2] to the "hand" of God, and this is in a quotation from Isaiah (Isa. 65:2, quoted in Rom. 10:21); nor does he mention the laying on of hands, even though it was he who laid hands on the twelve at Ephesus (Acts 19:1–7), and he himself twice received the imposition of hands (Acts 9:10–18; Acts 13:1–3). The occurrence of this motif in the Pastoral Epistles, and then only in connection with Timothy, should alert us to the possibility that there may be special historical circumstances attached to the laying on of hands in this case. For Luke, as we saw, the imposition of hands marked critical milestones in the history of the New Covenant people of God. Does this rite have the same significance in these letters?

---

1. Donald Guthrie, *The Pastoral Epistles*, Tyndale New Testament Commentary (Grand Rapids: Eerdmans, 1957), p. 98; E. K. Simpson, *The Pastoral Epistles* (London: Tyndale, 1954), p. 123; M. Dibelius and H. Conzelmann, *A Commentary on the Pastoral Epistles* (E.T., Philadelphia: Fortress Press, 1972), p. 71, and others.

2. That is, other than the "Pastorals." The question of the authorship of 1 and 2 Tim. and Tit. is complex. For the purpose of this study, it is assumed that these letters contain genuine Pauline instructions to Timothy and Titus. The methodology and vocabulary of these letters would suggest that the "hand" of Luke has played no mean role in the formation of the text as we have it.

THE ORDINATION OF TIMOTHY

The imposition of hands on Timothy can be understood only if we take into account Paul's background and sense of mission. Paul was a "Hebrew born of Hebrews" (Phil. 3:5), a "Septuagint-Jew"[3] steeped in Septuagint thought.[4] As a Pharisee, a disciple of the great Gamaliel (Acts 22:3), he had been trained to revere both the Torah and the "tradition of the elders."[5] As a first-century rabbi he was adept at midrashic argumentation, modes of thought Jewish to the core, and yet influenced by both the apocryphal literature of the age and the analogical interpretations of the Hellenistic writers. Paul's letters exhibit a theme common to rabbinic midrashim: God gave to Moses in both written and oral forms the answers to all religious questions.[6] When Paul admonishes Timothy, we see the interplay between his Judaistic presuppositions and practices and the Christian commitments he gained on the road to Damascus. We can expect, therefore, that when (as will be demonstrated) Paul envisions his relationship to Timothy as analogous to that of Moses to Joshua, he draws his correspondences in terms of his Pharisaic understanding of Joshua's position as the successor of Moses.[7] The Torah depicts Joshua's commission as one of military leadership in a holy war.[8] In the Pentateuch, Joshua is the successor of Moses as the leader of the Israelites, but not his successor in relation either to the cult or to the revelation of God,[9] for the Law came by Moses, and its safekeeping was the responsibility of the Levites. Paul retains the military theme of the Torah (2 Tim. 2:3, 4; 4:7), but in keeping with Pharisaic practice he expands and contemporizes Joshua's role. Through the association of Num. 11:14–29 and Num. 27:22–23, Judaism had broadened

3. Adolf Deissman, *Paul, A Study in Social and Religious History* (E.T., Gloucester, MA: Peter Smith, 1972), p. 90.

4. *Ibid.*, p. 99.

5. Richard Longenecker, *Biblical Exegesis*, pp. 113f.

6. Renée Bloch, "Midrash," in *Approaches to Ancient Judaism: Theory and Practice*, ed. William S. Green (Missoula: Scholars Press, 1978), p. 45. See also Rom. 4:3–25; cf. Gen. 15:6; 17:4–6; Gal. 3:8–14; cf. 12:3; 18:18; Joel 2:28; Rom. 9:6–13; 1 Cor. 15:54–56.

7. See Chapter 1.

8. Num. 27:17. Joshua is to be a man who shall "go out before them and come in before them, who shall lead them out and bring them in"; cf. 1 Sam. 18:13–16; 1 Kgs. 22:17; Acts 1:21.

9. There was a distinct shift in the understanding of the Moses-Joshua relationship in early Judaism. Commenting on Moses' ordination of Joshua, Philo reports Moses saying to the congregation of Israel, "Here is a successor to take charge of you" (*On the Virtues* xi:68).

Joshua's function to include both administrative and prophetic elements. Ben Sirach says that

> Joshua the son of Nun was mighty in war
> And was the successor of Moses in prophesying. (Sir. 46:1)

But Paul's orientation has been changed. His reasons for laying hands on Timothy are to be found in the context of the mission that dominated his life: to take the gospel to the Gentiles.

> Confronted with the immense problem of a change in economy—salvation by faith in Christ, the call of the Gentiles, the rejection by official Judaism—the Apostle, guided by the Spirit, searched ceaselessly in the ancient Scriptures to find divine answers to the questions posed by the new situation.[10]

Paul expressed one of his answers in the Moses-Joshua $s^e m\bar{i}k\bar{a}h$.

Thus, Paul sees Timothy as his successor, not only in the struggle for the new Promised Land (1 Tim. 1:18; 6:12; 2 Tim. 2:3, 4), but also as costeward of the gospel with him. Paul is himself a link in the chain of tradition (1 Cor. 15:3); his apostolic office has a priestly character, analogous to that of the Levites (cf. Acts 13:1–3). In instructing Timothy, Paul constantly uses the vocabulary of covenant initiation and renewal.[11] He sets his admonitions in the context of the Sinaitic event (cf. 2 Tim. 3:1–8) and his own death as a sacrifice for the Gentiles (2 Tim. 4:6–8). As Joshua was chosen as Moses' successor by divine decree, so also Timothy has been divinely chosen as Paul's (Num. 27:12–23; 1 Tim. 1:18).[12] Thus Timothy is to "guard" (φυλλάσειν) the faith (1 Tim. 6:20); while suffering imprisonments, with his own death an ever-present possibility, Paul sees in Timothy the one person to whom he can entrust the gospel.

So close is the relationship between Paul and Timothy that it verges on identification.[13] Timothy is Paul's "true child in the faith" (1 Tim. 1:2). In Jewish fashion, revelation is passed on from father to son: this includes Torah in its broad sense, that is, all matters whether of godly conduct (1 Tim. 4:6ff.; 2 Tim. 1:14ff.), cultic af-

---

10. Bloch, "Midrash," p. 48.

11. 1 Tim. 6:20; 2 Tim. 1:14. See Exod. 20:6; 23:13; Deut. 4– 8 *passim*; also Deut. 32:46 (Moses renews the covenant before his death); Josh. 1:7.

12. J. N. D. Kelly (*A Commentary on the Pastoral Epistles* [London: Adam & Charles Black, 1963], p. 108) views these texts as confirming that Timothy is a special *ad hoc* apostolic delegate and not a typical church leader.

13. 2 Cor. 1:1; Phil. 1:1; 1 Thess. 1:1; 2 Thess. 1:1. See also B. Van Elderen, "Timothy," *ZPEB* V:753.

fairs (1 Tim. 5; 2 Tim. 4:1–5), or more personal advice (2 Tim. 4:9, 22). Paul recalls the faith of his own forefathers (2 Tim. 1:3) and reminds Timothy of the faith of *his* (2 Tim. 1:5). He says "God did not give *us* a spirit of timidity" (v. 7), but "saved *us* and called *us* with a holy calling" (v. 9).[14] Both Paul and Timothy are to guard the truth entrusted to them *both* "by the Holy Spirit who dwells in *us*" (v. 14). Paul's instructions to Timothy are personal; they are given to him so that he will see himself as Paul's divinely chosen successor, and so that the early believers will accept him as such. The exhortations in the Pastorals presuppose this distinctive relationship between Paul and Timothy.[15]

Paul is, in a sense, delivering his last will and testament, and he is doing it in such a way that the authority of Torah is called upon to legitimize the instruction he gives Timothy (and incidentally, the early churches). To do so, Paul uses the intimate I-Thou form of the Sinaitic law (cf. 1 Tim. 1:3, 8–10). Paul, the New Covenant Moses, portrays himself as the authorized law-giver for the new Israel. He is now, through Timothy, giving *his* final exhortation to the people of God. The language of the Deuteronomist sets the stage for both 1 Tim. 4:14 and 2 Tim. 1:6. "Take heed" (προσέχω, Deut. 32:2, 46 LXX); likewise Paul says to Timothy, "Take heed" (προσέχω, 1 Tim. 4:13, ἐπέχω, v. 16). Moses reminds the people of God's saving acts and promises (Deut. 32); so also Paul tells Timothy to remember what God has done in *his* life (2 Tim. 1:3, 4, 6). Joshua "stands before" Moses (Num. 11:28) to perform special service; Timothy serves not just alongside Paul but with him (σὺν ἐμοί, Phil. 2:22), sharing a common task.[16] Thus as Moses lays hands on the "young man" Joshua (Exod. 33:11; Deut. 34:9), so Paul lays hands on the young man Timothy (1 Tim. 4:12, 14), the one divinely chosen to take *his* responsibilities after his death.

Paul's exhortations to Timothy reinforce the analogy he draws with Joshua's mission. Paul and Timothy, too, are engaged in a

14. Krister Stendahl's caution (*Paul Among Jews and Gentiles* [Philadelphia: Fortress Press, 1976], p. 12) that Paul's writings address historical situations is pertinent. "The 'I' in his writings is not 'the Christian' but 'the Apostle to the Gentiles'." The same applies to the "we" in Paul's letters to Timothy. "We" is Paul and Timothy, not all leaders in all ages.

15. B. Van Elderen, "Timothy," *ZPEB* V:753.

16. W. Grundmann, "σύν, μετά," *TDNT* VII:770.

"holy war" (cf. 2 Tim. 2:3, 4).[17] Paul encourages Timothy: "Be strong in the grace which is in Christ Jesus" (2 Tim. 2:1). Similarly, Joshua has been encouraged by Yahweh: "Be strong and of good courage" (Josh. 1:6; cf. vv. 7, 9). Timothy is to "command" (παράγγελε, 1 Tim. 4:11), a term Paul uses with careful reservations.[18] Paul entrusts (παρατίθεμαι) this charge (παραγγελία, apostolic instruction) to Timothy (1 Tim. 1:18). Paul uses such terminology for Timothy only. The same applies to Paul's use of διαμαρτύρομαι, to solemnly charge. As covenant mediator, Moses is to "solemnly charge" (δια-μαρτύρομαι) the people of God (Exod. 18:20; 19:10 LXX). He also "solemnly charges" them before "heaven and earth" when they are about to enter the Promised Land (Deut. 32:46). Also, Joshua is to "guard" (φυλάσσεσθαι, Josh. 1:7 LXX) the law of Moses, an injunction that parallels Paul's urgent exhortation to Timothy to guard (φυλάσσειν) the deposit of faith (1 Tim. 6:20; 2 Tim. 1:14). Paul charges (διαμαρτύρομαι) Timothy "in the presence of God and of Christ Jesus and of the elect angels" (1 Tim. 5:21), and Timothy, in turn, is to "solemnly charge" the people (διαμαρτυρόμενος, 2 Tim. 2:14). All of this is to encourage Timothy, who will be doing battle with emerging Jewish Gnosticism (1 Tim. 1:3, 4; 4:7; 2 Tim. 2:14ff.; Tit. 1:13f.). It is through the laying on of hands by Paul that he receives the authority to carry on Paul's mission.

The imposition of hands on Timothy by the presbytery (1 Tim. 4:14) is analogous to the rite in which Paul and Barnabas are given the imprimatur of the church in Acts 13:1-3. Timothy's gift is given to him "through prophecy" (διὰ προφητείας, 1 Tim. 4:14). This echoes the commissioning of Paul (and Barnabas) in Acts 13:1-3.

> Although the direction in Acts 13:2 to the leaders of the church in Syrian Antioch to release two of their number for a more extended ministry is not expressly said to have been uttered by a prophet, this is implied by the context. The five leaders mentioned were prophets as well as teachers, and if in the

17. Whether Paul intends the language of athletic contest or military conflict in 2 Tim. 4:7 is not clear. Both images are used in instructing Timothy. "Δρομός" (translated "race" in the RSV, 2 Tim. 4:7) is used in reference to Paul's commission to the Gentiles (Acts 20:24). In 2 Tim. 4:7 Paul says "I have fought the good fight" (τὸν καλὸν ἀγῶνα ἠγώνισμαι). For the use of ἀγών as a term of military conquest see "ἀγών," *NIDNTT* I:645.

18. Paul seems to differentiate deliberately in wording instructions to Timothy and Titus; cf. 1 Tim. 4:11, 12; 2 Tim. 5:7; and Tit. 2:1, 15. Titus is not told to "command," nor does he receive the imposition of hands, though this is often assumed.

course of their devotions they heard the Holy Spirit say "Come,
set Barnabas and Paul apart for the work to which I have
called them," we are most probably to understand that he used
one of them as his mouthpiece.[19]

Whether or not the dual account of the laying on of hands on
Timothy is to be explained as due to the differences in the character of 1 and 2 Tim.,[20] Paul has introduced a strand into the
imposition of hands on Timothy that links Timothy's office with
his own, and thus to the stewardship of God's revelation.[21] From
prison Paul testifies, "I have no one like him [Timothy], who will
be genuinely anxious for your welfare" (Phil. 2:20). Timothy shares
the divinely conferred responsibility of the apostle to the Gentiles;
he is equipped for his unique role through the laying on of hands
(διὰ τῆς ἐπιθέσεως τῶν χειρῶν μου, 2 Tim. 1:6), that is, the hands
of Paul as agent. Moses did the same for Joshua. The Lord says,
"lay your hands upon him" (ἐπιθήσεις τὰς χεῖρας σου ἐπ᾽ αὐτόν,
Num. 27:18 LXX). The use of the personal pronoun with χείρ,
hand, in both of these cases accentuates the personal transmission
of authority when Moses and Paul lay hands on their successors.
The personal pronoun is not used when Peter and John lay hands
on the Samaritans (Acts 8:17), when Paul lays hands on the Twelve
at Ephesus (Acts 19:6), or even when hands are laid on Barnabas
and Paul (Acts 13:3). Even in Acts 6:6, with its verbal analogy to
the commissioning of Joshua, the personal pronoun is not used in
the imposition of hands.[22] Moses commissions Joshua in the sight
of both the high priest and the congregation, so that the people
may recognize that these leaders have prophetic authorization for
office, an office that is, in a sense, mediatorial, and thus has a
duality of responsibility: to the God who authors the covenant and
the people who accept it. We do not know whether 1 Tim. 4:14 and
2 Tim. 1:6 speak of two separate occasions; evidently that is not
the author's concern. What *does* concern him is that the new people
of God understand that God is faithful, and, even at that point in

19. F. F. Bruce, "The Holy Spirit in the Acts of the Apostles," *Int* XXVII,
no. 2 (April 1973), p. 182.

20. Dibelius/Conzelmann, *Commentary on the Pastoral Epistles*, p. 71.
Such a rationale for the conflict in these texts is not convincing.

21. Num. 31:5ff.; Deut. 33:10. See also T. F. Torrance, "Consecration and
Ordination," *SJT* 11 (1958), p. 226.

22. Acts 6:6 reads "ἐπέθηκαν αὐτοῖς τὰς χεῖρας." The emphasis in the
imposition of hands in Acts is on critical events; in 1 and 2 Tim. it is on personal
commission.

time, was fulfilling his promises through his divinely selected and commissioned leaders.

There is no hint that Paul attaches any significance other than the special endowment for office (after the model of Joshua) and the sharing of his own unique commission, with the act of the imposition of hands in the case of Timothy's "ordination." It is unlikely that rabbinic ordination was customary at the time: Paul seems not to know it. Furthermore, extensive training in the written and oral Torah was evidently prerequisite to rabbinic ordination when it did become a practice. Paul bases Timothy's office on divine selection, not expertise in the Law. Paul calls Timothy a "man of God" (1 Tim. 6:11), a term indicating prophetic office, and used of Moses in Deut. 33:1. Because this term has been appropriated by church leaders throughout history one must beware of automatically associating it with pastoral office. Paul does not depict Timothy as the prototype of the pastor or elder, nor is he concerned with the quality of Timothy's performance in the pulpit (if an anachronism may be permitted). Rather, Paul places Timothy's office in a covenantal setting; if the historical context is stripped away, the office becomes vulnerable to manipulation. Paul is concerned with Timothy's stewardship of the deposit of faith, what he calls "my deposit" (παραθήκην μου, 2 Tim. 1:12). This is a "good" deposit that Timothy now "has" (ἔχε, has, not as in the RSV, that which he is to "follow," 2 Tim. 1:13). Paul apparently has a specific tradition in mind.[23] These are not generalized instructions for preaching the gospel,[24] no matter how applicable they may appear to be for that purpose.

The laying on of hands on Timothy is not a rite initiated by the apostolic church with a view to setting a normative pattern for induction into pastoral or missionary roles, nor is it an imitation of Jewish custom, patriarchal or rabbinic. Historically, Paul sets the imposition of hands on Timothy in the context of the entry of the Israelites into the land of Canaan (Deut. 32–34), and in that of his own commissioning for specific duty (Acts 13:1–3). By using the Moses-Joshua $s^e m\bar{\imath}k\bar{a}h$ and by linking Timothy's office to Levitical ordination through analogy with the laying on of hands on

23. It is not to be assumed that Paul is thinking in terms of canonical writings; just what this "deposit" consisted of is beyond the scope of this study.

24. That Timothy's office was unique and unrepeatable has been recognized by many. John Gill, for example, says that Timothy was an "extraordinary officer" with an "extraordinary gift" for an "extraordinary affair"; John Gill, *Body of Divinity* (Atlanta: Turner Lassiter, 1965 reprint), p. 869.

Paul, the writer of the Pastorals interprets the contemporary scene for the people of God.

"IN THE PRESENCE OF GOD . . ."

Paul's prohibition to Timothy about the laying on of hands in 1 Tim. 5:22 is prefaced by the solemn injunction "In the presence of God and of Christ Jesus and the elect angels I charge [δια-μαρτύρομαι] you. . . ." What Paul has to say to Timothy is apparently critical for the advance of the gospel. Again this is covenant vocabulary and the context is the Law. The early Christians who heard "διαμαρτύρομαι" (solemnly charge), and the witnesses in whose name the charge was being made, would be alerted to their traditions about the keeping of the Law. Not only was δια-μαρτύρομαι used when the covenant was given, but again and again it serves in warning the Israelites of the dire consequences of failure to keep the Law of God. Thus, a careful look at the Old Testament allusions helps to illuminate our New Testament text. In Deut. 30:19, Moses, calling on the witness of "heaven and earth," warns the people that to forsake the Law means failure to take the Promised Land, and death (see also Deut. 4:26; 8:19 LXX for similar contexts). By allusion, the writer of the Pastorals has placed the instructions of 1 Tim. 5:22 into a significant historical context. Before the Israelites entered Canaan,

> Moses came and recited all the words of this song in the hearing of the people, he and Joshua the son of Nun. And when Moses had finished speaking these words to all Israel, he said to them, "Lay to heart all the words which I enjoin [διαμαρτύρομαι LXX] upon you this day, that you may command them to your children, that they may be careful to do [φυλάσσειν LXX] all the words of this law. For it is no trifle for you, but it is your life, and thereby you shall live long in the land which you are going over Jordan to possess. (Deut. 32:44–47)

Paul is now charging Timothy before *he* enters the new territory to be taken for the gospel of Christ. Although these allusions are obscured in English translation, they would be immediately meaningful to Timothy. When Paul takes along four compatriots in fulfilling his Nazarite vow, it is to show just how careful *he* is to observe (φυλάσσειν) the Law (Acts 21:24), since his very mission was in peril because of those who felt he was blaspheming against

God in his attitude to the Torah.[25] It is distressing to observe the way some interpreters have jumped to conclusions as to the meaning of 1 Tim. 5:22. The New English Bible even goes so far as to read one particular interpretation into their translation: "Do not be over-hasty in laying on hands in ordination,"[26] this in spite of the fact that most commentators admit that the meaning of this text is obscure.[27]

1 Tim. 5:22 has been interpreted in three ways: as a reference to the imposition of hands in baptism,[28] to the restoration of sinners,[29] and to the ordination of elders.[30] Lohse, like many others,[31] is unsure of the meaning but favors either a reference to the rite

25. Φυλάσσω, "guard," is a term associated with the keeping of the Law of God, especially in Deuteronomy. See, for example, Deut. 4:2, 6, 9, 40; 5:1, 10, 12, 15, 29, 32; 6:2, 3, 17, 25; and *passim*. Paul sees himself as the custodian of the true Torah; as Moses had his Jannes and Jambres, so enemies of the revelation of God continue to plague his people. See 2 Tim. 3:1-11.

26. "In ordination" is wholly gratuitous; the Greek text says nothing about ordination, only the laying on of hands. A. T. Hanson (*The Pastoral Epistles* [Cambridge: Cambridge Univ. Press, 1966], p. 63) also reads ordination into this.

27. C. K. Barrett, *The Pastoral Epistles* (Oxford: Clarendon Press, 1963), pp. 80f.; Walter Lock, *A Critical and Exegetical Commentary on the Pastoral Epistles* (Edinburgh: T. & T. Clark, 1924), p. 64; Dibelius/Conzelmann, *Commentary on the Pastoral Epistles*, p. 80, though eventually coming down on the side of the restoration of sinners, admit the difficulty of the text.

28. Daube, *New Testament and Rabbinic Judaism*, p. 144; Kelly, *Pastoral Epistles*, p. 107; Tertullian, *On Baptism* XVIII.

29. Cyprian, *Letters*, XV.1; LXXXI.2; Dibelius/Conzelmann, *Commentary on the Pastoral Epistles*, p. 80; *ISBE* IV:2200.

30. By the fourth century Chrysostom was using 1 Tim. 5:22 as a weapon against the abuse of the priestly office. He remarks: "Many of the ordinations now-days do not proceed from the grace of God but are due to human ambition" (*On the Priesthood* IV.1). 1 Tim. 5:22 is then taken as a warning against ordination of unsuitable candidates (IV.2). In his *Homilies on the Statutes* I.1, after quoting the same text, "he explained the grievous danger of such a transgression by showing that so men will undergo the punishment of the sins perpetrated by others, in common with them, because they confer the power on their wickedness by the laying on of hands." Thus the meaning of the text was shaped early in church history by connecting it to a sacramental view of the laying on of hands in ordination. This text is thus still frequently taken to refer to ordination; Martin Bucer, *De Regno Christi*, Bk. 1, Chap. 4, quoted in *Melanchthon and Bucer*, ed. William Pauck (Philadelphia: Westminster Press, 1969), p. 239; William Hendriksen, *Exposition of the Pastoral Epistles* (Grand Rapids: Baker, 1957), p. 185; Joachim Jeremias, *Die Briefe an Timotheus und Titus* (Göttingen: Vandenhoeck & Ruprecht, 1975), pp. 42f., and many others. Even though 1 Tim. 5:22 is noted for its difficulty, Chrysostom's interpretation is often taken as though the meaning is straightforward.

31. See n. 27 above. H.-G. Schütz ("ἐπιτίθημι," *NIDNTT* II:152) believes that 1 Tim. 5:22 could refer to any one of these three.

of ordination or to the imposition of hands in the restoration of penitent sinners.[32] It has been pointed out by Bernard and others that to interpret this as the rite of restoration of sinners is anachronistic.

> Such reconciliation was doubtless attended with χειροθεσία in later ages ... but there is no evidence that it was an accustomed usage in Apostolic times, nor is χειροθεσία or any similar phrase used in such a context elsewhere in the New Testament.[33]

To term this "ordination" is equally anachronistic (cf. Chap. 20).

The immediate context of 1 Tim. 5:22 adds to the difficulties of interpretation. By modern literary standards the text appears to be heterogeneous, disorderly, containing many digressions. That is, however, *our* point of view; the author of the Pastorals was not primarily concerned with the literary aspects of his work. Dibelius/Conzelmann are of the opinion that v. 22 does not belong with the previous instruction concerning the elders (vv. 17–20).[34] The translators of the NIV have acknowledged the difficulty with a paragraph division after v. 20. Even if 1 Tim. 5:21–23 does refer to the elders, are we to assume that inadequacies in the characters of some potential elders was of such concern to Paul that he would employ this solemn vocabulary to instruct about ordination, and then go on to advise Timothy about his health (1 Tim. 5:21, 22)? Or is it possible that theologians and pastors, struggling with problems of church leadership, have, since the time of Chrysostom, been reading the anxieties of their own situations back into these texts?[35]

Since this text is enigmatic, perhaps several assumptions that have influenced the interpretation of 1 Tim. 5:22 need to be reexamined. The first, that 1 Tim. 5:21, 22 refers to the elders of v. 17, has already been mentioned. Nor is Timothy a type of the pastor, being charged to "keep these rules" (RSV) or "observe these things" (KJV). Διαμαρτύρομαι, "I solemnly charge," would bring to Timothy's mind the necessity for obedience to the Mosaic ordinances. Would Paul, trained as he was in rabbinic modes of thought, use

32. Lohse, "χείρ," *TDNT* IX:434; Jeremias, *Die Briefe*, pp. 42f. also acknowledges the obscurity of the text.

33. J. H. Bernard, *The Pastoral Epistles* (Cambridge: Cambridge Univ. Press, 1922), p. 88; Leon Morris, *Ministers of God*, p. 79.

34. Dibelius/Conzelmann, *Commentary on the Pastoral Epistles*, p. 80; Jeremias, *Die Briefe*, p. 42.

35. See n. 30 above.

this phraseology in connection with an aspect of induction to church office? We would do well to heed Stendahl's observation: "Again and again we find that there is hardly a thought of Paul's which is not tied up with his mission."[36] This text must first be viewed as advice to the latter-day Joshua who has the responsibility of continuing to lead the new people of God in the conquest of their Canaan. Only if there is no illumination from this vantage point should alternatives be sought out. We have no license to read present-day church patterns and concerns back into the apostolic age. If the failures of an elder were considered by Paul to be such a grave matter that he would use the urgent διαμαρτύρομαι, then we must assume that one-man leadership was the norm in the early Christian communities. We know, however, that this was not so (Acts 14:23; 15:4; 16:4; 20:17; 1 Pet. 5:4; James 5:14; Tit. 1:5; etc.). The only office magnified in the New Testament was that of the apostles, because it was they who transmitted the revelation of God. Paul uses διαμαρτύρομαι here because he wishes to remind Timothy that, as his successor, he will be carrying on for him. Nothing must be permitted to interfere with his subapostolic mission, the task given to him "by prophecy" (1 Tim. 4:14).

The assumption that this text speaks of ordination apparently underlies the translation of χωρὶς προκρίματος, μηδὲν ποιῶν κατὰ πρόσκλισιν (1 Tim. 5:21). The translators of the NIV make this an exhortation to Timothy to keep instructions "without partiality" and to do nothing "out of favoritism." Is Timothy really being cautioned against showing respect of persons? If so, it is indeed strange that the writer did not use προσωπολημψία, employed several times elsewhere in the New Testament for this concept (Rom. 2:11; Eph. 6:9; Col. 3:25; James 2:1; see also Acts 1:34; 1 Pet. 1:17). Furthermore, favoritism may well have been a problem centuries later when power structures had arisen among the hierarchy of the church, and when church and state were essentially one. But at a time when to be a Christian (and especially a Christian leader) could well bring persecution down on one's head, it would be doing a friend no favor to ordain him (as many suppose this text teaches). Both προκρίματος and πρόσκλισιν are *hapax legomena*, and both are legal technical terms. Προκρίματος means to prejudge an issue,[37] that is, to let one's prejudices or presuppositions rule. Κατὰ πρόσκλισιν, according to one's inclination,[38] has a similar meaning.

---

36. Stendahl, *Paul Among Jews and Gentiles*, p. 12.
37. W. Schneider, "κρίμα," *NIDNTT* II:363.
38. *BAG*, p. 723.

Both of these words apply to Timothy's attitude to the Law, a problem that was causing recurring friction between Jewish and Hellenistic Christians. Could we have here an echo of Ben Sirach 43:1, 2?

> Of the following things do not be ashamed and do not let partiality lead you to sin:
> of the law of the Most High and his covenant and of rendering judgment to acquit the ungodly.

R. H. Charles quotes Smend as explaining the meaning of this to be "an admonition to the Scribes not to be ashamed of the Law of their fathers (i.e. their ancestral religion) in the face of Greek fashion and influences."[39] In other words, Paul is cautioning Timothy about his attitude toward the Law. In passing, it might also be pointed out that a sacramental understanding of ordination seems to lie behind the translation of μηδὲ κοινώνει ἁμαρτίαις ἀλλοτρίαις as "nor participate in another man's sins" (1 Tim. 5:22b). ʿΑμαρτίαις ἀλλοτρίαις could just as well be taken as a reference to alien, perhaps Greek cultic practices; this would not be out of harmony with the context.

When Timothy is advised to keep himself "pure" (ἁγνόν, 1 Tim. 5:22c), we must ask if the term is being used in an ethical sense, or if this is a reference to ritual purity.[40] To answer this question, we need to clarify the role that purity played in Judaism, both normative and sectarian. In the Qumran communities, cultic and moral impurity were identified,[41] and even in other groups the concepts tended to merge. Cultic purity often had ethical and moral overtones, and both were related to illness, particularly leprosy. A sect's attitude to the purity laws served as a definition of its position in relation to Pharisaic Judaism. In the Second Temple period, a characteristic charge against a sect by its opponents was that it was polluting the Temple by failing to observe meticulously the purity stipulations.[42] Obsession with ritual purity was a characteristic of most of the factions in first-century Judaism. We should remember that the Christians of the first century were still essentially Jews. In fact, to outsiders they were a Jewish sect (Acts 24:14); to themselves they were the true Jews, the new Israel of God.

39. R. H. Charles, *The Apocrypha and Pseudepigrapha of the Old Testament*, vol. I (Oxford: Clarendon Press, 1913), p. 469.

40. *BAG*, p. 11.

41. Jacob Neusner, *The Idea of Purity in Ancient Judaism* (Leiden: E. J. Brill, 1973), p. 47.

42. *Ibid.*, p. 27.

Jewish worship in the Temple and in the synagogues was what they naturally looked upon as the worship pleasing to the one true God, the God of Abraham, Isaac, and Jacob—and, now, the Father of the Lord Jesus Christ. The outward form of Jewish life was the immediately obvious form of living in accordance with the commands God had given his people.[43]

In a time when differentiation between Judaism and Christianity was taking place, tensions over the adherence to the Law increased. The observance of ritual purity regulations showed in an obvious way where a Jew stood in relation to respect for the Law of Moses and hence to Yahweh himself. During his ministry, Jesus had been careful about this very thing, lest he be arrested prematurely and be unable to complete his mission. Paul, too, had faced the same threat to his own commission.

Thus, when Timothy is instructed to keep himself pure, the concern with the question of ritual purity in early Judaism must be taken into account. Ἁγνόν, pure, occurs together with the laying on of hands, an act generally associated at this time with Temple sacrifice.[44] When Timothy is instructed to "lay hands suddenly on no man [μηδενί]" (1 Tim. 5:22a KJV),[45] the translators have assumed that μηδενί is a masculine pronoun and the reference is to an ordination rite. The morphology of this word permits, however, that it be taken as *either* masculine or neuter. If μηδενί is neuter ("nothing," "not anything"), then the instruction reads "Do not hastily lay hands on anything" and could conceivably be a reference to Temple sacrifice. But why should Paul caution Timothy about cultic practices? Would he be likely to participate in Jewish ritual?

For all the impressions one might get from some of the statements in Romans and Galatians, Paul's attitude to his Jewish heritage is far from negative. He evidently took great care to continue to observe the precepts of the Law, not in any way to minimize the work of his Lord, but so that the gospel might not be hindered by the creation of unnecessary antagonism from his Jewish brethren.

---

43. R. A. Markus, *Christianity in the Roman World* (London: Thames and Hudson, 1974), pp. 20f.

44. References to the laying on of hands in the talmudic literature are infrequent. There are, however, many references to "hand" or "hands" in connection with ritual purity.

45. Μηδενί is translated "any one" in the NASB and is not translated at all in the NIV, the RSV, and the NEB. The NASB paraphrases 1 Tim. 5:22 as follows: "Do not lay hands upon any one too hastily and thus share responsibility for the sins of others; keep yourself free from sin."

Stephen had been martyred over the question of the relationship of the Law to the gospel (Acts 6:11–14; 7:58–60); most of the leadership problems in the early churches had to do with this issue, as evidenced in the dispute between Peter and Paul (Gal. 2:11–21). This may have been the cause of John Mark's defection,[46] which resulted also in the separation of Paul and Barnabas. Questions brought before the Jerusalem Council (Acts 15) and accusations brought against Paul (Acts 21:8) all had to do with conformity with the Mosaic ordinances.[47] Paul had even circumcised Timothy so that no offense might be given to the Jews (Acts 16:3). Paul himself was still obeying the ceremonial law (Acts 14:17, 18; cf. Acts 20:5, 6; 24:14; 25:8), and the Temple was still the divinely appointed center of worship for God's people.[48] The making of vows and the giving of alms were still very much a part of the religious life of the people. According to Josephus,

> It is usual with those that had either afflicted with a distemper, or with any other distresses, to make vows; and for thirty days before they are to offer their sacrifice, to abstain from wine, and to shave the hair of their head.[49]

According to the law for the Nazarite (Num. 6:13–21), upon completion of vows the priest was to put part of the Nazarite's offering on the latter's hands, after which he could drink wine (v. 20). The practice of making a Nazarite vow was common.[50] Josephus tells of Herod Agrippa sponsoring a large number of Nazarites,[51] and later, a whole tractate of the Mishnah was devoted to the traditions and regulations connected with the Nazarite vow.[52]

Jewish Christians also undertook Nazarite vows. On his second missionary journey, Paul "cut his hair, for he had a vow" (Acts 18:18). Whether this had anything to do with Paul's "thorn" (2 Cor. 12:8), or any of the other weaknesses he mentions,[53] we do not know. We do know that in order to discharge his vow, Paul had to return to Jerusalem and sacrifice in the Temple.

Evidently religious fervor and ritual had become considerably

46. Richard Longenecker, *Ministry and Message of Paul*, p. 43.

47. In Corinth Paul was accused of persuading the people to worship in a way contrary to the Law: Acts 18:13; cf. Acts 21:28; 24:5, 6.

48. C. Brown, "τὸ ἱερόν," *NIDNTT* III:793.

49. Josephus, *Wars of the Jews* II.15.1.

50. Jeremias, *Jerusalem*, p. 129.

51. Josephus, *Antiquities* XIX.6.1.

52. M. Nazir.

53. Paul mentions his weaknesses (ἀσθένειαι) in 1 Cor. 2:3 and 2 Cor. 10:10. He also calls his "thorn" a weakness; 2 Cor. 12:5; cf. Gal. 4:13–15.

more rigid within the Jerusalem church since Paul's "famine visit". . . . And although James and the Jerusalem apostles never went on record as favoring such a development, they seem to have been hard pressed to control it. Thus they suggested to Paul that in an endeavor to alleviate the fears engendered by the malicious rumors about him, he publicly show his respect for Jewish customs and piety by joining in the temple rites of Nazarite purification about to be performed by four Jewish Christians.[54]

This Paul agreed to do (Acts 21:20–26), to show that he "guarded the law" (φυλάσσων τὸν νόμον, Acts 21:24). The Law (Num. 6:9) required that seven days had to elapse before a Nazarite who had been defiled could complete his vow by offering his sacrifice in the Temple.[55] Paul had almost fulfilled this requirement when the Jews, convinced that he had defiled the Temple, attacked him (Acts 21:27–31). As a result, Paul was imprisoned.

The vocabulary of 1 Tim. 5:21–23 indicates that Timothy also may have undertaken a vow, for he had been abstaining from wine.[56] He, too, had many illnesses (τὰς πυκνάς σου ἀσθενείας, 1 Tim. 5:23).

As his successor, Paul might expect Timothy to follow his example in purifying himself. Gentile converts were not, of course, required to adopt Jewish ritual as necessary to salvation. Nevertheless, with their union with Christ they had inevitably acquired union with the religion of Israel. The roots from which Christianity had sprung were not now suddenly to be destroyed.

Paul was not drawing men out of Judaism or Hellenism so as to form a new religion. His Jewish converts remained within Judaism and his gentile converts were drawn into Judaism, the "true" Judaism. . . . When a gentile was converted to the "Christian" belief, he thereby in that same change became a Jew, a "true" Jew.[57]

Timothy is, then, to "take a little wine," and yet is to "keep himself pure" (ἁγνόν, 1 Tim. 5:22). When a person (man or woman) made a special vow (Num. 6), he was to separate himself "with purity to the Lord" (ἀφαγνίσασθε ἁγνείαν κυρίῳ LXX) and to "purely

54. Longenecker, *Ministry and Message of Paul*, p. 79.

55. M. Nazir vi.6.

56. Proselytes undertook Nazarite vows; M. Nazir iii.6; vi.11; cf. Acts 21:28.

57. Kenneth W. Clark, "The Israel of God," in *Studies in the New Testament and Early Christian Literature*, ed. D. Aune (Leiden: E. J. Brill, 1972), pp. 167f.

abstain" (ἁγνισθήσεται LXX) from wine and strong drink (Num. 6:2, 3 LXX). If the reference in 1 Tim. 5:22 is to a vow that Timothy has undertaken,[58] Paul's instruction to Timothy not to lay hands on prematurely (ταχέως) could well be an exhortation that he meticulously fulfill the Law. The full seven days must elapse after defilement (such as drinking wine while under a vow) before completing his vow by sacrificing in the Temple. Paul is, perhaps, thinking back to the time when he was arrested and imprisoned on charges of teaching against the Law and of defiling the Temple (Acts 21:28) and of how others were involved with him (Acts 21:28). Timothy must be careful lest he, too, is accused of "blaspheming against Moses" by treating the Law frivolously, especially because he was a Gentile. For Paul, looking to Timothy to carry on the mission to the Gentiles, this would indeed be a matter of grave concern, one in which he might well invoke the "presence of God, and of Christ, and of the elect angels" (1 Tim. 5:21).

Up to this point, in every case in the New Testament where mention is made of hands being laid on persons (with the exception of Acts 9:10–18), the writers have interpreted the act by the use of verbal analogy with either the consecration of the Levites or the Moses-Joshua $s^e m \bar{i} k \bar{a} h$. No such analogy is used here in spite of the abundant Old Testament allusion. Reference has been made to the Old Testament in 1 Tim. 5:18, 19, and 20 and, in a different context, in vv. 21 and 22. Evidently, Paul's caution to Timothy is to be taken in a manner that would be understood naturally by his listeners. The sense most familiar to these early Christians would be that of a reference to Temple sacrifice. Timothy is to be careful that he fulfills his vows meticulously, lest he give offense to Jewish religious leaders, and imperil his own mission as Paul's successor.

Whatever the interpretation of 1 Tim. 5:22, it is evident that this text cannot be used to buttress any argument for the laying on of hands in ordination to church office. To claim that 1 and 2 Timothy offer a "clear picture of Christian ordination as it was adopted by the Pauline churches from the Jewish-Christian church in Palestine"[59] is manifestly a misstatement. The power of the unquestioned assumptions underlying this type of assertion has been apparent throughout the history of the church. The mark of such thinking has been felt in our translations and has thus been perpetuated throughout the rank and file of Christianity. The per-

---

58. The noun ἁγνεία is used in 1 Tim. 4:12 and 1 Tim. 5:2 for moral uprightness. The change to ἁγνός, used absolutely, could be significant.

59. Lohse, "χείρ," *TDNT* IX:433.

son who does not know the biblical languages is dependent on the care, skill, and integrity of those who have translated the version he or she uses. For those who insist on the authority of the Scriptures, such misleading translations are not to be lightly dismissed as of little consequence.

Chapter 11

THE LAYING ON OF HANDS
IN THE APOSTOLIC AGE

The laying on of hands in connection with leadership roles in the
New Testament is contextualized by Luke and Paul according to
three Old Testament analogies. Paul, as the mediator of the gospel
to the Gentiles, sees his own life as a sacrificial offering (Acts
9:10–18; cf. Phil. 2:17), in a sense continuing the mission of his
Lord, the Lamb of God, without blemish or spot, who gave his life
for his people (1 Pet. 1:19). Second, the offices of the Hellenists
(Acts 6:1–6) and Timothy (2 Tim. 1:6) are likened to the role of
Joshua whose responsibility it was to continue to implement the
Sinaitic covenant. Finally, the missions of Paul and Barnabas (Acts
13:1–3) and Timothy (1 Tim. 4:14) are linked by analogy (in Timothy's case indirectly) with the representative office of the Levites,
those who had been given the priestly responsibility of preserving
the covenant documents and of mediating the covenant stipulations to the people. As has been indicated, the meaning of 1 Tim.
5:22 is obscure; the context suggests a reference to contemporary
cultic practices.

The laying on of hands for induction into office evidently was
peculiar to Hebrew traditions. There is no reference to such a rite
in Greek mythologies or in the religions of Israel's neighbors. Neither in Philo, Josephus, nor in the Qumran documents is the imposition of hands spoken of in connection with those holding office
at this time. Even in the talmudic literature, the laying on of
hands is mentioned only rarely, and then mainly in connection
with Temple sacrifice. What few references there are may or may
not be an indication of practices known to first-century Judaism.
Even the Pharisaic sage Paul, not generally backward in asserting
his scholarly achievements, says nothing about having received
the laying on of hands in rabbinic ordination. Such paucity of evi-

dence has its advantages in that it narrows the sources to manageable proportions. Historically, however, those who have sought to build a doctrine of ordination on the available evidence have had to rely on flimsy foundations indeed.

It is notable that the laying on of hands occurs in those New Testament writings that emphasize the continuity of Christianity with its historic origins. The New Covenant in Jesus Christ is modeled on its prototype at Sinai. A new Exodus is taking place under the guiding hand of the risen Savior; the Moses-Torah is now the Jesus-teaching (διδασκαλία); the shadowy forms of the past provide the pattern for present reality.[1]

With consummate skill and creativity, the New Testament writers use the laying-on-of-hands motif in its Old Testament context to interpret current personalities and events for the new people of God. The new Torah, the Jesus-teaching, rooted though it is in the great faith events of ancient times,[2] is nonetheless conveyed in the contemporary modes by which that faith was expressed among first-century Jews. Since the time of the great scribe Ezra, midrashic methods of interpretation had gradually taken over where prophetic inspiration had left off.[3] Under the inspiration of the Spirit of God, Luke and Paul do not hesitate to use these methods to communicate the covenant faithfulness of God to his people. So it is that by means of midrashic exposition and the mnemonic techniques so effective and familiar in the synagogue setting, Paul and Luke capture for their readers the significance of the momentous events they are witnessing.

The churches to which Paul and Luke were writing still displayed many features of their Jewish heritage; it took several centuries for even the externals of Judaism to vanish from the Christian churches.[4] The fall of the Temple (A.D. 70), the Bar Kochba revolt

---

1. David Daube develops this theme in *The Exodus Pattern in the Bible* (London: Faber & Faber, 1963). The "teaching" (διδασκαλία) is not to be thought of as *replacing* the Torah anymore than the Exodus events of the Pentateuch are replaced by the new Exodus. See Lloyd Gaston, "Paul and the Torah" in *Antisemitism and the Foundations of Christianity*, ed. Alan T. Davies (New York: Paulist Press, 1979), pp. 51f., 62ff.; and Charlotte Klein, *Anti-Judaism in Christian Theology*, trans. Edward Quinn (Philadelphia: Fortress Press, 1978), pp. 39ff.

2. See K. Wegenast, "διδάσκω, διδασκαλία," *NIDNTT* III:759–771. In Sir. 39:8 and Prov. 2:17 the law and the teaching are equated. Cf. 2 Chron. 7:17ff.

3. M. Gertner, "Midrashim in the New Testament," *JSS*, vol. 7 (1962), p. 276.

4. See Adolf Deissman, *Paul, a Study in Social and Religious History* (E.T., Gloucester, MA: Peter Smith, 1972), pp. 104f., and Henry M. Shires, *Finding the Old Testament in the New* (Philadelphia: Westminster Press, 1974), pp. 38f.

(A.D. 135), and the triumph of the "Great Church" all contributed to the emergence of Gentile Christianity. We might expect, therefore, that all the early Christians, even the Gentile Christians, were addressed as though they were Jews or Jewish proselytes. The four men under Nazarite vows whose Temple expenses Paul undertook to pay were designated "Greeks" (Acts 21:28), and he seems to have taken Jewish customs in Gentile churches for granted (1 Cor. 11:2–16).[5] With the laying on of hands a part of both the Temple ritual and the designation of office in the Old Testament, we might expect to find references to both in the New Testament. Such is indeed the case.

The Bible of the early Christians was the Septuagint. Paul and Luke use the vocabulary of this version for purposes of recall and association of ideas. The priority of these writers was the dynamic of salvation; they were not concerned with establishing norms for church government. Just as it is evident from Acts 8:14–17 and 19:1–7 that Luke is not delineating an *ordo salutis*, neither is he in Acts 6:1–6 and 13:1–3 setting forth an ordination theology for "the ministry." The laying on of hands in the New Testament must be evaluated in conjunction with its Old Testament connections. If the similitude to the Old Testament sources is missed, so also is the significance of the laying on of hands in the New Testament writings.

The diversity of the situations in which the imposition of hands occurs in the New Testament is evident. We have seen that the laying on of hands may be accompanied by miraculous signs (Acts 8:17; 9:17, 18; 19:6), though often it is not (Acts 6:6; 13:3). In some texts the apostles lay on hands (Acts 8:17; 19:6; 2 Tim. 1:6); in others they do not (Acts 9:1–7; 13:1–3; 1 Tim. 4:14); and in still others the construction of the Greek is ambiguous, and who lays hands on is not conclusive (Acts 6:6; 13:3). The rite is variously associated with baptism (Acts 8:17; 19:6), the sacrifice of animals (Heb. 6:2; 1 Tim. 5:22[?]), temporary ministry of a practical nature (Acts 6:6), itinerant evangelistic ministry, also temporary (Acts 13:3), and person-to-person mediatorship of a spiritual gift (2 Tim. 1:6). In two enigmatic texts (Acts 9:10–19; 1 Tim. 5:22), it is difficult to determine which of several possible circumstances underlie the rite. In such a situation, those who have attempted to construct a consistent doctrine of ordination have had to resort to one of two possible expedients. Either they must base their doc-

---

5. Georg Strecker elaborates on some of these points in Appendix I of Walter Bauer's *Orthodoxy and Heresy in Earliest Christianity* (E.T., Philadelphia: Fortress Press, 1971).

trine on the teaching of the church, or they must be selective in choosing the texts they wish to use to validate their stance. In either case, the historical contexts so carefully introduced by Luke or Paul are neglected. With the loss of context there is a corresponding loss of meaning; the Old Testament "control" can no longer operate and the texts, whether by accident or intention, are at the mercy of the exegete's presuppositions. Under such circumstances, conflicting doctrines of ordination, which are forged in the polemical atmosphere of denominational rivalry (or worse), are not likely to be resolved by appeals to a Scripture that has been shorn of its historical-theological foundations. Surely, if Paul and Luke had been concerned in these texts with legislating procedures for induction of church officers, they would have presented their instructions with consistency, or they would at least have avoided the apparent grammatical ambiguities that have confounded theologians for centuries.

The distinctive character of the laying on of hands in the New Testament does not lie in the conveyance of special powers through tactual transmission, or the lack of such conveyance. God could equip his servants with or without[6] the imposition of hands. The motif signifies the "hand" of God powerfully at work in covenant fulfillment according to the times of *his* choosing; it is linked to the dynamic of salvation history. The times and seasons are under the control of a sovereign God; they are not under the jurisdiction of his servants. Both Paul and Luke employ this motif as a figure to explain the events of the new age in terms the early Christians would understand. This dramatic rite would have a powerful impact on those familiar with their Jewish heritage. These writers have carefully chosen their allusions according to the meanings they wished to convey, and it is through these allusions that the texts receive their orientation. The events of the new age in which the imposition of hands occur are unique, once-for-all situations. The laying on of hands has nothing to do with routine installation into office in the church, whether as elder, deacon, pastor, or missionary. Rather, that action confirmed to the new people of God that Yahweh, the God of the covenant, was even now faithfully implementing the fulfillment of his covenant promises to his people.

---

6. Acts 6:1 – 6; 2 Tim. 1:6; there is no record of hands being laid on any of the apostles (except Paul), or on Silas, Apollos, Titus, or others (with the exception of Barnabas who was teamed with Paul, Acts 13:1 – 3).

Part III

ORDINATION AND THE THEOLOGY OF MINISTRY

Chapter 12

ORDINATION, OFFICE, AND MINISTRY

The decisions of the Apostolic Council (Acts 15) gave concrete expression to those elements of discontinuity between the Old and the New Covenants that were to be demonstrated in the cultic associations of the new people of God. For a generation the "royal priesthood" had coexisted with the Levitical priesthood. The separation of Christianity from Judaism enforced certain aspects of radical change; still, old ways were not easily abandoned. The spiritual sacrifices of the new people of God were not bound to Jerusalem, nor their worship to the Sabbath. They required no mediatorial caste between themselves and God; men and women now had an Advocate in heaven, and the indwelling Spirit as their helper on earth.

This radically new society called for a new pattern of leadership. The key concept in the structuring of the new communities was to be service, διακονία. Service to God was no longer the prerogative of priest and Levite, but was to be the privilege of all believers. Jesus Christ had not only pioneered the new community, but had set the example of perfect service in giving his life for his people. Jesus sought to impress the new model on his followers by both example and precept. When James and John aspired to prestigious positions after the worldly pattern, Jesus reminded them that even he came "not to be served, but to serve, and to give his life as a ransom for many" (Mark 10:45). Lest those who had been honored to be in the inner circle during his earthly ministry forget this principle, Jesus performed the lowliest of services by washing their feet (John 13:1ff.). They would be reminded that the essence of their calling as Christians was διακονία, service, every time they were refreshed in this manner. No one was exempt. Just as voluntary lowliness had typified the office of our Lord (Phil. 2:5–8), so also should all those who name the Name of Christ have the same spirit (Phil. 2:3–5). There was to be neither hierarchy nor false egalitarianism among the new people of God, but a mutuality of service, a spirit of διακονία pervading the body of Christ. "As each has received a gift, employ [διακονοῦντες] it for one another, as good stewards of God's varied grace" (1 Pet. 4:10). With the coming of the Spirit, all the believing community have been empowered to serve Christ and to serve each other. These are the Levites of the New Covenant with a dual responsibility: to serve God through their High Priest, Jesus Christ, and to represent Christ to the world.[1] Jesus Christ has fulfilled the office of the mediatorial priesthood. He is our Prophet, Priest, and King. The indwelling Spirit has united the service of the people of God; the privilege of service now belongs to all believers.

VOCABULARY AND OFFICE

The principle of mutual dependency among believers is reflected in the vocabulary chosen by the New Testament writers. Words in secular Greek for civil and religious authorities are consistently avoided in connection with the ministries of the church.[2] Τιμή, for example, is used in secular Greek to describe the honor and dignity of office. Not once is it used of office holding in the New Testament,[3] nor are ἀρχή or ἄρχων used in reference to leadership in the Christian community.

> Ἀρχή, which always implies a primacy, whether in time ("beginning," "first principle") or in rank ("power," "authority," "office"), means, in connection with office, a leading, a precedence or rule. The Septuagint uses the word in secular contexts ... and in religious ones (for high priests, Levitical doorkeepers). The New Testament uses it for Jewish and Gentile authorities, and in a different sense for Christ (Col. 1:16 ...), but never for Church ministries of any sort. Similarly the title ἄρχων (ruler, prince) is used for demonic powers, Roman and Jewish officials, and also for Christ (Rev. 1:5, "ruler of the kings of the earth"), but never for office in the Church.[4]

1. See Chapter 1, "Old Testament Origins."
2. Hans Küng, *The Church*, p. 388.
3. In Heb. 5:4, τιμή, honor, is applied to the high-priestly office, not to Christian ministry. Even so, it is not uncommon to find this text wrested out of context and applied to the "call" of Christian ministers to office in the church.
4. Küng, *The Church*, p. 389.

Words used of the Old Testament cult (ἱερεύς, λειτουργός) are like-wise avoided in connection with the office of individuals in the Christian communities.

> It is simply staggering in view of the background of these New Testament writers, steeped as they were in the priestly system of the Old Testament, that never once do they use the word *hiereus* of the Christian minister. The Aaronic analogy for their ministry lay obviously to hand. But they refused to use it. It is hard to overrate the significance of this point when we notice that they *did* use it of the *whole Christian community*.[5]

The ἱερεύς, priest, was the one who offered sacrifices, who per-formed mediatorial offices between God and man. But there was no place in the New Testament communities for a mediator—such a role was Christ's alone. In the early centuries of the church, however, this role was assumed by church leaders.[6] They used the priestly vocabulary of the Old Testament, and their sacrifice was made at the mass. What is more troubling is that this same idea in a slightly different form is now flowing from the pens of Prot-estant writers. Purkiser, for example, has this to say:

> Only in a secondary sense is the minister ever referred to as a *priest* in the New Testament. . . . Yet in a particular way the minister may serve as the representative of his [!] people with God, that is, as their priest, when he intercedes for them in either public or private. As William Barclay has pointed out, the Latin for priest is *pontifex*, literally, "bridge-builder," and the minister must build bridges between God and man.[7]

The "minister" is now a pontiff, a mediator!

Robert Paul denies that ordination concentrates on one mem-ber's religious experience, capacities, and vocation; that properly seen in the context of the church's ministry and that of our Lord, it serves a high purpose in bringing to focus the nature of the church's own ministry. Yet he admits that it is our Lord who per-sonifies all ministry and incorporates within himself the ministry of God's people, the true Israel.[8] Any representative view of "the ministry" cannot avoid creating a third priesthood, functioning

5. Michael Green, "Called to Serve," in *Christian Foundations*, vol. I, p. 78.

6. The use of Old Testament priestly terminology for New Testament of-fice-bearers was becoming common as early as the second century. Cf. Chapter 3.

7. W. T. Purkiser, *The New Testament Image of the Ministry* (Grand Rapids: Baker, 1974), p. 51.

8. Robert Paul, *Ministry* (Grand Rapids: Eerdmans, 1965), pp. 134f.

between Christ's and the believers'. While not intentionally mediatorial, in practice it tends to infringe on either the divinely assigned office of Christ, or the commission given to the church as a whole, or both. Robert Paul believes that ordination is important,

> ... not because it gives an aura of special dignity to the office, but only because it re-presents sacramentally to the Church the nature of the Church's own corporate ministry. ... The Minister should be the representative in the local congregation of the One Great Church of Jesus Christ.[9]

The line between representation and mediation is very fine indeed. The only mediators the New Testament knows are Christ who mediates to his own, and the church which mediates to the world. The New Testament provides for no Levitical function to the believing communities such as was necessary in the old system. The selection of a representative person in each local community presupposes the embodiment in one person of a special enduring relationship that sets him apart as having a superior position to which other believers may not attain.[10] Yet if New Testament believers are all "sons" and heirs (Rom. 8:17; Gal. 4:7; Eph. 1:5; 3:6), what closer relationship could one envision? Nor have the sons and heirs the right to delegate their God-given responsibilities to one of their number so that they may shirk their own sphere of service to God and to the world. *Every* Christian has a representative role. The principle of *mutual* service is to be implemented on the basis of the gifts for ministry given to each believer (1 Pet. 4:10), as distributed sovereignly by the Spirit of God.

Kenneth Hamilton links the representative function to ordination, however.

> The ordained "professional" minister is a symbolic person. His function is to represent the presence of the church in the world. ... Other Christians may be commissioned by the church for

9. *Ibid.*, pp. 156, 159.

10. The encroachment on the priesthood of all believers that results from a representative view of the ministry can be detected in "A Statement on the Doctrine of the Ministry Agreed by the Anglican–Roman Catholic International Commission," prepared by H. R. McAdoo and Alan C. Clark (Canterbury, 1973). They say that at the Eucharist in particular, ministers are "representative of the whole Church in the fulfilment of its priestly vocation of self-offering to God as a living sacrifice (Rom. 12:1)" (Johannes Feiner and Lukas Vischer, *The Common Catechism* [New York: Seabury, 1975], Appendix, p. 679).

special kinds of Christian service; he is commissioned to represent the church as a whole.[11]

If the ordained professional minister is to represent the church as a whole to the world, the erosion of the believer's mandate has already begun. In time he sees his Christian activity as that which he performs when the people of God meet in community. He perceives his gifts in the same way: he is called to teach Sunday School or to sing in the choir. The field is so limited (especially for women) that he may feel he was behind the door when God distributed his gifts for service. A representative view of ordination is not an improvement over the sacramental view.

Is there really any great harm in seeing the "minister" as the embodiment of the ministry of the church? Does the "minister" as representative infringe on the mediatorial office of Christ? Lightfoot distinguishes between the representative role of the minister and the vicarial role of Christ:

> He [the minister] does not interpose between God and man in such a way that direct communion with God is superseded on the one hand, or that his own mediation becomes indispensable on the other. . . . The Christian minister is representative of man to God—of the congregation primarily, of the individual indirectly.[12]

No grading of the mediatorial roles can do away with the fact that this *is* mediation, and indispensable mediation at that. What Lightfoot calls the "doubly representative" character of office[13] belongs to all the people of God, that is, the Levites of the New Covenant; their office is bound up in the priesthood of all believers. "Ordination," if by such is meant induction to service, is the privilege of all who name the name of Christ, and is signaled by the conversion-baptism experience.

OFFICE AND ORDINATION

The diversity in the designation of the ministries in the apostolic churches veritably defies any attempt at rigid classification. The

11. Kenneth Hamilton, *To Turn From Idols*, p. 208. Human mediation in various forms is characteristic of heathen religions. John V. Taylor (*The Primal Vision* [London: SCM, 1963], p. 127) points out that the tribal leaders in African pagan societies represent man to the divine and mediate the divine to man.

12. J. B. Lightfoot, *St. Paul's Epistle to the Philippians*, 8th ed. (London: Macmillan & Co., 1888), p. 267.

13. *Ibid.*

lists of gifts differ; the offices through which they function cannot be precisely defined. For example, it is often difficult to decide whether the term "apostle" refers to office or function. Jesus is called an apostle (Heb. 3:1), and the term is used of the Twelve, especially in Luke and in Revelation. Paul, however, applies the word to many others, and never to the twelve disciples as a group.[14] Διάκονος, servant, presents similar difficulties.

There does seem to be a broad classification of gifts into those that equip others to serve and those of a more general nature (Eph. 4:11, 12; 1 Cor. 12:28). Customarily, the church has reserved ordination for some of those who are gifted to equip others;[15] in practice, it has not been possible to make any rigid distinctions between those who, for example, teach, or preach, or counsel. Nevertheless, the attempt is made to differentiate these two types of gifts by the rite of ordination. This has served to foster a dichotomy in the body of Christ unknown in the New Testament; the flow of mutual service between believers is seriously hindered. Careful attention to the tenses of the verbs that Paul uses in Eph. 4:11 and 1 Cor. 12:28 would suggest that he is relating how, under the guidance of the Holy Spirit, certain patterns of leadership had already emerged in the apostolic church. God placed (ἔθετο, aorist) first[16] apostles (1 Cor. 12:28);[17] he gave (ἔδωκεν, aorist) apostles, prophets, evangelists (Eph. 4:11).

> The pattern of leadership that actually existed in the early church formed the basis of what Paul later taught concerning the gifts in his Epistles. For this reason Paul's teaching in Ephesians and 1 Corinthians should take priority over the descriptions in Acts of the various leaders which were in fact emerging. In his evangelism Paul saw the need for leadership and, led by the Spirit, appointed elders in the churches he founded. Later, writing to these churches, Paul reflected on what had happened and gave an interpretation showing what God had done. . . .[18]

14. D. Müller, "Apostle," *NIDNTT* I:130.
15. With exceptions, as, for example, teachers, lecturers, writers, to name a few to which rigid classifications cannot be applied.
16. Küng, *The Church*, p. 353, interprets this as first in point of time. Rather than "first" indicating the start of either a hierarchical or a chronological list of offices, perhaps this word should be taken as denoting the primacy of the foundational work of the apostles, prophets, and evangelists.
17. L. Coenen, "πρεσβύτερος," *NIDNTT* II:198, is of the opinion that it is unlikely that the numbering of the first three gifts in 1 Cor. 12:28 is intended to show any basic contrast.
18. Howard A. Snyder, *The Community of the King* (Downers Grove: InterVarsity Press, 1977), p. 82.

Taken historically, these texts show that leadership patterns were emerging in the churches according to the needs of the multifarious communities, and were provided through the gifts given by the Holy Spirit.

The purpose of office was to facilitate the functioning of the churches as they sought to fulfill the gospel mandate in the society of their day. The Spirit did not provide the Corinthians with leaders identical in function to those he gave to the church at Ephesus.[19] Indeed, neither then nor now could the needs of a changing society be met for long with any one pattern of office. The fountainhead of spiritual leadership was the Spirit of God, in whom alone was the wisdom to bestow gifts best suited to the common good (1 Cor. 12:7). The Spirit alone, as the superintendent of the affairs of the church through the ages, could provide patterns of leadership that would function optimally in whatever political or sociological milieu the church found itself. When the emerging patterns of office are extracted from their New Testament historical settings and made into a mold to shape the contours of ministry for all situations in all times, the result is a rigid church leadership that is unable to equip the saints or coordinate their gifts to cope with a changing society.

The principle of ecclesiological pluralism is evident also in the use of those terms so characteristic of Christian ministry, διάκονος, servant, and διακονία, service. The apostle Paul calls both himself and Timothy διάκονοι, servants (2 Cor. 6:4; 1 Thess. 3:2; 1 Tim. 4:6). Epaphras, a preacher of the Word, is a faithful servant, διάκονος (Col. 1:7). The office of "deacon" (again διάκονος, 1 Tim. 3:8ff.) is described in very general terms. The qualifications for this office read very much like a list of qualities all believers should exhibit. Furthermore, these διάκονοι, servants, are not to be "double-talkers," and are to "hold the mystery of the faith with a clear conscience" (1 Tim. 3:9); the latter almost certainly refers to the teaching function.[20]

Office of some kind is necessary for the smooth functioning of any group, social or religious. But because the church is a living, growing organism, static conceptions of office will not meet its needs. For example, the Seven of Acts 6:1–6 were given a specific task to perform; only as long as widows needed to be provided for

19. R. A. Cole, "The Body of Christ," p. 45, in *Christian Foundations*, vol. I, believes that this is a representative list; cf. 1 Cor. 12:27–31; Eph. 4:11, 12; Rom. 12:3–8.

20. E. Earle Ellis, "Paul and his Co-workers," *NTS* XVII, no. 4 (July 1974), p. 442, n. 4; cf. *Didache* XV.1; Ignatius, *To the Philadelphians* XI.1.

would such an office be required. If there were no destitute widows, or if the state provided for them, such an office would vanish. An office designed to minister to the material needs of widows would be anachronistic in today's churches; just because a position such as this was essential in the apostolic age does not mean that we must have one like it. We claim that we use 1 Tim. 3:8–13 as a pattern for the office of deacon, yet in many denominations the implications of vv. 9 and 11 are ignored and the office of deacon is fashioned to suit the needs of our present-day situation. When this is done, the office functions reasonably well. To seek to justify our version of it on the basis of 1 Tim. 3 is, however, another matter. Acts 6:8–10 and 8:4–40 indicate that office is dynamic, not static in character. In these cases, Stephen and Philip had begun serving in a wider ministry.[21]

The terminology used in connection with other church roles warrants equal caution in defining any church office. The church at Antioch had prophets and teachers (Acts 13:1), but we also know that some of these were apostles.

> Distinctions are not clearly drawn even within the permanent ministries in the community; the prophet can also be a teacher, the teacher a prophet; Paul himself embodies several ministries. Finally, the different lists of charisms . . . do not agree. From all this we may conclude that although each member of the community, at all places and at all times, will receive his own special call, there is no way of knowing in advance what ministries God in the freedom of his grace will see fit to call upon in specific places at specific times.[22]

The gifts and the offices through which they functioned were diverse; office could no more be fettered than could the Spirit of God who supplied the gifts for office.

Yet, ordination to office presupposes a static, readily definable church leadership role, a state of affairs that did not hold in the apostolic communities.

> If we find ourselves thinking of the ministry in terms of office and status, of authority and validity, we go far away from the thought of the Bible . . . nowhere do we meet the suggestion that clergy and laity (the very terms are not only anachro-

21. Snyder, *Community of the King*, p. 85, remarks: "One must . . . be extremely hesitant to assume the so-called office of deacon was a fixed leadership role in the New Testament."
22. Küng, *The Church*, p. 395.

nisms, but distortions of the New Testament position) have realms into which the other is not permitted to venture.[23]

The Corinthians particularly had difficulty in adjusting to authority in the form of the indwelling Spirit, in learning to give place when a gift one of them lacked was exercised by someone else.[24]

With the early loss of the New Testament service-oriented ethic, leadership styles soon reverted to Old Testament models.[25] Priestly terms reappeared very early in the language of the Fathers.[26] The succession of "faithful men" (2 Tim. 2:2) became interpreted as apostolic succession. A distinction between clergy and laity was inevitable, especially as the giving of the Spirit was increasingly bound up with office holding,[27] and office holding with ordination. We need to be alert to the fact that Roman Catholic theologians are now not merely claiming apostolic succession for their clergy, but are placing this within the framework of the apostolic succession of the church as a whole and of each individual member of it.[28] The clergy are a special part of this succession, the door to which is ordination and the special grace for office that it confers. Schillebeeckx's statement on the relationship between church office and ordination is reminiscent of the consecration of the Levites whose mediatorial role is evident in Num. 8:10–13.

> When the Church bestows office on one of her members, she is at the same time bestowing grace on him—his solidarity with Christ and with the community of believers is the fruit of his ordination, in other words, his reception of office in the Church in and through a sacrament. The effect of ordination is not simply an office, a status within the community of the Church. It is also a special inward and existential orientation towards Christ and towards the community of believers.[29]

This is Aquinas' doctrine of ordination in modern garb.[30] Such an

23. Green, "Called to Serve," p. 27.

24. Schweizer, *Church Order*, p. 102. The Corinthians seemed to be more interested in establishing a hierarchy of gifts than in recognizing their common source; cf. Snyder, *Community of the King*, p. 85.

25. J. Coppens, "Imposition of Hands," *NCE* VII:402; Lampe, *Seal of the Spirit*, p. 224.

26. *1 Clement* 42f.; *Didache* 13.3; 15.1; etc.

27. G. C. Berkouwer, *Second Vatican Council*, p. 160.

28. McAdoo and Clark, "A Statement on the Doctrine of the Ministry . . . ," *The Common Catechism*, p. 679.

29. Edward Schillebeeckx, *The Mission of the Church* (New York: Seabury, 1973), p. 176.

30. Fransen ("Orders and Ordination," p. 1146) says that "The essentials of the doctrine of Aquinas are simply that ordination places the ordinand 'in the face of the community in the name of Christ'."

understanding of church office makes a special clerical class the successors of the Levites, the ones who had replaced the firstborn in the stream of redemption. Instead of the "royal priesthood," the firstborn of the New Covenant, representing Christ (cf. Heb. 12:23) in the world, we have the clergy representing Christ to the "faithful." Mediation took one of its most iniquitous forms in the institution of the confessional. Abuses that grew out of the assumption of a mediatorial role by an elite within the body of Christ eventually forced schism.

Ordination to office presupposes a stable, readily definable church leadership role, a role distinct from other ministries in the church. Under the rigid institutional forms that developed in Roman Catholicism, ordination became not only a possibility and a fact, but an essential part of the hierarchical structure. When aberrant forms of ministry arose in spite of organizational strictures, the church managed to accommodate most of them within its monastic system. The *Tridentine Confession* (A.D. 1563) reaffirmed the bestowal of "character" in ordination and denied the priesthood of all believers.[31] The hierarchy would continue to be the "almoner of supernatural powers" and the "gatekeeper of the celestial world."[32]

Backed by centuries of tradition in the form of canon law, ordination had effectively safeguarded the privileges of the Roman Catholic clergy. The rite survived the radical ecclesiological changes of the Reformation era with merely a shift in emphasis. The priests of Catholicism had indeed been the gatekeepers of salvation, but the Protestant clergy were now the trustees of the revelation of God. According to the *Augsburg Confession* (A.D. 1530), the highest office in the church was the preaching office. The similarities to the emergence of authority patterns in Judaism are not to be missed. Alongside the ancient sacerdotal system had come the rabbis, interpreters of Torah and custodians of the mysteries of God. The church, too, could adapt its mediatorial patterns under the pressure of cultural and political change.

Due to increasing literacy, the Protestant minister found himself in a vulnerable position. Ordination could provide stability and conformity within denominational ranks, especially with the assistance of the state, but it could not prevent the formation of dissenting sects, most of which also fenced off their theological positions with confession of faith, or ordination, or both. So the

31. Seeburg II:445.
32. *Ibid.*, p. 449.

clergy continued to lay claim to apostolic authority, through various ways. One way was to see the office of elder or pastor as included in the apostolic office, the difference being more one of degree of authority rather than of kind. Such an understanding was, of course, open to the possibility of a fair amount of manipulation, and could even claim an apostolic succession of a kind. Under the pressures of controversy, the Scriptures were also combed for normative organizational structures to authenticate the diverse ecclesiologies that were emerging. The resulting fragmentation of the biblical text often meant that contextual factors were ignored. Significantly, this was the kind of error that earned Simon Magus his rebuke (Acts 8:20–24). He was not only guilty of wanting to buy the power to confer the Spirit, but he also failed to take into account the historical implications of the imposition of hands on the Samaritans by Peter and John. The church has made much of his first error. It has, on the whole, failed to note the second.

The assumption that Timothy's office was typical of the pastoral role also confused the issues surrounding ordination and office holding. Timothy's special relationship to Paul after the Moses-Joshua model set him apart from the general elder/pastor/bishop office of the local churches. Both he and Paul had the authority to command ($\pi\alpha\rho\alpha\gamma\gamma\acute{\epsilon}\lambda\lambda\epsilon\iota\nu$). Apart from its use in a secular sense, this authoritative word is used only by our Lord himself and by Paul, and as that which Timothy may also do.[33] Even then, Paul, by appeal to God and Christ, makes it abundantly clear that he is not speaking on his own authority.[34] Taking its historical setting into account, the imposition of hands on Timothy by Paul for the reception of his *charisma* cannot be cited as a precedent for ordination, whether episcopal or any other kind.

ORDINATION AND MINISTRY

The distinction in Eph. 4:12 between gifts that equip or coordinate and those of a general nature has been used as a wedge to divide the new people of God into two classes of citizens. This division is entrenched in the vocabulary of the church. The Anglican bishop, addressing the priest at ordination, tells him of his responsibilities to the congregation he serves. He reminds him that *they* are Christ's sheep.[35] Pastors speak of *their* people, an understandable way of

33. W. Mundle, "$\pi\alpha\rho\alpha\gamma\gamma\acute{\epsilon}\lambda\lambda\omega$," *NIDNTT* I:340f.
34. *Ibid.*, p. 341; cf. 1 Cor. 7:10; 1 Tim. 6:13f.
35. *Book of Common Prayer*, "The Form and Manner of Ordaining Priests."

speaking, perhaps, but nevertheless potentially misleading, especially if the people should also start to think of themselves as *his*.
The "ministry" is the privilege and duty of all believers, not that
of a few. Attention to the context of Eph. 4:12 could serve as a
much needed corrective. Paul is addressing all believers when he
says "I . . . beg you to lead a life worthy of the calling to which you
have been called" (Eph. 4:1). He then makes some strong statements about unity in the body. There is "one hope that belongs to
your call, one Lord, one faith, one baptism, one God and Father of
us all" (Eph. 4:5, 6). After listing apostles, prophets, evangelists,
and pastor-teachers (in historical order?), Paul again stresses unity.
The goal of all gifting of such people is unity *within* the body:
". . . until we all attain to the unity of the faith and of the knowledge of the Son of God" (Eph. 4:13). There is no hint that those
who "equip" are to be set apart from the rest. All gifts are of grace
from our one Lord (v. 7) that we might all grow up into him (v. 15).
These texts are often applied to the "church universal," when making a plea for organizational unity. Denominational diversity is
treated as the great shame of Christendom. It is indeed significant
that the ecumenical movement has had to deal with the questions
revolving around orders and ordination before any degree of unity
could be attained. The success of this movement depends on agreement on a doctrine of "the ministry." Perhaps attention should
first be directed to attaining unity within the local bodies.

When statements such as "The Ministry is the highest of all
callings" are applied to *all* who minister, to all whose ethic is
διαχονία, service, we will be on the way to restoring the unity
spoken of in Eph. 4.[36] Christ expressly forbids vertical relationships among his followers. "You know that the rulers of the Gentiles lord it over [καταχυριεύουσιν] them, and their great men
exercise authority over [κατεξουσιάζουσιν] them. It shall be not so
among you" (Matt. 20:25, 26). Yet of the preacher Alexander Whyte
it was said, "Whyte's pulpit was his throne."[37] Lawrence Eyres,
writing about the elders of the church, says that they are "those
who are exalted to the position of Christ's assistant restorers of
what sin has destroyed";[38] of the presbytery he remarks: "When

36. W. D. Davies (*Christian Origins and Judaism* [London: Darton,
Longman, and Todd, 1962], p. 237) points out "There are no higher or lower
ministries in the church of the New Testament."

37. Warren Wiersbe, *Walking With the Giants* (Grand Rapids: Baker, 1976),
p. 90.

38. L. R. Eyres, *Elders of the Church*, p. 26.

the elders are 'up there' in session, their minds and hearts must
be fully aware of all that goes on 'down there' where the church
lives in the world."[39] What a contrast to the teaching of our Lord!

> But you are not to be called rabbi, for you have one teacher,
> and you are all brethren. And call no man your father on
> earth, for you have one Father, who is in heaven. Neither be
> called masters, for you have one master, the Christ. He who
> is greatest among you shall be your servant; whoever exalts
> himself shall be humbled, and whoever humbles himself shall
> be exalted. (Matt. 28:8–12)

Thus Jesus taught the crowds and disciples. How startling this
must have been to those familiar with the pride and arrogance of
their own religious leaders, those so used to showing deference to
their rabbis.

In the New Testament, church leaders are never called "rulers" (ἄρχοντες), but many translators do not hesitate to use the
word for them. In the King James translation Heb. 13:17 reads
"Obey them that have the rule over you, and submit yourselves
. . ." (Πείθεσθε τοῖς ἡγουμένοις ὑμῶν καὶ ὑπείκετε . . .). The subtle-
ties of the Greek are destroyed in this translation. There is a distinct difference in being told to "obey your rulers" and being
exhorted to be persuaded by your leaders.[40] The result of either
approach may be the same, namely, obedience to leaders. However,
the vocabulary of the Greek New Testament permits the believer
the dignity of responsible and intelligent response; blind obedience
to human leadership is not required of those in Christian community. Elders who "rule well" (1 Tim. 5:17) are really elders who
have been placed before (προεστῶτες) their congregations to lead,
not over them to rule. Even the apostle Paul, called for a unique
mission by God and given apostolic authority, never sets himself

---

39. *Ibid.*, p. 16.

40. The middle and passive form πείθομαι stresses the outcome of being
persuaded, that is, willing obedience. The contexts of all uses of πείθομαι (I
am persuaded) in the New Testament stress the voluntary aspect of the word,
except perhaps in James 3:3, which deals with the matter of persuading a horse,
and we are told not to be like the horse. The use of this verb in Gal. 5:7 is
followed by "this persuasion" in v. 8. See *NIDNTT* I:591. Ἡγουμένοις means
simply "leaders," and ὑπείκετε, a *hapax legomenon* in the New Testament,
means "yield." Since this is its only occurrence in the New Testament, the exact
sense is difficult to pinpoint. It may be worth noting that the usual words for
"obey" and "submit" (ὑπακούω and ὑποτάσσω) are not used here.

up above the lowliest saint.[41] 1 Thess. 5:12 reads: "But we beseech you, brethren, to respect those who labor among you and are over you in the Lord and admonish you." Here too, the nuances of the Greek have been lost in translation. "Those who . . . are over you" are the προϊστάμενους, the ones set before you; this participle stresses the function of several, not the office of one.[42] The word for "admonish" is νουθετεῖν, an appeal to the νοῦς, the faculty of understanding and intelligent judgment.[43] The tone of the word can be derived from its use in Acts 20:31 where Paul describes his appeal in the gospel as "tearful"; or in 1 Cor. 4:14 where he entreats the Corinthians as he would entreat much-loved children.[44] The word suggests an appeal in love, not the deliverance of an authoritative edict. The language of New Testament leadership is a language of horizontal relationships, of leading and following, of voluntary submission and service to one another. Even the risen Lord, the head of the church, who is in the "heavenlies" and is "far above all rule and authority and power and dominion" (Eph. 1:21), is, in relation to the church, said to build it (Matt. 16:18), give gifts to it (Eph. 4:11), bestow grace on it (2 Cor. 8:1), nourish it (Eph. 5:29), love it (Eph. 5:25), and by giving himself for it, sanctify it (Eph. 5:25, 26). He has set the pattern of διακονία, service, for us to emulate. It is by this criterion that we must test our doctrine of ministry, and in so doing evaluate the practice of ordination.

41. Paul is the "least of all saints" (Eph. 3:8); the Galatians are "brothers with me" (Gal. 1:2). Paul does not demand respect on personal grounds, or because he is a New Testament church officer, but because he is the bearer of apostolic authority, in analogy to that authority which Moses possessed as the mediator of the Old Covenant; cf. 2 Cor. 2:17; 3:4–18.

42. L. Coenen, "πρεσβύτερος," *NIDNTT* I:197.

43. *BAG*, "νοῦς," p. 543.

44. See also Rom. 15:14. In this context, where all the brethren are said to be able to νουθετεῖν one another, some versions (RSV, NIV) translate this as "instruct," but in the context of leadership, as in 1 Thess. 5:12, they use "admonish." These may seem to be minor details; one wonders what would prompt the change.

Chapter 13

AUTHORITY AND ORDINATION

When any major doctrine of the Christian faith is formulated, it is generally recognized that evidence must be adduced from the whole Bible. It is then possible to see that the shadows of the Old Covenant become the realities of the New, and that the promises of God are of sure fulfillment. There is comfort and hope in the knowledge that God's plan in history is moving on to its consummation. This progressive character of revelation is often neglected when the doctrine of ordination is considered, and few are willing to permit all the texts in which the laying on of hands occurs to contribute their share of meaning to the subject. By means of verbal analogy, Paul and Luke both allude to those Old Testament incidents in which hands are laid on the Levites and Joshua. By doing so, the New Testament events are illuminated by the Old; the "hand" of Yahweh is still performing mighty deeds in the redemption of his people.

ORDINATION: DESCRIPTIVE OR NORMATIVE?

Confusion results when texts that relate events in the flow of redemptive history are isolated from the context of the Bible as a whole and are treated as prescriptions to be imitated by the church in all ages. Thus to see a Paul-Timothy relationship without also seeing its Moses-Joshua prototype is to misunderstand what is happening when Paul lays hands on Timothy in the presence of the elders. When we try to make these texts into rules of order, we run into contradictions that somehow have to be explained away. So it becomes necessary to deny that the laying on of hands on Timothy in 2 Tim. 1:6 confers a *charisma*, because the laying on of hands in Acts 13:1–3 evidently did not confer gifts on Paul and Barnabas. It then also follows that διὰ τῆς ἐπιθέσεως τῶν χειρῶν μου ("through the laying on of my hands") cannot really mean what it seems to say. Διά, through, does not mean agency in this case, it is explained, even though any other meaning is exceptional.[1] This preposition is said to have a circumstantial force; Timothy received his gift at the time when hands were laid on him, but there was no direct relationship between the imposition of Paul's hands and the reception of the gift. Such an argument is not only unconvincing, but quite unnecessary.

The question of whether or not "grace" is conveyed through the laying on of hands has continued through the ages. When the texts in which this motif appears are examined without attention being given to their historical context, the argument tends to focus around the force of διά, through, when used governing the genitive case. With the genitive of the person[2] this preposition may refer to the agent or intermediary, or even the originator of the action.[3] Some[4] have argued that διά, when used in connection with the laying on of hands, implies "attendant circumstances," not agency.[5] Robertson, however, asserts that "the notion of 'between' is always present,"[6] and that "the etymological force in the word is very persistent."[7] Luke always uses διά with the genitive of the person to indicate agency; as has been pointed out,[8] he chooses some other prepositions when he intends metaphor. Paul also is careful of his use of prepositions in the context of the laying on of hands. It is through (διά) the hands of Paul that Timothy's prophetic gift is mediated (2 Tim. 1:6); it is through (διά) prophecy with (μετά) the laying on of hands of the presbytery (1 Tim. 4:14). Of the 386 occurrences of διά with the genitive in the New Testament, only a few (Rom. 2:27; 4:11; 8:25; 14:20; 2 Cor. 2:4; 1 Tim. 2:15) could signify attendant circumstances, and these are διά with the genitive of the *thing*, not the *person*.[9] In most examples of διά with the genitive of the person, the notion of agency or even mediation is very strong indeed. Honesty with the text of 2 Tim. 1:6 demands that we accept that Timothy's gift was received through the agency of the hands of Paul. In the final analysis it is the hand of God that equips his servants Joshua and Timothy; yet in a certain sense

1. M. J. Harris, "Prepositions and Theology in the Greek New Testament," *NIDNTT* III:1182f.; cf. *BAG*, pp. 179ff.

2. The temporal and locative uses do not concern us.

3. *BAG*, pp. 178f.

4. For example, M. J. Harris, "Prepositions and Theology . . . ," pp. 1182f.

5. Cf. Bernard, *Pastoral Epistles*, p. 72.

6. A. T. Robertson, *A Grammar of the Greek New Testament in the Light of Historical Research* (Nashville: Broadman, 1934), p. 583.

7. *Ibid.*, p. 580.

8. See Chapter 9.

9. *BAG*, p. 179.

Moses shared some of his authority (or as the LXX expresses it, "glory," Num. 27:20, or "wisdom," Deut. 34:9) with Joshua. In a similar manner Paul shares a measure of his commission with Timothy. The sense of the original requires that we accept the reality of the transference of "grace" through the laying on of hands, and not dismiss this as mere symbol.

Taking the laying-on-of-hands texts as prescriptive raises historical problems, also. Why is there no evidence for the ordination of pastors or elders in the first two centuries of the church? This also must be explained away. One writer does it this way:

> In Acts 14:24 we are told that Paul and Barnabas appointed elders in every church, and after prayer and fasting "committed them to the Lord in whom they believed." Although the laying on of hands is not specifically mentioned, the word translated "appointed" is the verb *cheirotoneo*, which in later ecclesiastical usage means "the laying on of hands."[10]

This "later ecclesiastical usage" was third- and fourth-century usage. In New Testament times, and for some time thereafter, χει-ροτονεῖν meant simply "to select."[11] Perhaps aware of the anachronism, the writer goes on to remark:

> Literally, the word means "to choose by the raising of hands." . . . If it does not mean that they [Paul and Barnabas] raised their hands to vote, it could mean that the apostles lowered their hands, and laid them on the new elders. But we cannot be sure of it.[12]

Actually, the practice followed on the heels of the rise of infant baptism,[13] and the even earlier appearance of the monarchical episcopate.[14] The development of rigid power structures in the church has often been attributed to reaction against heresy, or what the early Fathers considered to be heresy. If the church was to survive, it would have to pattern itself after the centralized political structures of secular society. There is no doubt that the laying on of hands in ordination served to strengthen and define leadership. When infant baptism became customary in the churches, baptism lost much of its theological significance. Supplementary rites were introduced to take care of deficiencies. Just as the baptized infant was incapable of exercising faith, neither could he

10. Michael Harper, *Let My People Grow* (London: Hodder and Stoughton, 1977), p. 229.

11. See Chapter 3.

12. Harper, *Let My People Grow*, p. 229.

13. See Paul Jewett, *Infant Baptism and the Covenant of Grace*, pp. 16ff.

14. Kenneth Strand, "The Rise of the Monarchical Episcopate," in *Three Essays on Early Church History* (Ann Arbor: Braun-Brumfield, 1967), p. 18.

exercise spiritual gifts for the edification of the believing community. The doctrines that developed around the rite of confirmation answered to the first problem; the sacrament of ordination solved (for a few) the second. Confirmation was for all at the age of accountability; ordination was for the spiritual elite.

The doctrine of ordination has been beset by arguments from silence and the selective use of texts. The church, with a quite natural concern to maintain order and preserve lines of authority, has, at times, seemed to have a greater commitment to the stability of the *status quo* than to the primacy of taking the gospel to the ends of the earth. In 1954, the Baptist Union in Britain commissioned a study on ordination. When published in 1957 it was acknowledged to contain "useful biblical and historical sections" and to make several "wise practical suggestions."[15] Its chief value was said to be in the "stimulus it provided for further serious theological thinking."[16] The theological thinking produced no changes; the report was shelved.[17]

AUTHORITY FOR OFFICE

The church has always recognized that authority for office is vested primarily in the Spirit of God. The church, as the body of Christ, plays a secondary role, confirming and structuring the divine choice. The problems that have arisen within these parameters are legion.

The theory of endowment through succession from the apostles has served the church for centuries; the laying on of hands gives objective and suitable expression to dogma, for the priest (or bishop) *has* been endowed with the Spirit at ordination and is thus equipped to perform his office. The shift of emphasis at the Reformation to the subjective "call" as evidence for the authority of the Spirit for church office opened the door to diverse claims, and again necessitated the elevation of office to preserve its sanctity and to protect it from invasion by undesirables. "Call" was attached chiefly to the preaching function, though the conduct of church ordinances was accepted as part and parcel of the minister's role. The claim to special call was based chiefly on Old Testament examples (partic-

15. E. A. Payne, *The Baptist Union: A Short History*, p. 252.
16. *Ibid.*
17. *Ibid.*, p. 253. The argument that ordination helps to preserve orthodoxy will not stand up to historical inspection; it failed to prevent the General Baptists of Great Britain from sinking into Arianism and Socinianism.

ularly God's calls to Isaiah and Samuel), and to Paul's call to minister to the Gentiles.[18]

Failure to recognize that Old Testament leadership patterns were an integral part of a now obsolete sacerdotal system characterized the early church struggle for organizational stability. By analogy with the Old Testament priesthood, the offices of bishop, priest, and deacon were established and Old Testament vocabulary used to designate these offices. Lightfoot remarks that the "sacerdotal view of the ministry is one of the most striking and important phenomena in the history of the Church."[19] Once this sacerdotal vocabulary hardened into tradition, the perpetuity of the sacerdotal view of the ministry seemed assured, and a mediatorial priesthood eventually emerged within the believing community. Again, failure to distinguish the *modus operandi* of the Holy Spirit in the lives of Old and New Testament believers[20] confused the concept of "call"; special call to specific ministry (in the monastic sense) was separated from the holistic view of call as a constituent of every believer's salvation. From this point on, the view of the minister as a prophet after the style of a Jeremiah or a Samuel, charismatically entrusted with divine revelation, is often tacitly assumed as though the divine Prophet himself had never come. Quotations from the New Testament, shorn of their historical context, were often indiscriminately employed. Thus the call of a high priest such as Aaron for service in the Temple is often assumed to apply to New Testament office. When the writer to the Hebrews, in discussing the Aaronic priesthood, says, "And one does not take the honor upon himself, but he is called by God, just as Aaron was" (Heb. 5:4), contextual considerations preclude equating Aaron's call with the "call" of a New Testament believer to a nonsacerdotal office. Unlike his Old Testament counterpart, the New Testament believer is indwelt by the Spirit of God from conversion, and his call to ministry and his gifting for it is not to be thought of as a distinct event separate from his salvation.

18. Torbet, *History of the Baptists*, p. 56; Strong, *Systematic Theology*, p. 919. In many Baptist groups, dual testimony to "call" is required for ordination. The candidate is to have had a subjective experience of being "called" to a specific ministry (generally pastoral or missionary in nature), and the church that has asked for his ordination bears witness that he has demonstrated the gifts necessary for the task. In practice, because the ordained minister generally moves from charge to charge, the subjective constituent of "call" assumes the more predominant aspect of the two.

19. Lightfoot, *Saint Paul's Epistle to the Philippians*, p. 144.

20. See Lloyd Neve, *The Spirit of God in the Old Testament*, pp. 56f.

The fact that God is the καλῶν and that Christians are the κεκλημένοι with no qualifying addition makes it clear that in the New Testament, καλεῖν is a technical term for the process of salvation.[21]

God does not limit the call to serve him to a few, nor is there any indication in the New Testament that "call" can be attached to one kind of gift and not to another, or that one may be called to preach but not to administrate or to give personal service to others. Simply put, the indiscriminate use of Old Testament models perpetuates Old Testament patterns of leadership. Some apply the expression "man of God" to preachers, thus implying a continuity, or at least a similarity of office between the inspired prophets of the Old Testament and the modern preacher.[22] Edmund Clowney leans heavily on Old Testament thought to dramatize the role of the pastor. According to him, "God does call workmen in the Word with deepened insights to perceive the outlines of sound words and with anointed lips to declare them."[23] The reference here is to the call of Isaiah (Isa. 6:6–9). The use of an Old Testament figure in connection with a New Testament office tends to blur the very vital distinction between Old and New Testament office, a distinction inherent in the revelation of Jesus Christ as our Prophet, Priest, and King. The authority of the Holy Spirit, which the Roman Catholic priest could claim through the laying on of hands in ordination, has now slipped in through the back door, so to speak, by way of the concept of the special "call." An experience of the Holy Spirit subsequent to conversion now becomes the rationale for ordination. Instead of the laying on of hands conferring the authority of the Holy Spirit, it now confirms it. We might well question whether the authority that inheres in the activity of the Spirit of God requires public recognition in some cases and not in others, or indeed whether authentication of the Spirit's work by man is either necessary or possible. The obsession with authority that characterizes much writing on the ministry[24] carries with it more of the tone of an Ignatius than the lowly διακονία of our Lord. In reference to ordination Clowney says, "Public recognition is necessary, for the reason that the stewardship of Christ's Word must be exercised with authority."[25] This again places the locus of authority in one

---

21. K. L. Schmidt, "καλέω," *TDNT* III:188.

22. Edmund Clowney, *Called to the Ministry* (Philadelphia: Presbyterian and Reformed, 1976), p. 56.

23. *Ibid.*, p. 50.

24. See, for example, *ibid.*, pp. 40, 45, 47–49, and *passim*.

25. *Ibid.*, p. 56.

person. Such attempts to confer authority are really attempts to confer grace. This is a sacramental view of ordination.

Unless we claim continuity between the office of apostle and that of elder or pastor, great caution must be exercised in taking texts that apply to Paul's mission to the Gentiles and applying them to present-day leadership offices. Paul was indeed a "chosen vessel," but he was a vessel chosen to carry the gospel to "the Gentiles and the kings and the sons of Israel" (Acts 9:15). Paul's commission was unique, as was his preparation for it (2 Cor. 12:2ff.; Acts 9:1–19). What the Scriptures say of Paul cannot be applied *carte blanche* to ministry in general.

AUTHORITY FOR ORDINATION

The cry that the authoritative preaching of the Word demands that the one with this function be set apart ceremonially in public needs to be entertained with caution. Quoting Dietrich Bonhoeffer, Robert Paul says, "This hankering for false authority has at its roots a desire to re-establish some sort of immediacy, a dependence upon human beings in the Church."[26] Rome bases the authority of her priests on the giving of the Spirit at ordination, that is, authority is invested in a particular individual by this rite. As Protestants who deny that ordination is a sacrament of the church,[27] but instead vest that authority in the Spirit-directed Word of God, just why do we find it necessary to lay hands on one person in public? Are we sure that there is no idea of transmission of authority and mediation in all of this? Commenting on John 3:29, John Calvin remarks: "This is a great and excellent thing for men to be set over the Church, that they may represent the person of the Son of God."[28] The New Testament knows only Christ set over the church.

26. Quoted in Robert Paul, *Ministry*, p. 188.

27. This does not mean all Protestants deny that grace is conferred through the laying on of hands. Classic Pentecostalism had its roots in just such an interpretation of Acts 8 and Acts 19. In 1900, Agnes Ozman, then at Bethel Bible College in Topeka, Kansas, asked a Holiness preacher to lay hands on her so that she might receive the Holy Spirit after the pattern in Acts. See Richard Quebedeaux, *The New Charismatics* (Garden City: Doubleday, 1976), p. 28. Quoting Edward O'Connor, "The Laying on of Hands" (Pecos, NM: Dove Publications, 1969), pp. 3, 4, Quebedeaux writes (p. 12): "The adoption of this gesture has been inspired by biblical precedents, especially those in which the Holy Spirit was given to someone through the laying on of hands. However, its continued use is motivated above all by the power it seems to have."

28. John Calvin, *Commentary on the Gospel According to John*, vol. I (Edinburgh: Calvin Translation Society, 1847, reprinted from 1630), p. 134. Perhaps sensing the danger of this remark he goes on: "ministers may not appropriate to themselves what exclusively belongs to the bridegroom."

Even overseers have been set *in* the church, not *over* it (Acts 20:28). Nor does the New Testament teach that some Christians represent the Son of God and some do not. All are referred to as the "laity of God" (1 Pet. 2:10). Stewardship of the Word is not portrayed as the exclusive right of a clerical caste (1 Pet. 2:9; 3:15). There are about thirty words in the New Testament that describe the activity of spreading the gospel: proclaim, announce, teach, explain, speak, testify, confess, persuade, preach, and admonish are only a few of them.[29] There is no way these can be rigidly segregated into public and private categories. The different kinds of "preaching" allow everyone to make his or her contribution toward the proclamation of the gospel.[30] When this is permitted to happen, the results are exciting. Writing of the rapid growth of Baptist churches in Britain during the time of Cromwell's Model Army, Whitley says:

> The mobility of the Army contributed to this rapid growth. Colonels Ride and Deane traversed South Wales to stamp out a rising in Pembroke, and Baptist churches sprang up along their route. A Lincolnshire rising in May was quelled by Robert Lilburne, and within a month John Wigan had planted a Baptist church in Manchester.[31]

This is the "royal priesthood" functioning as it should. These are the Levites of the New Covenant, representing God and his Christ to the nations.

Unfortunately, the statements of many Protestants differ little from the Roman Catholic position. They speak of the "ministry" as a mediatorial body set within the body as a whole. Charles Bridges gives the typical definition. "The ministry," he says, was established by God "as the standing ordinance in his Church and the medium of the revelation of his will to the end of time."[32] T. F. Torrance would move "the ministry" (the ordained) into a special category, placing it within the realm of Christ's high-priestly work. "The ordained are to be regarded as drawn in a special way within the sphere of Christ's self-consecration so that it is only as they share in his self-consecration that they can minister the Word to

29. Küng, *The Church*, p. 375. See also F. F. Bruce, *Tradition Old and New* (Grand Rapids: Zondervan, 1970), p. 65.

30. Küng, *The Church*, p. 375.

31. Underwood, *History of the English Baptists*, p. 87, quoting from W. T. Whitley, *A History of British Baptists* (London: Chas. Griffin & Co., 1932), pp. 78f.

32. Charles Bridges, *The Christian Ministry* (Edinburgh: The Banner of Truth, 1976 reprint [1830]), p. 5.

others in His Name."[33] The foundation for this teaching is not clear. The creation of a privileged class of believers presents a danger to the priesthood of believers *and* to the mediatorship of Christ. An old problem has taken on a new form.

Confusion over function and office is an indication of other hermeneutical and ecclesiological problems relating to the subject of ordination. The emergence of the charismatic renewal movement has shown just how muddy the waters are. The energy and authority of the Spirit of God are apparently manifesting themselves outside the traditional channels in a manner that simply cannot be ignored. Clerical authority seems to have a rival and is hard-pressed to explain and accommodate this new threat to its spiritual prerogatives. Some fundamentalists condemn the movement outright as representing the intrusion of an alien and divisive authority threatening the precincts of orthodoxy.[34] Roman Catholics and Episcopalians have had to come to some rather uneasy terms with the phenomenon of spiritual gifts. Just what forms in the church are legitimate expressions of the authority of the Spirit of God who rules the church? When hands are laid on for the reception of spiritual gifts the resemblance to the ordination rite is not likely to be missed. Furthermore, problems are created when laypeople perform the rite and then the recipients of the baptism in the Spirit seek avenues of service not usually permitted without ordination. Some Roman Catholic theologians see the work of the Spirit in charismatic manifestations as distinct from the Spirit's governance through ecclesiastical structures, that is, they see both hierarchical and charismatic gifts in the church.[35] The authority received by priests in the laying on of hands in ordination stems from the apostles by succession and confers office that makes its bearer a personal representative of Christ. Thus charismatic activity does not compete with the hierarchical, but supplements it.[36] The authority problem is solved by dichotomizing office and function. This enables the church to incorporate enthusiastic lay involvement into its traditional authority structures.

33. T. F. Torrance, "Consecration and Ordination," *SJT* 11 (1958), p. 241. See also Robert Paul, *Ministry*, pp. 156f.

34. Those who take this position assert that "tongues have ceased" and that therefore present-day glossolalia cannot be identified with biblical tongues-speaking. The coming of the "perfect" of 1 Cor. 13:10 is identified with the completion of the New Testament canon.

35. This view was endorsed at Vatican II. See Edward D. O'Connor, *The Pentecostal Movement in the Catholic Church*, p. 283.

36. *Ibid.*, pp. 228f.

This theological solution has other merits. In the past, the church channeled feminine zeal into the monastic orders. Now it can be relegated to the sphere of charismatic activity, and thus be controlled and regulated by males who have received hierarchical authority through ordination. So long as the laying on of hands is thought to bestow representative "character" on the ordinand, and so long as it is assumed that only men can represent Christ, then there is not much room for argument. The assumption that representation is the function of a sex-differentiated class within the believing community instead of the responsibility of every believer effectively limits the work of the church in the world. It is a limitation the church can ill afford.

Today, women are pressing for entry into the power structures of the church through ordination. Yet, if they are granted the right to ministerial office, this would serve merely to reinforce unbiblical hierarchical organizational patterns. But authoritative positions once attained are not willingly relinquished. There is no reason to believe that the recognition, privilege, and security afforded by the laying on of hands in ordination should be any less appealing to women than to men.

Ultimate authority in the church resides in the Spirit of Christ, and cannot be distributed or delegated except by the sovereign Spirit himself. The church may not, whether by majority vote, ordination, the imposition of hands, or any combination thereof, delegate the authority that Christ has given to the church as a body. It does not have the authority to designate one person from its midst as its representative, either of itself to Christ or of Christ to the church. Effective kingdom work requires competent leadership, but the forms devised for this purpose must not be permitted to encroach on the rights of the Head of the church nor to hinder the work of the Spirit in the community of believers. If, by illegitimate claims to what is considered to be a scriptural norm, or by reluctance to challenge traditional structures, leadership forms are granted an authority they do not rightly possess, they will end up by thwarting the functioning of the body they should be serving.

Ordination with the laying on of hands has been one such form that the church has used to facilitate church government. We have seen how, in the early centuries, ordination was permitted to become the key to authority in the church. Only the ordained office-bearer could dispense forgiveness and salvation. Though deprived of some of this authority, ordination was retained by the post-Reformation churches, and served to centralize the authority of the church in one person who alone could administer the ordinances and interpret the Scriptures. Church officers performed mediatorial duties *within* the believing community. As long as the laying on of hands (symbolic of the transfer of the power and authority of God) was retained, forms of church office tended to assume such a role.[37] Even if ordination is considered to be merely recognition that God has bestowed on an individual certain gifts for ministry, the imposition of hands is historically and symbolically inappropriate. In such cases, its use contributes to a concentration of the authority that belongs to the church as a whole in one person. Peter Schouls suggests that "to the extent that one gains insight [i.e., spiritual understanding], to that extent one possesses authority."[38] The source of such understanding is the Spirit. Thus the communal authority of the church, though a shared authority, is not shared equally, but according to the individual believer's capacity to serve the body as a whole. The authority of any one member of the believing community is not an independent authority, but exists only in its relationship to the authority held by the members in common. The purpose of such authority is service, διακονία.

Only if ordination facilitates the legitimate use of authority in the church is it a valid form. If, in the laying on of hands, there is any attempt (well-meaning though it may be) to manipulate divine authority, whether through succession theory or through delegation of communal authority, the rite of ordination is illegitimate. The practice of ordination with the laying on of hands must be tested by these criteria.

37. Both a sacramental understanding of ordination and the theory of apostolic succession that accompanies such an understanding tend to reappear, as, for example, in the Landmark movement in the Southern Baptist Convention. See William Wright Barnes, *The Southern Baptist Convention 1845–1953* (Nashville: Broadman Press, 1954), p. 101.

38. Peter Schouls, *Insight, Authority, and Power* (Toronto: Wedge Publishing Foundation, 1972), p. 14.

POSTSCRIPT

When God redeemed for himself a people out of Egypt, he found it necessary to stipulate in detail that which he required of his own. He mediated his rule through a priestly caste and gave his people the Law. With the coming of the Christ and the gift of the Spirit to every believer, the mediation of priest (and prophet and king) was no longer required. Mediatorial office within the believing community had been fulfilled in the person of Jesus Christ. There remained, however, the need for a clear understanding of how believers were to relate to each other. Our Lord plainly stated the principles during his ministry.

> Among the disciples no office was to be allowed which would correspond to that of the political rulers (Mark x:44 par. (Matt.); cf. Mark x:35 (par. Luke)) or to that of the Scribes (Matt. xxiii:11, cf. vs. 8–10). The one is constituted by right and power, the other by right and knowledge.[1]

Yet the church has always been inclined to slip into one pattern or the other. The cry has been for "order," a cry that has masked the struggle for authority in the church. Those who held office magnified their positions.[2] Not only was the Old Testament vocabulary adopted by the New Testament communities, but failure to accord the New Testament leaders the obedience they thought their right even brought down threats of divine wrath after the example of Nadab and Abihu.[3] The Great Church added the traditions of

---

1. Leonhard Goppelt, *Apostolic and Post-Apostolic Times* (E.T., Grand Rapids: Baker, 1970), p. 178.
2. For example, see Ignatius, *To the Ephesians* 6.2–3; *To the Magnesians* 6.1; *To the Smyrnaeans* 9.2–3; Chrysostom, *On the Priesthood* 3, 4; etc.
3. *Early Latin Theology*, ed. S. L. Greenslade (Philadelphia: Westminster Press, 1956), quoting Irenaeus, *Against Heresies*, p. 72; cf. Cyprian, *The Unity of the Catholic Church*, p. 136; Ambrose, *The Episcopal Election at Vercellae*, p. 271.

the Fathers to canonical authority; the edicts of the ecumenical councils and the codifications of canon law all, it was insisted, evidenced the authority of Christ speaking to and through his church. Ordination played a key role in consolidating clerical power, so that the priesthood of the church could now lord it over both the "faithful" and the secular authorities. One would have thought that the return to the Scriptures as the sole authority for faith and practice at the time of the Reformation would have restored a semblance of the community relations that had been taught by Christ. Some indeed tried to implement New Testament principles of church government, but they were hounded unmercifully and their leaders killed. Claims to religious authority over others persisted, claims based on the theory of apostolic succession, or on special divine "call," or on the delegation of authority by the community itself. The doctrine of ordination was adapted to accommodate these diverse ecclesiologies.

The church of Jesus Christ has continued to seek its patterns for church office in the society in which it is placed, in spite of our Lord's warnings that he is initiating a new society with its own unique authority structure. The fact that some churches are now run "democratically" makes it no less an offense against the edict of Christ. We hear, too, that the hierarchical structuring of any human community is inevitable, that such is "natural," for man is *homo hierarchicus*. This is secularism, not Christianity. If we are convinced that the individual believer can be or is being transformed by the Spirit of God, then the church too must demonstrate to the world that it is the community of the redeemed. Its political structures must reflect the transformed character of the community as a whole if the world is to take its gospel seriously. Robert Paul points out that

> ... the credibility of the Church has a direct relationship to the *way* authority is exercised and manifested in the Church: what the Church does and the way it does it demonstrate to everyone what manner of Spirit rules the Church.[4]

Jesus gave the church an authority structure based on his Lordship of the church and the indwelling authority of the Spirit in the believers. In striking contrast to the detailed provisions given to the Old Covenant people at Sinai, neither Jesus nor Paul imposed any fixed organizational forms on the new Israel. They left no

4. Robert Paul, *The Church in Search of Itself* (Grand Rapids: Eerdmans, 1972), p. 265.

instructions about the laying on of hands; in fact, even Jesus' own apostles were simply "made" (Mark 3:14). The vocabulary of New Testament leadership permits no pyramidal forms; it is a language of horizontal relationships, of leaders and followers, of those set before others as models (1 Cor. 11:1; 2 Thess. 3:9; 1 Tim. 4:12; 1 Pet. 5:3), of mutual service one to another for the sake of the kingdom. Ordination can have no function in such a system, for it sets up barriers where none should exist, that is, between one Christian and another, and hinders the mutual service by which the church is edified.

As has been demonstrated, the laying on of hands heralds key moments in the history of redemption, moments when the "hand" of God is manifestly shaping the destinies of his people. Its essence is of the "times and seasons" that are under the authority of God alone (Acts 1:7; cf. 1 Thess. 5:1). The church is exceeding its jurisdiction when it divests this rite of its kairotic essentiality and uses it to confer office in the church. Even in the political realm we do not sanction lifelong positions of power—how much less should we permit this in the realm of church government? In a democratic society, competition for political office serves as a check on the acquisition of excessive power by our political representatives. In ordination, the "man of God" is elevated above such mundane (but essential) controls. Only the most flagrant misbehavior can remove him from his representative status. Often, by virtue of the aura conferred on him through the laying on of hands, the ordained minister is unable to serve as a model of the Christian life so that others may emulate him. Personal aggrandizement may be abhorrent to him, but he cannot rid himself of the remnant of economic and prestigious advantages still accruing to him from state concessions to the clergy in earlier ages. We may well question the wisdom of retaining a rite that can so easily be abused.

If authority in the church should be based on capability to serve, then leadership roles must be based on a biblical understanding of the functioning of spiritual gifts in the New Covenant communities. F. Roy Coad remarks:

> When it is understood that "gift" extends to every necessary task within the church's life and witness, and that the ideal is that every member of the church should have his or her function within that life and witness made plain, then recognition becomes the open acknowledgment by the congregation of the formal place of each of its members. In this way the churches can be revolutionized by a partnership of grace in which every member has his or her own function to fulfil,

without jealousy or frustration, and where the Holy Spirit will weld the individual gifts of the many into a united testimony to His power.[5]

When the Spirit of God "lays hands on" men and women at conversion, this is their consecration, their call to serve their High Priest, Jesus Christ. They become members of the royal priesthood; they are the Levites of the New Covenant. God has made provision for their ordination at baptism. They need no other.

5. F. Roy Coad, *History of the Brethren Movement*, p. 270. A Reformed expression of this principle may be found in Albert F. Gedraitis, *Worship and Politics* (Toronto: Wedge Publishing Foundation, 1972).

SELECTED BIBLIOGRAPHY

Ahlstrom, Sydney E. *A Religious History of the American People.* New Haven/ London: Yale University Press, 1972.

Aland, K. *et al. The Greek New Testament.* 3rd ed. The United Bible Societies, 1975.

Albright, Raymond W. *A History of the Protestant Episcopal Church.* New York: Macmillan, 1964.

Ante-Nicene Fathers. Edited by Alexander Roberts and James Donaldson. Grand Rapids: Eerdmans, 1951.

Barnes, William Wright. *The Southern Baptist Convention 1845–1953.* Nashville: Broadman Press, 1954.

Bauer, W. *Greek-English Lexicon.* Translated by W. F. Arndt and F. W. Gingrich. Chicago: The University of Chicago Press, 1957.

Bender, H. "Ordination." *Mennonite Encyclopaedia.* vol. 4, pp. 72–73. Scottdale: Mennonite Publishing House, 1955.

Ben-Sasson, H. H., editor. *The History of the Jewish People.* Cambridge, Mass.: Harvard University Press, 1976.

Bettenson, Henry. *Documents of the Christian Church.* 2nd ed. Oxford: Oxford University Press, 1963.

Bloch, Renée. "Midrash." In *Approaches to Ancient Judaism: Theory and Practice,* edited by William S. Green, pp. 29–50. Missoula: Scholars Press, 1978.

Blass, F., Debrunner, A. and Funk, R. W. *A Greek Grammar of the New Testament.* Chicago: University of Chicago Press, 1961.

Brightman, F. E. "The Sacramentary of the Serapion of Thmuis, Part III, Ordinations." *Journal of Theological Studies* 1 (1900), pp. 247–258.

The Book of Common Prayer. London: Cambridge University Press, n.d.

Bruce, F. F. "The Holy Spirit in the Acts of the Apostles." *Interpretation* 27 (April 1973), pp. 166–183.

Calvin, John. "Ecclesiastical Ordinances." In *Calvin: Theological Treatises,* translation, introductions and notes by J. K. S. Reid, Library of Christian Classics XXII. London: SCM, 1954.

———. *Institutes of the Christian Religion.* Philadelphia: Westminster Press, 1960.

Chadwick, Henry. *The Early Church.* Grand Rapids: Eerdmans, 1967.

Chadwick, Owen. *The Reformation.* Grand Rapids: Eerdmans, 1965.

Chown, S. D. *The Story of the Church Union in Canada.* Toronto: Ryerson Press, 1930.

Coad, F. Roy. *A History of the Brethren Movement.* 2nd ed. Exeter: The Paternoster Press, 1976.

Coppens, J. "Imposition of Hands." *New Catholic Encyclopaedia,* vol. 7, pp. 401–403. New York: McGraw-Hill, 1967.

Daube, D. *The Exodus Pattern in the Bible.* London: Faber & Faber, 1963.

———. *The New Testament and Rabbinic Judaism.* London: Athlone Press, 1956.

189

Davies, W. D. *Paul and Rabbinic Judaism*. London: SPCK, 1948.

Dictionary of Christian Antiquities. Edited by William Smith. London: John Murray, 1875.

Dimitrovsky, Haim, editor. *Exploring the Talmud*. New York: Ktav, 1976.

Ehrhardt, Arnold. "Jewish and Christian Ordination." *Journal of Ecclesiastical History* 5 (1954), pp. 125–138.

Ellis, E. Earle. "Paul and His Co-workers." *New Testament Studies*, vol. 17, no. 4 (July 1971), pp. 437–452.

Encyclopaedia Judaica. 16 vols. Edited by Cecil Roth. New York: Macmillan, 1962.

Eusebius. *Ecclesiastical History*. 2 vols. Translated by Kirsopp Lake. London: Heinemann, 1958.

Feiner, Johannes and Vischer, Lukas, editors. *The Common Catechism*. New York: Seabury Press, 1975.

Ferguson, Everett. "Eusebius and Ordination." *Journal of Ecclesiastical History* 13 (1962), pp. 139–144.

———. "Jewish and Christian Ordination: Some Observations." *Harvard Theological Review* 56 (1963), pp. 13–19.

Filson, Floyd V. "The Journey Motif in Luke-Acts." In *Apostolic History and the Gospel*, edited by W. Ward Gasque and Ralph P. Martin. Exeter: The Paternoster Press, 1970.

Fowler, Stuart. "The Continuance of the Charismata." *The Evangelical Quarterly*. vol. 45, no. 3 (July-Sept. 1973), pp. 172–183.

Fransen, Piet. "Orders and Ordination." *Sacramentum Mundi*, pp. 1122–1148.

Frend, W. H. C. *The Donatist Church*. Oxford: Clarendon Press, 1952.

Frere, W. H. "Early Ordination Services." *Journal of Theological Studies* 16 (1915), pp. 323–372.

Garrison, Ernest and De Groot, Alfred T. *The Disciples of Christ, A History*. Revised edition. St. Louis: Bethany Press, 1958.

Gavin, F. *The Jewish Antecedents of the Christian Sacraments*. New York: Ktav, 1969.

Gertner, M. "Midrashim in the New Testament." *Journal of Semitic Studies* 7 (1962), pp. 267–292.

Greaves, Richard L. "The Ordination Controversy and the Spirit of Reform in Puritan England." *Journal of Ecclesiastical History* 21 (1970), pp. 225–241.

———. "The Organizational Response of Nonconformity to Repression and Indulgence: The Case of Bedfordshire." *Church History* 44 (1975), pp. 472–484.

Harris, M. J. "Prepositions and Theology in the Greek New Testament." *New International Dictionary of New Testament Theology*, pp. 1171–1215.

Hastings' Encyclopaedia of Religion and Ethics. 27 vols. Edited by James Hastings. New York: Scribners, n.d.

Hatch, E. "Ordination." In *A Dictionary of Christian Antiquities*, edited by William Smith, pp. 1501–1520.

Hatch, Nathan O. "The Christian Movement and the Demand for a Theology of the People." *Journal of American History*, vol. 67, no. 3 (Dec. 1980), pp. 545–567.

Hengel, Martin. *Acts and the History of Earliest Christianity*. E. T. Philadelphia: Fortress Press, 1979.

Hiscox, Edward T. *The New Directory for Baptist Churches*. Philadelphia: American Baptist Publication Society, 1894.

Jewish Encyclopaedia. 12 vols. Edited by Isidore Singer. New York: Ktav, 1901.

Johnsson, William G. "The Pilgrimage Motif in the Book of Hebrews." *Journal of Biblical Literature*, vol. 97, no. 2 (June 1978), pp. 239– 251.

Jones, C. P. M. "The Epistle to the Hebrews and the Lukan Writings." In *Studies in the Gospels*, edited by D. E. Nineham. Oxford: Basil Blackwell, 1967.

Josephus, Complete Works. Translated by William Whiston. Grand Rapids: Kregel, 1960.

Kelly, J. N. D. *Early Christian Doctrines.* Revised edition. San Francisco: Harper and Row, 1978.

Küng, Hans. *The Church.* E. T. New York: Sheed and Ward, 1967.

Lambert, Malcolm. *Medieval Heresy: Popular Movements from Bogomil to Hus.* London: Edward Arnold, 1977.

Lampe, G. W. .H. "The Holy Spirit in the Writings of St. Luke." In *Studies in the Gospels*, edited by D. E. Nineham. Oxford: Basil Blackwell, 1967.

_____. *The Seal of the Spirit.* 2nd edition. London: SPCK, 1967.

Lauterbach, J. Z. "Ordination." *Jewish Encyclopaedia*, vol. 9, pp. 429– 429.

Levitats, Isaac. "Semikhah." *Encyclopaedia Judaica* XIV, pp. 1142– 1143.

Lightfoot, J. B. *The Apostolic Fathers.* Grand Rapids: Baker Book House, 1956.

Littell, Franklin H. *The Origins of Sectarian Protestantism* (formerly *The Anabaptist View of the Church*). New York: Macmillan, 1964.

Lohse, Eduard, "χείρ," *Theological Dictionary of the New Testament*, vol. 9, pp. 425– 437.

Longenecker, R. N. *Biblical Exegesis in the Apostolic Period.* Grand Rapids: Eerdmans, 1975.

_____. "Paul, the Apostle." *Zondervan Pictorial Encyclopaedia of the Bible*, vol. 4, pp. 624– 657.

Lumpkin, William L. *Baptist Confessions of Faith.* Revised edition. Valley Forge: The Judson Press, 1969.

Luther's Works. Edited by T. H. Lehman and J. Pelikan. St. Louis: Concordia, 1973.

Maclean, A. J. "Ordination: Christian." *Hastings' Encyclopaedia of Religion and Ethics*, vol. 19, pp. 540– 552.

Mantel, Hugo. "Ordination and Appointment in the Period of the Temple." *Harvard Theological Review* 57 (1964), pp. 325– 346.

McAdoo, H. R. and Clark, Alan C. *Ministry and Ordination: A Statement on the Doctrine of the Ministry Agreed on by the Anglical–Roman Catholic International Commission, Canterbury, 1973.* London: SPCK, 1973.

McClellan, Albert. "Southern Baptist Roots in Practice and Polity." *Review and Expositor*, vol. LXXV, no. 2 (Spring 1978), pp. 279– 293.

Mennonite Encyclopaedia. 4 vols. Edited by H. S. Bender and C. H. Smith. Scottdale: Mennonite Publishing House, 1955– 1959.

Metzger, Bruce M., editor. *The Oxford Annotated Apocrypha (RSV).* New York: Oxford University Press, 1973.

The Mishnah. Translated by H. Danby. London: Oxford University Press, 1933.

Moore, R. I. *The Birth of Popular Heresy, Documents of Medieval History I.* London: Edward Arnold, 1975.

Moulton, J. H. *A Grammar of New Testament Greek, Vol. I: Prolegomena.* Edinburgh: T. & T. Clark, 1908.

Neusner, Jacob. *The Idea of Purity in Ancient Judaism.* Leiden: E. J. Brill, 1973.

New Catholic Encyclopaedia. 15 vols. New York: McGraw-Hill, 1967.

New International Dictionary of New Testament Theology. 3 vols. Colin Brown, General Editor. Grand Rapids: Zondervan, 1975– 1978.

New Schaff-Hertzog Encyclopaedia of Religious Knowledge. 13 vols. Grand
   Rapids: Baker Book House, 1950.
New, Silva. "The Name, Baptism, and the Laying on of Hands." In *The Begin-
   nings of Christianity*, edited by F. J. Foakes Jackson and Kirsopp Lake.
   . Grand Rapids: Baker Book House, 1966. See vol. 5, pp. 121– 140.
Nicene and Post-Nicene Fathers. Edited by Philip Schaff and Henry Wace
   Grand Rapids: Eerdmans, 1952.
O'Connor, Edward D. *The Pentecostal Movement in the Catholic Church.* Re-
   vised edition. Notre Dame: Ave Maria Press, 1971.
"Ordination, Nonconformity and Separation." *Church Quarterly Review* XIX
   (1884), pp. 37– 59.
Oulton, J. E. L. "The Holy Spirit Baptism and the Laying on of Hands in Acts."
   Expository Times 66 (1954– 1955), pp. 236– 240.
_____. "Second Century Teaching on Holy Baptism." *Theology*, March 1947,
   pp. 86– 91.
Parratt, J. K. "The Laying on of Hands in the New Testament." *Expository Times*
   80 (1968– 1969), pp. 210– 214.
Paul, Robert S. *The Church in Search of Itself.* Grand Rapids: Eerdmans, 1972.
Robertson, A. T. *A Grammar of the Greek New Testament in the Light of
   Historical Research.* Nashville: Broadman Press, 1934.
Robinson, H. W. "Hebrew Sacrifice and Prophetic Symbolism." *Journal of Theo-
   logical Studies* 43 (1942), pp. 129– 138.
Ross, J. M. "The Appointment of Presbyters in Acts XIV:23." *Expository Times*
   63 (1951– 1952), pp. 288– 289.
Rothkoff, Aaron. "Semikhah." *Encyclopaedia Judaica*, vol. 14, pp. 1140– 1147.
Sacramentum Mundi. Edited by Karl Rahner. New York: Seabury Press, 1975.
Sanders, E. P. "Patterns of Religion in Paul and Rabbinic Judaism." *Harvard
   Theological Review* 66 (1973), pp. 471– 476.
Schaff, Philip. *The Creeds of Christendom.* New York: Harper and Row, 1919.
Schweizer, Eduard. *Church Order in the New Testament.* London: SCM, 1961.
Scott, J. Julius, Jr. "Parties in the Church in Jerusalem as Seen in the Book of
   Acts." *Journal of the Evangelical Theological Society*, vol. 18, no. 4 (Fall
   1975), pp. 217– 227.
Smith, H. Shelton, Handy, Robert T., and Loetscher, Lefferts A., editors. *Amer-
   ican Christianity: Interpretation and Documents 1820– 1960.* Vol. II. New
   York: Charles Scribner's Sons, 1963.
Southern, R. W. *Western Society and the Church in the Middle Ages.* Har-
   mondsworth: Penguin Books, 1969.
Spinka, Matthew. *Advocates of Reform.* Philadelphia: Westminster Press, 1953.
Strack, Hermann L. and Billerbeck, Paul. *Kommentar zum Neuen Testament
   aus Talmud und Midrash.* Munich: C. H. Beck'sche Verlagsbuchhandlung,
   1974.
Theological Dictionary of the New Testament. 10 vols. Edited by Gerhard Kittel
   and Gerhard Friedrich. Translated by G. W. Bromiley. Grand Rapids: Eerd-
   mans, 1964– 1972.
Toews, J. A. *A History of the Mennonite Brethren Church.* Hillsboro: Mennon-
   ite Brethren Publishing House, 1975.
Torrance, T. F. "Consecration and Ordination." *Scottish Journal of Theology* 11
   (1958), pp. 225– 253.
Turner, C. H. "The Ordination Prayer for a Presbyter in the Church Order of
   Hippolytus." *Journal of Theological Studies* 16 (1915), pp. 542– 547.
_____. "Χειροτονία, χειροθεσία, ἐπίθεσις χειρῶν." *Journal of Theological Stud-
   ies* 24 (1923), pp. 496– 504.

Underwood, A. C. *A History of the English Baptists.* London: The Baptist Union of Great Britain and Ireland, 1947.

Verduin, Leonard. *The Reformers and Their Stepchildren.* Grand Rapids: Eerdmans, 1964.

White, R. E. O. *The Biblical Doctrine of Initiation.* London: Hodder and Stoughton, 1960.

Zondervan Pictorial Encyclopaedia of the Bible. 5 vols. Edited by Merrill C. Tenney. Grand Rapids: Zondervan, 1975.

AUTHOR INDEX

SUBJECT INDEX

DATE DUE